I COULD HAVE BEEN A KILLER

The Benjamin Smart Story

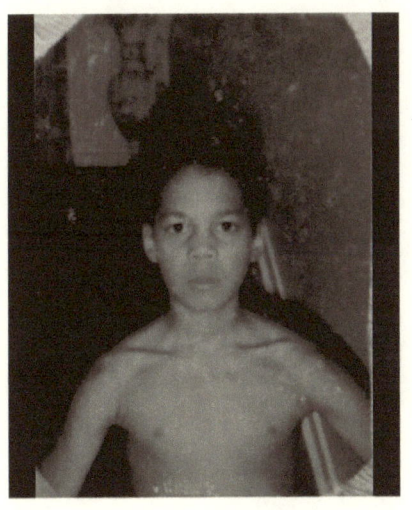

BENJAMIN SMART

Copyright © 2024 by Hulett Publishing

All rights reserved.

No part of this book may be reproduced in any form or by any electronic or mechanical means, including information storage and retrieval systems, without written permission from the author, except for the use of brief quotations in a book review.

For all correspondence, email hulettpublishing@gmail.com .

Dedicated to my beautiful, brilliant, intelligent, and very talented daughter, Anjolie

CONTENTS

Foreword — vii
Laurie McDonald, CHT

Prologue — ix

Chapter One — 1
The Choice

Chapter Two — 3
Earliest Memories

Chapter Three — 11
DEADbeat

Chapter Four — 27
Recognizing Depression

Chapter Five — 37
My Horrible Teen Years

Chapter Six — 47
A Lost Love

Chapter Seven — 53
Buffalo Won't Leave Me

Chapter Eight — 59
I'm Goin' Back to Cali

Chapter Nine — 85
The Industry

Chapter Nine – Bonus — 125
Gift of Gab, Tim Parker

Chapter Ten — 131
I Won't Forget What You Did

Chapter Eleven — 141
A Degree Doesn't Mean Intelligent

Chapter Twelve — 151
Narcissistic

Chapter Thirteen — 171
Lies & Betrayal

Chapter Fourteen — 183
180° to Crazy

Chapter Fifteen *Back to Benny*	203
Chapter Sixteen *Loyalty*	227
Chapter Seventeen *TJ*	243
Chapter Eighteen *Kidnapped*	251
Chapter Nineteen *Getting to Know Your Heroes*	259
Chapter Twenty *If I Could Be Where You Are*	277
Epilogue	291
The Author	297

FOREWORD
LAURIE MCDONALD, CHT

"I Could Have Been a Killer"

In the depths of human experience lies a narrative that transcends the boundaries of conventional understanding. The book you hold in your hands, "I Could Have Been a Killer," beckons you into the tumultuous journey of a soul teetering on the edge of darkness, yet ultimately choosing the path of resilience and redemption. With a knowing of the spiritual world that surpasses the mundane.

The author's revelation that their pseudonym is, in fact, their real name sets the stage for a tale woven with the threads of truth and introspection. A life shrouded in complexities stemming from familial secrets and societal neglect unfolds with raw honesty and unfiltered emotion.

From the shadows of a childhood marked by abandonment and emotional isolation, emerges a poignant exploration of the human psyche grappling with the forces of betrayal, abuse, and profound loneliness. Benjamin's voice echoes with the weight of experiences that transcend mere words.

Fatherhood, a beacon of light and a pillar of strength, holds profound importance for Benjamin. Through his poignant reflections on the role of fatherhood in his own life, to becoming the best father that he could be.

"I Could Have Been a Killer" is not merely a recounting of personal struggles; it is a testament to the indomitable nature of the human spirit in the face of adversity. It challenges us to reexamine our perceptions of pain, resilience, and the inherent capacity for transformation that resides within us all.

I have known Benjamin for over a decade and am happy to call him my friend.

Laurie McDonald,
Clinical Hypnotherapist

PROLOGUE

Believe it or not, my pseudonym is my real name. I've been using a name that isn't mine for my entire life. I wasn't being deceptive. This was because my mother was using a last name from a man that wasn't her real father, or maybe he was. I'm still confused about that. But the main reason is, because my father was too old for her and they didn't want to risk any connection between him and my sister, in which my mother was definitely underage when my sister was conceived. She may have also been underage with me. This story is 100% true. Names have been changed to protect everyone only because innocent people may get caught in the cross-fire. This is a story of a young boy that was purposely left behind by society and family. That young boy was me. I have harbored my emotions since I was five, never having anyone to talk to about what was going on in my head and in my heart. This story details thoughts and memories that I have had ever since I was an infant, and believe it or not, before then. I detail the struggles between science, religion, spirituality, and believing in God or a god. This is the ultimate story of betrayal, selfishness, revenge, neglect, abuse, abandonment, sickness, and loneliness. My hope is to shed light into the world of how not to treat people, especially those too young to speak up for and defend themselves. The sheer number of things I will speak about and the extent of things that happened will seem like too much to be real. All of these things have happened to people all over the world throughout history, but I have my doubts that more than a handful of people in the entirety of existence have experienced all of these things for themselves. There are triumphs and failures. I'm not saying that I have experienced the worst single thing in the world. There are those that have been tortured and killed, and between my experiences in totality, and something like that, is left up for debate as to which would be a better ending. There is an old saying, "There are things worse than death." Now let me tell you what those things may be...

I COULD HAVE BEEN A KILLER

CHAPTER ONE
THE CHOICE

This may seem like nonsense, but this is my earliest memory. This is a memory I have had since I was an infant. Yes, you read that right, since an infant. That's kind of a lie, only because that's the easiest way for me to soften the blow of me saying this memory predates my birth. This is also where my struggle with religion, God, and spirituality begins. It was a home in Buffalo, NY. There was very little furniture in it. I recall what were supposed to be white walls, but laden with handprints and dirt from neglect of cleaning. I recall the floors being brown. I do not recollect if they were carpeted or hardwood. We were between the front entrance of the house, the bedroom which was to our adjacent right, and behind us was the living room which went at a 90° angle. I don't recall where the kitchen was because this is as far as my spirit was when this took place. There were two entities. I can only speculate who they were. One was above me, and the other was above it. They felt like male spirits, and the one highest felt like the one with the most authority. I do recollect the lower spirit asking me if I was sure if this is whom I wanted to be my mother.

They both spoke. It was explained to me that I can choose whom I'm born to, and I could choose a wonderful life full of love, a life full of wealth, a life of poverty, a life full of pain, or I could experience all the hardships I could imagine in one life, but I would eventually live each one of those. I chose to get all of the hardships out of the way. I was asked if I was sure, and I said yes. I was sent into the room. I had no physical form, but I was just sent there. I have to assume I was sent into the act of my parents conceiving me. Exactly 2 months to the day after I wrote the above, a friend sent me a text and asked if I saw Terrence Howard on the Joe Rogan Podcast. I immediately went to watch it because when she suggests something, it's for good reason. In it, he described something very similar to what I experienced, and in it, he suggested that the entity was his future self. I now believe this may have been the two entities I experienced. Two alternate futures or realities.

It was nothing but redness, and there was another presence there with me. This person was my sister. Evidently, she made the same decision that I had made. What I'm about to tell you is something that I cannot explain. I am a man of science, and there is no explanation that I can give you. One of the spirits told me to climb, so I started climbing the red lined wall that led to somewhere that I wasn't familiar with. As I started climbing, my sister pulled me down and started climbing in my place. I was confused, but the spirit told me that it was ok, and it didn't really matter who was born first, so to let her go.

CHAPTER TWO
EARLIEST MEMORIES

I do not recall every moment in my life as an infant, nor in any stage of my life, believe it or not. I will just highlight some of my memories, as I could write an entire book based on memories alone. I'll just share some of the ones that I think about the most.

I remember a small room, white walls and a bed. It appeared to be well kept, and there were toys on the floor in the corner under where the window was. There was a small gap, but large enough for me to play between the bed and the wall. There was a toy airplane, like a 747 jumbo jet with a row of windows and a door that flipped down to give access to the inside. The airplane was primarily white, blue wings, and red parts, and bits of yellow. I had figurines that I could put inside the plane. The body of the figurines were cylindrical and had a head about the same size as the body. No legs or feet, as they were shaped like a circle on the bottom in order to fit into the airplane to stay secure. I had no concept of time back then, but it seemed like a very long time every time I was left in there. I remember sometimes it was light outside when she left me, and it was dark when she came back.

This was a different house. Come to think of it, and as I'm writing this, the layout seems a lot like where my grandfather lived on Jefferson Ave. Once again, there was very little furniture. There was a mattress on the floor in the living room, but not in the bedroom. I was being breastfed while on the mattress. I had enough and wiggled around for my mother to put me down, which she did. I crawled into the bedroom which was empty, and I crawled into the closet where there was another baby, a girl, there who appeared to be caucasian. She was only laden in a diaper, and she was sitting there in very runny poop which flowed out of her diaper and all over the floor around her in the closet. I crawled next to her and waved my hands around in the poop. She smiled and did the same. My mother then came into the room, not mad, but more so of a sigh and picked me up to wash me off before cleaning the girl off. To this day, I have no idea who the little girl was.

There were very few memories of my sister and I together with my mother. It was a city bus. My mother was holding me and she pulled the cable to signal she wanted off. We got off from the back door, and as she stepped down, the door closed on her. My mother was irate and accosted the bus driver. When we got off, there was a guy that appeared much older than my mother who recognized her. He asked her if they could get together for a drink, and she politely said no thanks, and that she doesn't drink anymore. I thought to myself, how does one stop drinking and still live? Alcoholics probably have the same question, but for different reasons. We walked through a quiet neighborhood. There were few cars on the road, which now that I think of it, means it was probably

Sunday. It was still bright and sunny. I could hear music blasting from a red-clay brick house at the corner of two streets. I specifically remember the words to the song that was playing, well, at least the chorus of the song. "She's a brick ...HOUSE, she's mightay mightay, lettin' it all hang out..." I do remember some of the other lyrics that came after that, but that's neither here nor there. I had no idea what we were there for, but she took me into a room and left me there. I now know that she must have been turning a trick.

My next memory is inside of a grocery store. This was a rare occasion that I can remember my sister and I being together with our mother. It was like she only liked to take us out separately or something. She was carrying the both of us. She grabbed a can opener and opened up the can. I can recall very specifically that they were scalloped potatoes with herbs and spices. She fed us while she walked in the store. I had no idea she was stealing, or what stealing even was, but I do remember her being confronted by someone in the store.

Now this is the first memory that I have of when I was no longer a baby and I actually remember the name of the street I lived on. Mind you, I'm only sticking to the memories I have with my mother and not the many others that I have with other people. Keep in mind that I'm telling you all of these for a reason, and they will come into play 43 years later. I'm now on Schauf Street and I'm somewhere between 3½ and 4 years old. My mother would send my sister off to school, and she would read to me on a chair in an empty living room, the same book, over and over again, pointing to each word that she read as she read it. It was a small Disney book with the gold spine. It was Huey, Dewey, and Louie. It got to the point that I recognized all of the words in the book. It didn't stop there though. I now was interested in how she knew what the words were and how to say them. I listened to her as she pointed out all of the words and pronounced each one.

I now remember going to school and being in kindergarten. I remember the layout of the entire classroom. I remember where the coat closet was, the cubby shelving where we kept our personal belongings, the mat that we played with the building blocks on, the sink, and much more. I remember the first time I discovered how Elmer's glue dries to your hands and you can peel it off like skin. I also learned a couple of tricks to get out of class. I would mix orange juice with milk and drink it to make myself throw up, just so I could have a trip to another part of the school and see different things. I even used to staple the palm of my hand so that I could be sent to the nurse. Eventually, they figured me out and saw that I was just bored. I would get sent to my sister's 1st grade class to learn with them. I was advanced and already knew how to read and was interested in math, so whenever my sister's class would begin their math lesson, the teacher would send for me, and I would learn with them. I recall the abacus that I learned on. At this point, I had caught up with my sister as far as actual knowledge goes, but I was never advanced to her grade.

I remember the very same book that my mother read to me from, with me at my other grandmother's house and reading it in the kitchen. "A dismal island swamp" I read, but I pronounced it "iz-land". When my aunt heard me say it that way, she said "how did you pronounce that?" I showed her, and that was the very moment that she knew I knew how to read, and that was the first time I knew that it was an odd accomplishment at my age. She told me she thought that I memorized the book, until I said that word the way it was spelled. She also reminded me that I was walking at 7 months old, and I was obviously advanced. So the story of me playing with poop in the closet, I must have been less than 7 months old, because I crawled, and I remember my size. This is when my aunt took a special interest in me. Nothing bad, but she now saw me as someone that she could mentor, and aside from one other aunt, she was my favorite. I'm refraining from naming anyone as of yet, as it is not important at this time, because this isn't about them in this chapter. My sister and aunt will come into play later on, where I shall make up names for them.

One thing I always struggled with is how few memories I have of my mother. My time with her seemed rather inconsistent. I will only give a few more memories of her before I get into my childhood. I will give the character in this next story a name. My mother used to take me to the dentist's office quite often. He was a rather large Black man, and by large, I mean rotund. He had a dusty office with old equipment even for the time. This was the 70s. I recall she would get dental work done, and I would also get my teeth taken care of. When he would clean her teeth or do whatever it is he was doing, I would be in the waiting room. Chairs lined 3 of the walls and the center of the room was empty, and there was a thin carpet that laid on the floor. It was brown and old. This waiting room had many spiders, mostly what I called "daddy long legs." I had no fear of spiders. I would watch them walk across the carpet in amazement of how they walked with all of those legs. I would catch some of them and their legs would easily fall off. I didn't mean to hurt them, but they didn't seem to feel pain, at least that I knew of. They would still scamper away even with a couple or a few legs missing. In this office on Bailey Avenue, there was an upstairs. A very long set of stairs led to a room up there where there was a small television. I don't recall it being a color tv, but it worked, and that small upstairs room was where I got my first taste of Godzilla movies. My mother would bring me upstairs, turn on the television, and for some reason, Godzilla movies would always seem to be on. I think that maybe Dr Tanner had a VCR or something and had the tapes in there ready for me so that he could tend to my mother with no interruptions. I saw him back then as her boyfriend who looked far too old for her, but they spent a lot of time together, and he treated us very nicely and took us places. He once took us to a gloomy restaurant where I had my first taste of crab legs. I ordered snow crab, which was spikey and what I called white, but was actually blue. He asked me what grade I was in and I don't recall my answer, which is weird, because I asked him what grade he was in, and he giggled and thought for a minute, then said "34th" which the older me realizes he must have been about 39 years old. My mother must have been about 23, if my memory serves me correctly, she was 19 when she had me. Maybe even 18. Dr Tanner took us to Toronto, OT, Canada. I remember riding in the elevator of a tower and the elevator had a glass floor, and it was exciting, yet very scary. This was my first experience with heights and where my fear of heights developed. He bought me a battery operated monster truck. I was so excited about that. He also bought me a Chevrolet Impala police car with the red and blue lights on top, you know, the old circular style. I loved that car. It was a blueish color. One day, my mother and I were sitting in an apartment that I had very few memories of. I used to play with that car a lot. One day while playing with the car, my mother was taking out the garbage. It was a very nice apartment and it was upstairs. She told me I had to come with her to take the garbage out, and as we were going out the door, the garbage bag swung and hit her leg. There was broken glass in the bag, and it gave her a really nasty gash. I somehow thought it was my fault because I think I hit the bag or something. She went back in the door to bandage her leg up. On another occasion, I was playing with the electric monster truck that Dr Tanner bought me, and I didn't know any better, but my mother had really long, silky hair like Native Americans, due to the fact that she had Native American heritage. I had the truck powered on, and the wheels were rotating. I took the truck and made it climb up her arm, and I made it go into her hair. This was a big mistake because her hair got tangled into all of the wheels, and she had to cut her hair to get it out of the truck. This was the first and only time I ever recall her being upset at me. My next memory of her was her packing suitcases. Mine was a cloth one with an army green background, and leaf green and purple flowers on it. I remember being in a yellow cab with her and my sister, and bringing us to our grandmother's house on my father's side. The cab drove down the driveway to just past the walkway to the back porch. I knew something abnormal was going on, and when we got out of the car and she walked us up the stairs of the back porch and rang the doorbell, I just knew I wasn't ever going to see her again. I cried so loud and long. There was nothing anyone could say to soothe me. She didn't come in to see us away, and she left without saying bye. I felt as though the incident with my toy truck was the reason she left. I remember a lot of people being at the house on Minnesota Ave, and my grandmother telling her that she can leave and we'll be alright. I ran to the front window to try to peek over the window seal to catch a final glimpse of my mother, but it was dark and I couldn't see her as the cab drove away. From this moment on, it was time for me to grow up. Days would go by. Days turned into weeks, and weeks turned into months, but every single day, whenever I heard someone walking by, I would run to the window of the sun porch and see if it was my mother coming back to get us. The winter was no different. I could hear footsteps in the snow, and every time I heard footsteps, the same thing, I'd run to the window, only to be disappointed that it was usually my aunt that I liked the least because she was scary and had mental issues. I heard stories of how she got possessed while being there when a demon was cast out of someone else at a church, and the demon went into her because she had the weakest soul. Oh, how I did not like my Aunt Wendy. I despised her with every fiber in my body. I have absolutely zero good memories of her. She would throw my toys away because she said they were made by the devil. She would hide my books, including my coloring books and art books on the top shelf that was in the closet of my bedroom. I was far too small to even climb on anything to get to them. My sister bought me a book of magic tricks for kids, and Aunt Wendy hid that from me on the top shelf. She would make me memorize verses from the Bible every day and test me on it. I couldn't do anything until I memorized the verse and passed her tests. I remember she would wash me and scrub my anus until it bled, It was so painful. I recall the many times she would straddle me, stomach down on her lap and wash me until I bled in my grandmothers' upstairs bathroom.

Then, my first day of kindergarten. I transferred schools a lot, so I experienced kindergarten at maybe 3 different schools, depending on who was willing to keep me at the time. These days, we were allowed to do so as 5 y/o kids, to walk to school alone. The school was 3/4 of a mile away, but someone my size, it felt like 5 miles. I walked to school wearing my sister's white snow boots. I was late, and the class was next to the walkway where the entrance was. The teacher saw me standing there and came out to get me. I was sad and she asked me why. I told her that my mother left and never came back. I ruined the teacher's day, as I saw her holding back tears as she escorted me to class.

CHAPTER THREE
DEADBEAT

My father wasn't around a lot. I do remember he did try at times to be a father, and I saw him slowly become poisoned by the family as time went on and how he transformed into a bad person. He had job instability, but was a collision mechanic by trade. He was considered by many to be the best. He was creative and a literal genius. He was always designing and inventing things. I could never blame him for not always being around, because unlike my mother, he was at least around sometimes, and he did try to raise us like a normal family. It was just his instability that prevented that from happening. I do recall living with him on a few occasions. My earliest was when I was a toddler and he had a Caucasian girlfriend. Her race becomes relevant later, and she will remain unnamed for now. Even though I couldn't have been more than 2 years old, I remember he worked at a factory and we lived in a high-rise condo. I remember his girlfriend used to hold me in her arms and look out the window, and I would see metal stairs or fire escapes leading down, and neon signs at night. The entire apartment was white. White carpet, white furniture, everything white. I remember his girlfriend would have a male visitor come over while he was at work. For reasons of how the brain works, I only have this one specific memory of being at the apartment, but I have a memory within that memory, kind of like a lucid dream of being somewhere that you carry full lifetime memories of. I remembered the place, and I remember in that one memory I have, that I had been there many times, though I didn't really live there, and I remember seeing his girlf....ok, I'll name her...I remember seeing Karly's (not her real name) friend on a few occasions. He would bring her favorite chips, and she'd share them with me. It would either be cheddar popcorn, Cheeto's, or Doritos, and also onion ring chips. At least while I was there, she would not allow him to go past the kitchen. The layout of the apartment was, you walk in, and you're in the kitchen. It went the full width all the way to the window she would look out of with me. The table was right next to the window, and there were two large openings to the living area, which was big by comparison to how someone my size sees things. I don't remember any bedrooms or where they could possibly be located.

 I remember Karly living with us on Schauf St during the era of the 22 Caliber Killer, or Joseph Christopher. It was late night right around midnight, and my sister and I were playing in the upstairs room which was mostly empty. There were a couple of chairs there, and that's it. My sister and I heard something outside, then saw the figure of a man when we looked outside the window. We screamed, and Karly quickly ran up the stairs and into the room. She grabbed the telephone and sat us on her lap while she called the police. It was incredible how quickly the police arrived at the house. It wasn't even minutes. It was less than a minute, as they must have been right in the neighborhood. My only frame of reference to how quickly they arrived is because they got there before he could get into the window, and he was trying to open it when

Karly called them. They arrested the man before he could break in. Don't ask what we were doing up so late, as I have no idea. Maybe we were watching Doctor Who, as that was my introduction to sci-fi, and it seemed to always come on late. I only remember it was around midnight based on his exchange with the police officers and his lame excuse as to why he was on the lower roof of the house. He said he was retrieving a frisbee, and the police said "at midnight?" He had a knife on him, and that's all I can remember. I do remember after that, Karly told us that he was the 22 Caliber Killer, but the police weren't aware that it was him, so he went through the system not being brought up on charges for the murders that he committed. This is why I felt the need to bring up the race of my father's girlfriend. I can just imagine some of you saying "why do you feel the need to mention that she was Caucasian?" You see, it's because Joseph Christopher was targeting Black men that dated or married White girls, and my father was next on the list. As badly as I will talk about my father later in this chapter, I do have some good memories. Like I said, he did try, but when your family is run by a monarch with secrets that could tear the family apart, the eldest son just may know these secrets, and the monarch and eldest son may harbor ill feelings towards each other, and sometimes things surface. One example of this is an incident that occurred on my 12th birthday. I was on the swim team, and I won first place in my event, the backstroke. My father wanted to celebrate my victory at the same time as taking me out for my birthday. Never having a birthday party or dinner in the past, I was looking forward to this. This was one of the few times my father didn't have a car. Well, he often didn't have a car, but by him being a collision mechanic, he always had access to a car, but this time, he did not. He asked his mother if he could use her car, and she would not let him. He argued and pleaded with her and said it was a special occasion because it was my birthday and I just won my swim competition. She was totally unfazed. It got ugly. He was so hurt that she would not let him use one of her three cars for such a momentous occasion. You see, she had 12 children, and we grew up thinking they all had the same parents, though it was obvious that they couldn't have had the same parents. We know Black people come in many shades, and many anomalies can occur. We have seen Black couples producing White children, and White couples producing Black children. We know how strong genetics works, but these 12 siblings ranged from high yellow, to midnight. Evidently, there were 3 men involved. My grandmother was at the time, married to her youngest son, El's father. They looked very much alike, and there was no denying the paternity. They had the same looks, and body structure. My father went on to air out her dirty laundry right there, of how he would catch her sneaking out the window with different men all the time. I now realize that because I was now privy to this information, why my grandmother started treating me a lot worse than she ever did. I guess some people treat you nicer when you know things about them that they don't want you to know, and others treat you worse in hopes that you lash out, so that anything I say can be attributed to me being a bad person and untruthful. The truth is, I always thought that the 12 of them had different fathers, but I didn't care. I knew a lot more about my grandmother than she thought. What really hurt about her not letting him use the car is, she would freely let other people drive it with no problem. The Pastor of her church had a house fire, and they lost everything, so she literally gave them her prized 1986 Lincoln Town Car (it was a signature edition or something, but it wasn't the basic one). On top of that, she gave them several thousand dollars. That hurt deeply, because she would never give me any money for school trips, and all the kids thought I was poor. When they would see the house I lived in and the nice, expensive cars in the driveway, or come in and see how the house was laid out with lavish expensive furniture and antique items, such as a $10,000 mirror and frame with the large base, something you'd find in the bedroom of a desolate Princess, the antique silver tea pot and accessories collection, the marble table and matching coffee tables, brand new carpet, etc..., they could not understand how it was that I was so poor. My grandmother wasn't always cruel to me. She did some nice things for me. I was in total shock when she rented a new car and tuxedo for my senior prom. 32 years later, I'm still in disbelief. My grandmother did later in life apologize for all the bad things she did to me, and I had long before that, already forgiven her. We went over 10 years without speaking, so that was plenty of time to get over things. She even went as far to tell me what it was she wanted me to have upon her death, as she probably felt she didn't have long to go. I shall get into that and the greed of my family later.

My father was an avid bowler and chess player. He rocked the platform shoes. He was also a very physical disciplinarian with very little tolerance outside of his own reasoning. But let me start with some good memories. I'll preface this by saying I can count on my two hands how many times he bought me a gift, but they were always good ones. My favorite thing he ever got me was a rubber molding set. You would pour this liquid into this heated oven that was about the size of a toaster. You poured it on top of whatever mold you inserted into it. And after it cooled, you had a rubber spider, octopus, bat, or whatever. I honestly think it was his more than it was mine. I really loved the smell of the hot rubber, and whenever I smell it today, I have good memories. He bought me a Casio keyboard. You know, the cheap one with pre-installed melodies and drum kits and the green and red lights that ran the length of it to show which key was making the note. I loved that thing. I loved anything he would buy me to be honest. My new favorite thing he bought me was a Robotix set. If I still had it, I would probably still play with it. You piece different parts together, connect the wires between the parts and the control board, and you could move those parts. I may have to find one on eBay now. The melody and words to the commercial are in my head as I write this. If anyone wants to buy me a gift, send me one of those.

I remember living at these apartments called "Raintree Island Apartments" in Tonawanda, NY. I had a girlfriend, even though I was probably only 4 or 5. I will give her real name just in case she's reading this. I would love to just say hello to her. Her name is Cherry. I recall going outside just to play with her. We were best friends. Seeing her was the highlight of my day. If she wasn't outside when I went out, I didn't want to be out. It was Christmas season, and my father and Karly took me to the mall to see Santa Claus. Santa asked me what I wanted for Christmas, and I told him I wanted a race car track. When I got the race car track for Christmas, my father acted like he was upset because I didn't deserve it. I swear, this is the first time I thought about this, but... come to think of it, I don't think he bought it for me at all, and that Karly bought it for me. Why would he be so mad that I got what I asked for? Another good memory I have of him was that he did actually teach me how to ride a bike. When my daughter and I moved back to Buffalo for a short 3½ years, I would go to Schauf St to see the house we lived in, and where I learned to ride a bike. For those of you familiar with that street, I know it was Avenue, but I always called it Street, so it shall stay that way. My father also bought me a Matchbox set and a Hot Wheels set. Yes, the era of the all metallic toy cars and giant metal Tonka trucks. I had those for a very long time and I hid them in the pantry under the stairs of my grandmother's basement, only to find that she had put them in a box of donations to sell at a church yard sale. I was hurt, and that collection is worth tens of thousands today. I can't be too mad, I gave away my Transformers collection to my cousin that either broke, lost, or traded them. You see, the only way I acquired them was because I would steal them from the CVS up the street. I gave them away because I learned my lesson of stealing and didn't want to have them because I didn't earn them. This is how I stole them. I would walk in the CVS with the Casio keyboard my father bought me and let it be seen that I walked in with it. I would go to the toy aisle and look up at the mirrors to make sure the employees were watching other people. I would then stuff the large transformer box inside my windbreaker. I would use the Casio keyboard to hide the bulge, and walk out. I learned my lesson after my best friend and his brother got caught stealing while I was with them. I actually didn't steal anything that time. I told them how I did it, and they wanted to try. They didn't need to steal. Their parents bought them all the latest things. They had everything. All the latest, most expensive of everything. Well, they got caught that day, and they checked us all for stolen items. I didn't have anything, but they did. I can't recall which one of them snitched, but I think it was the younger brother that said "why isn't he getting in trouble? He steals from here all the time. He taught us how to do it." I stopped going to that store for at least a couple of months, and when I did go, I was making a purchase. Funny thing is, I think they got caught because of me, and that could have easily been me. They must have done an inventory and found hundreds of dollars of Transformers missing, so decided to watch all the kids that came in. To my luck, I had already decided to quit and passed the torch. I honestly can't remember if it was because they got caught that I quit, or if I decided to quit before that. Ok, so we'll call them Andrew and Marcus. Andrew was one year younger than I, and Marcus was two years younger. Andrew was one of my best friends, and he got this really nice trick bike, which at the time was expensive, but now can be bought for cheap at Walmart. It was a beautiful white and green Mongoose. Well, one day, it was stolen. We would search several neighborhoods for that bike, and one day, guess who they saw riding a bike that resembled his, but dirty and stickers peeled off? My cousin that I gave my Transformers collection to. It hadn't been but a week or so since we saw the bike after it was stolen, and I saw my cousin with it before that, but I didn't think it was the same bike. It was the same color, but it looked too old to be it. My friends insisted it was. They didn't get the bike back. I asked my cousin if he stole the bike, and he denied it.

The last thing I recall my father buying me was after a long time of me not seeing him. I knew he didn't have much money, and he would avoid coming around because he thought he needed money to see us. That just wasn't true. I was into Voltron at the time, and I knew he couldn't afford the real thing, so I told him there was one that I wanted that was much smaller and plastic. He took me to go buy it. I don't know if he was disappointed that I was that age and still wanted a toy (I may have been eleven or twelve), or if he was shocked that he didn't have to spend a hundred dollars on me to make me happy.

Ok, this isn't buying me anything, but I consider it more valuable. Out of the dozens of times he'd promise to come pick us up, 99% of the time, he wouldn't show up, and my sister and I would wait on the back porch for him for hours. He would even say he's on his way and still never would show up. I remember once he actually showed up and took us to Beaver Island. Another time he showed up and tried taking us to Toronto, OT, in Canada. I take that back, this was his second time taking us there, because I remember the first time, he bought each of us a Whopper. That was the biggest burger I had ever seen, and I could only eat half of it. Ok, so the second attempt, we got stopped at customs, which was at the bridge. Mind you, his girlfriend was Karly, and racism is a thing. He was smoking a cigarette as they asked him if he had anything to declare. He said no. They told him to pull over for inspection. He was upset because he knew what was going on and this was delaying our trip. They searched the vehicle and found a pack of cigarettes. It may have even been a carton. They arrested him and later allowed Karly to take us home, but our father had to stay.

Now I'm going to get into the darker side of life with my father as a child and some of the things he had to deal with that molded him into the person he became. I previously told you about how he and my grandmother had a huge falling out over her not letting him use her car to take me out for my birthday, and that belongs in this section, but it flowed more with the story I was telling at the time.

We used to live on Woodlawn Ave. It was the last house at the dead end across the street from the empty field that I used to catch spiders at. There was a Twin Fair grocery store in the lot adjacent to us. My father scrapped together parts and hand built a 1965 Chevy Impala convertible. He worked on it for at least a couple of years. He even mixed paint and painted it a color that no one else had ever used on a car before. It was like a violet, purple, silver light blue mixture. Long story short, my grandmother confiscated the car because he owed her money, though he did work on her house to make up for it. But she took the car from him and gave it to her youngest son. This was the first time I ever saw him cry when his youngest brother traded the car for a 1984 Camaro and paid extra money to the guy he traded with, on top of that. It wasn't even a higher end Camaro. Ok, but let's rewind. I remember getting whooped a lot by my father for things my sister did, but she would lie and say I did it. For example, whenever Karly would make cake, there would always be slices missing, and I got the blame and the whooping. One time, I got tired of getting whooped and not even having the benefit of having cake, so I snuck downstairs and got myself a piece of cake. I tripped going up the stairs and busted my chin open on the metallic trim. I still got a whooping and was told that they knew it was me all along sneaking the cake. What can I say at this point? This reminds me of when Andrew and Marcus got caught stealing the one time I didn't steal. Another bad memory on Woodlawn, we were really poor. As children, you really don't know what that means, but one time, we had pizza for dinner. We had some left over for the next day and it was kept in the oven. Maybe we didn't have a refrigerator at the time. Well, the next day, it was time to eat, and Karly and my father opened the oven, and several rats ran out of the oven, and we ate the pizza anyway. It's a wonder we didn't get any diseases from that. Speaking of rats, It was while standing in front of that house that my sister and I saw the largest rats we have ever seen. One was about the size of a cat, and it had a bunch of smaller ones running behind it. It was behind a fence in the parking lot adjacent to Twin Fair. I will admit, it could have been an opossum, but they looked like rats to us. One last memory I had was my first fight, if you want to call it that. I was at the field across the street where I used to collect spiders, and one time, I caught this really really huge and gorgeous black and yellow spider that was in the middle of a spiral web. I put it into a big jar. One of the neighborhood boys didn't like that I caught the spider and told me that I should leave them alone. He punched me in the stomach and took my jar. He was a lot bigger than I was, so I just cried as I tried to catch my breath. My father came out and didn't say anything to me or the boy. He did a lot of hitting, but never taught me how to fight. It wasn't until high school that I ever even began to learn to fight. In stark contrast to this story, I remember when I was maybe 14, I had a brand new pair of Jordans. They were white with purple trim. A guy I knew in the neighborhood saw them on me and he had on a pair like mine, but older, and white, black and red. He asked if he could try them on. He was several years older than me and much bigger, but I knew him and where he lived, though I didn't want to let him try them on, I did. He ran off with them and left me with his. I told my father what happened, and we went to his house to get the sneakers back. His brothers were there, but he wasn't and we were unable to get them. Lesson learned, but the entire neighborhood knew what happened. His real name is Vance, and he lived in a blue house on Comstock, just past Hewitt. He was rarely seen after that, and evidently a lot of people were looking for him for other robberies he pulled. I think he ended up moving to another part of the city. He's one of maybe three people that if I saw today, regardless of how long ago it was, I would get into a physical confrontation with.

I used to pee in the bed all the way until I was about 8, and once, my father humiliated me by making me walk down the street wearing a diaper. Once, I was caught playing with my sister's dolls because I didn't have any toys of my own, and he made me wear a dress up the street.

The worst thing my father ever did, but it started out good was when we moved to Florida when I was 8 years old. We drove all the way there in his beloved '59 Ford Thunderbird. It was cherry red with black and white interior. That engine purred something awesome. I remember he said it was a 5 speed automatic, though I had no idea what that even meant. People stared at it whenever he drove it. It was a big attention getter. The muscular sounds it made were to die for. The only problem is, the driver side window actuator was broken and it was stuck in the open position, so we were cold once the sun went down. Upon arriving at the house, it was night time. Finally, we arrived in St Petersburg, FL. Our father showed us the BBQ grill that was made entirely out of cinder blocks. I reached in it and my arm was covered in baby frogs. That was cool. Florida had a lot of creatures I never saw in Buffalo. I never saw lizards before, and there were plenty. Tree frogs, pelican birds, and a lot of other animals that I have never seen. When we first went inside the house, there was the biggest roach I have ever seen, on the ceiling. Karly grabbed a broom, stood on the chair, and crushed it. Well, at least that's what it sounded like. The damn thing just flew away.

My father immediately left because he had business to take care of in Buffalo. He did come back, and he had his brother with him, my uncle Arnold. They partied at the side yard, got drunk and ate cherries off of the tree. I remember in the morning, they were really sick, not because of a hangover, but they saw maggots crawling inside of all the cherries. We had a house on the beach. Well, it wasn't directly on the beach. There was a small road that separated us. We used to wake up at 5 in the morning to go and flip over horseshoe crabs to see all of their claws. We had a few good memories from living in Florida, but a few bad ones too. When school started, I was in the 3rd grade. It was a school unlike one that I had ever seen before. It was flat and spread out into different sections and had a lot of lawn. Like acres of it. It was pretty, but I did not have a pleasant experience there. Physical Education wasn't basketball, fun and games. It was like boot camp. "One two, rah rah rah..." I will never get that out of my head. Well, that was not the bad experience. There was this little girl, 8 years old, that let me know who ran things around there. It was her. She pulled a knife on me to let me know. Strangely enough, I don't have any more memories of that school. I think it was because Karly may have stopped sending us. I do know we only lived in Florida for 6 or 7 months. It wasn't long after Halloween that we moved back to Buffalo. Karly did some questionable things, or said some questionable things. I remember she pointed to some mushrooms and warned us not to eat them because if we do, we'd see

Smurfs. My sister and I were too smart to fall for that. We wanted to see Smurfs, but we knew better than to take drugs. Maybe it stemmed from the time my father was hanging with his friend across the street from us on Schauf St, and they were having so much fun. His friend was the coolest. He had a 1977 Pontiac Trans-Am Firebird just like the one on Smokey and the Bandit. My sister and I went across the street and joined them on the balcony. We were 4 and 5 years old at the time. I told my father that I wanted to smoke and drink too. He said ok, and made me drink an entire beer and smoke an entire cigarette. I was so sick, and I think that may have contributed to me not being a smoker or a drinker to this day. Two more stories on this street before I jump back to the Florida story. Two doors down from my dad's friend, my sister was trying to pet an American Bulldog, and someone started throwing rocks at the dog, and it bit her on the lip. She blamed me of course. A bad memory I will always have about that street other than the 22 Caliber Killer, is my Uncle Dino, and that's his real name, was doing a gig at a party. He was super talented and played every instrument like Prince. On his way home, he was jumped and left for dead. His body wasn't found until after all the snow and ice from the blizzard melted.

Ok, back to Florida. I will have to eventually jump back to Schauf Street later on in this memoir. My father had to leave back for Buffalo maybe two months after we had arrived. He said he had to take care of important business and would be back in a couple of weeks. I learned that he sold his precious '59 T-Bird for pennies on the dollar. $4,000. I think I was in my twenties when the internet first came online temporarily, and I looked up the value of his car. He said it was a rare 1959½. It was different because the hood scoop was facing a different direction than the earlier models of that year. So when I googled it, the car was worth much more than that. He didn't come back, and of course, this brought up abandonment issues. I remember Karly saying that he only left her with $200. That may be about $500 with today's inflation. She burned through that within a couple of weeks, thinking he would be back. Honestly, he was probably in jail. At least I was hoping he had a good reason for not coming back. We were starving. We lived off of popcorn, tea, and water for the next couple of months. We got so skinny, that our ribs were showing like kids in a third world country. Our grandmother paid for plane tickets for the two of us to fly back. I remember one of the airline attendants treated us so well. We ate and she looked after us as if we were her children. The plane had to make an emergency landing and we had to exit on the inflatable device that deployed. I have no idea what happened. But Florida traumatized me. I was unable to eat popcorn until I was well into my 30s. The smell and sound of popcorn literally made me throw up. I remember sleeping on the couch in the sun porch and my uncle Arnold was smacking on popcorn. I honestly think he did it on purpose. I woke up and started throwing up. He discovered that I wasn't faking about popcorn sickness. That was one of two times that I ever heard him apologize to me. The other time was after I had a boil lanced, the same day, he picked me up by my under arms, and burst open my wound. I had to have it lanced with no anesthetics because they were afraid that I might have a reaction to it because of my illness. At least he even apologized at all. I never got one from my father for him getting irate after I finally beat him, a champion, in chess. He and my Uncle Sal belonged to a league and they won several titles, and yes, I beat my father. He wasn't the type to let me win at anything, as you will learn later.

 Looking back, I feel badly for Karly, because she still had no money, but then again, maybe she could hook back up with her NHL hockey player boyfriend. She used to take us to practices and we would be in the back with the players as they practiced.

Oh, I almost forgot. The other questionable thing she did was, when she took us trick or treating, she told us not to eat any candy unless she inspected it first. That wasn't strange. The strange thing is, she said she found a razor blade in one of our chocolates. Maybe she was telling the truth, but it reminded me too much of what she said about the mushrooms.

One time, I almost died. We were at the beach, and I ventured too far into the water. The current started carrying me out. This was not long after Karly ran into the water and grabbed me just before I touched a jellyfish. I thought it was a fish egg sack. I used all the energy I had, to swim back to where my feet could touch the seafloor. Karly didn't do very well watching me. She probably was too busy meeting her new boyfriend. A good time I used to have there was a bunch of us kids used to help this man catch blue crabs. I remember I scooped up a bunch of baby crabs and my hands filled with blood. I didn't feel it, but the baby blue crabs sliced my palms up. I didn't cry or wasn't scared. I do have one good memory of my father while in Florida. He took me fishing off of the pier. It was the first and only time I have ever gone fishing in my entire life. I caught one fish. It was a puffer fish. It was blown up with all of its spikes on full display. My father dried it out and shellacked it. I wish I still had it. My father used to go fishing with his friend, James, a lot. James ironically lived in Jamestown. He had a really nice house and he had giant fish tanks for walls. No, his walls in the hallways were literally fish tanks. They were done professionally, so it's not like they were several fish tanks that were stacked to make walls. I'm talking about thousand gallon walls. I remember being there with my sister and James' kids and we watched the musical "Grease." It was our first time ever seeing it. Well, one time we were over there with James' family while he and my father went fishing in an inflatable boat. They didn't come back when they were supposed to. Finally, they came back, soaking wet and said their boat was attacked by alligators and they were chased by alligators and out-swam them to shore. Wild story, right? But we used to eat fish a lot and that's when I first learned that you had to eat fish with bread just in case the tiny bones got stuck in your throat. I don't know what kind of fish it was, but it was really delicious, maybe especially because they were fresh out the lake.

CHAPTER FOUR
RECOGNIZING DEPRESSION

I received nothing but discipline as a child. The men in my family, and strictly speaking of my uncles, weren't nurturing. I did have one Uncle that seemed to care and took me with him to places, and I will forever appreciate that. Even the time he made me hot chocolate and accidentally spilled the boiling water onto my arm, directly from the kettle. I cried, but guess what? It was worth the fact that someone was finally showing me positive attention. It didn't matter that he made a mistake. It's like I always tell my daughter, "If you notice, I have never fussed at you for making expensive mistakes, because they're learning experiences. I didn't even get mad when you broke my expensive phone or got your brand new clothes dirty, but notice how I will fuss at you for what you consider small things. They're not small things because I had to repeatedly tell you the same thing over and over again. These small things can save your life or save you heartache later in life, as with a phone, I can get a new phone." Uncle El was the youngest of my grandmother's twelve children. He was spoiled, and money that was supposed to be spent on me, went towards his

Adidas collection, leather jackets, fly gear in general, drum set, cars, etc..., but at a young age, I was wise enough not to blame him for that. He was still my favorite uncle and the only one that gave to me rather than took from me. Well, my other uncle we shall call "Sal", he never took from me, and he did quite often take us to the skating rink as part of his church skating group "The Holy Rollers." I can't say that he ever mistreated me as a child other than not being there for me in my younger years. He would give you the shirt off of his back, but you'd have to ask him, and he's the type to have conditions, but still, I considered him a great person. My other uncle, Arnold, was a great person. He was very talented in music, but could never hold down a job and always stole my socks. He did employ me when I was in high school to help him paint houses. Those were fun times. I'm not going to go through the list of all of my aunts and uncles just yet, as you'll slowly be introduced to them in other stories. I just wanted to give you a small example of personality traits that run within my family and how they affected me. One other person worth mentioning is my at the time, favorite aunt. We will call her Sonya. She would every now and then buy me a shirt, or a jacket. She would let me wear her full length leather coat and gold chain, and she had colored contacts that she would let me wear. I always realized that was big of her to do. My sister had the opposite experience. All of our aunts would always take her places and buy her things. They were heavily involved in her life whilst ignoring mine (with the exception of sometimes aunt Sonya helped me). As an example, she got all the praise in the world when in high school, she was elected Class Secretary, and praised for making the cheerleading team. She was awarded for her good grades and was thrown birthday parties. Me, by stark contrast, never received a single "congratulations" for being elected Senior Class President, making the track and cross country team, and actually getting better grades than my sister. It was safe to say that I did have some resentment.

Uncle El and Aunt Sonya were the only two that showed any care and concern for my disposition in life. I showed very obvious signs of depression. I was extremely depressed and suicidal at this age. I had this weird urge to pull my eyeballs out of my head because of all the evil I have seen in such a short time. One of the obvious signs was that my grandmother's house was fairly large with many hiding places. Each one of the three bedrooms were also large. They were all located upstairs. The closets were about 20 feet in length and maybe 4 feet in width. My grandparent's room had two of these closets. My room had one of them, and inside that closet was the door to get into the closet, and adjacent to that door, another door which led to another bedroom that not only had its own closet of the same size, but shared my closet, making it a secondary master bedroom. Well, at 5 years old all the way up to maybe 7 or 8, I would hide inside one of the closets, usually mine, all the way in the back, and usually under a pile of clothes, with the doors closed. I would cry myself to sleep. My grandmother used to find me, and she usually yelled at me and whooped me for hiding. It got to the point that Aunt Sonya and Uncle El would get to me first, and I could see that they felt badly for me and saw that I was extremely sad. They would take me downstairs and make me something to eat or something to make me feel better. There were certain songs that triggered me into a depression. For some reason, "We Are the World" by Michael Jackson was one of them. "Suddenly" by Billy Ocean was another song that got me depressed, then there was "Tomorrow" by The Winans. I remember finally getting the nerve to tell Aunt Sonya about my thoughts of hurting myself, and she would let me sleep in her bed with her.

The year is 1981. I'm 7 years old at the time. I remember I

used to get canker sores in my mouth and on my lips quite often, but everyone thought it was normal and that I just happened to get them more often than other people did. I'm in the sun porch and my grandmother is in the living room on one of her swivel chairs, talking on the phone to one of her church friends. I suddenly started feeling really sick. My throat started to swell up. I started finding it really difficult to breathe. It was a cardinal sin to interrupt my grandmother while she was on the phone, so I would never do that, but this time, I did. I was gasping for air as I told her that I couldn't breathe. She shushed me away, so I started heading up the stairs while trying to stay conscious. I had the wherewithal to know I might not make it up the stairs where my sister was in her room, so I banged on the walls as I ascended the first flight of stairs. Luckily for me, my sister, whom we shall call "Belle", heard me and came to the stairs. I could hear her as I was passing out, yelling to our grandmother that something was wrong with me and that I was passed out on the stairs. I don't even recall how it is that I got to the hospital, but I woke up there with a tube going down my throat and in a private room down a dark hall. It was very quiet. I later learned that I was in the cancer ward. I was in some type of coma. I don't recall if it was induced, or if I slipped into it. Evidently, whatever was wrong with me, was very serious. I didn't know it at the time, but I later found out as a teen that they did a bone marrow biopsy, along with a gamut of other tests to try and figure out what was causing me to be so sick and to cause my neutrophil count to literally go down to zero. I don't know exactly how long I was in the hospital, but I lived there. I used to get play time where they had a room down the hall for all the kids to go play in. I would wonder why I would stop seeing certain friends that I made, but no one would tell me it was because they were dying. I had to be there for at least 3 months. I remember being admitted there for Thanksgiving, Christmas, and New Years. In all that time, the only people that came to visit me were my grandparents (grandmother and her husband, Grandaddy Gene), Aunt Sonya, and Uncle El. I would mention this later on in life to my family and they would tell me they had no idea I was ever in the hospital, which shows you just how much attention it was that I received from anyone. I was literally not there unless I was in their face, but I digress. The doctor and the medical staff gave up hope on finding out what was wrong with me. Finally, they flew in a doctor from Germany, and a doctor from Japan. I don't recall both of their names, but one of them was Dr. Benjamin. Take a gander as to how I remember his name. They figured out what it was that I had after seeing my blood tests run on me over the course of several weeks. Cyclic Neutropenia. It's a very rare disease. Every 21 days... not 20, not 22, but every 21 days, my neutrophil count would go down to zero, and my body would stop producing white blood cells. Factory closed for cleaning. Everyone, time to go home. It never failed. People thought I was crazy when I would tell them I couldn't go to Crystal Beach, Darian Lake, or their birthday party because I was planning to be sick. Not out of the ordinary, but as I write this, I'm in the middle of a sick cycle with a giant canker sore on my lip and a small boil on my face just under my right eye next to my nostril.

Imagine how hard it is to overhear the doctor telling your grandmother that her grandson probably wouldn't make it past 18. I found it hard to understand what the point of having goals was. Let me jump to after high school. I didn't even plan to go to college. What's the point if I'm going to die anyways? I told myself that I had to do something while I was alive. I wanted to fly planes and possibly become an astronaut, so I tried joining the Air Force. I was denied because of my illness. I tried becoming a firefighter. You guessed it. I was denied because of my illness. Lets just say I learned to lie about having an illness in order to get a job. I do realize that even had I lied to the Air Force and fire department, my illness would catch up with me sooner rather than later.

I don't want to skip too far ahead, so let's go back to when I was living in the cancer ward of the hospital. Christmas came, and Uncle El brought me a gift. I remember he asked me what I wanted for Christmas, and I said that I wanted a toy helicopter. I didn't think much of it, but Christmas came, and I didn't realize it was even Christmas. Keep in mind, even though my grandparents, aunt and uncle came to visit me, it wasn't often. I swear, that helicopter he bought me trumped anything anyone else had ever gotten me ever. It was white, with black blades, and had a black trigger on the tail that activated a blue claw that would pick up a payload. It had another trigger that would cause the blades to rotate. I don't recall how long after that, I was able to go home, but it was definitely after New Years. I think it was sometime in February. Either way, we knew what was wrong with me, and I was scared. I was told what an immune system was, and that I didn't have one that worked properly, and that anything could kill me. Did I tell you that I was scared? Well, that was an understatement. The understatement of the century. I was already invisible not by choice, but now I had to disappear so that I didn't die. Imagine that. I don't want to downplay the time I lied to my Aunt Claire that it was my birthday, and she immediately left the house and went and bought me a giant red fire truck. When she got back, I told her I was just kidding. I tried to tell her I was kidding, but she ran out so quickly that I literally couldn't stop her. She did peak my interest in wanting to become a firefighter though.

As I said, my sister had all the support in the world. It was bad enough I already wasn't getting any attention nor the help I needed, but I then had to compete with Foster children living in the home. I even had to give up my bedroom so that my grandmother could get that foster care money. If I remember correctly, it was like $800/mo per child, but I could be wrong. She always had at least two kids at a time. Everyone from toddlers, to teenagers. Oh, but she didn't stop there. She eventually got into keeping troubled adults. I could give examples of how the adults were treated, but I will refrain from that. I will stick with how I was treated. It got worse as she started taking in foster children. She kept two little boys. They were maybe 5 years old or somewhere close to that age. I was already upset that they took my room and now I was displaced in my own house, but they started leaving their toys in the sun porch where I slept on the couch. I grew tired of cleaning their stuff up just to lay down. Remember that big die cast metal Tonka truck I mentioned? Well, that belonged to one of the boys. I brought it up the stairs and put it in my old room and told one of the boys to not leave their things in the sun porch. My grandmother was in her room and heard me saying this to him. She got irate at me and yelled at me. I was on the mid platform between the two sets of stairs, exactly where it was when I passed out from my throat swelling up, and she was standing at the top of the stairs. She went in on me about how she's not going to let me mess up her chances of keeping foster kids and that if the case worker isn't happy with how the boys are treated, they'll take them away from her. She was cherry red and she didn't say it nicely, then she threw that big metal Tonka truck down the stairs at me. I don't recall if it hit me or if I was injured from it, but I was hurt. I knew then and there that she did not love me more than she loved the money she was getting, and that was the moment that my relationship with my grandmother had soured and how it would be defined. I moved back and forth between my two grandmothers, and that may have been one of the times that I moved. My mother's mother never mistreated me physically, nor did she ever really yell at me. I never felt like I belonged there though because my uncle felt a way about her showing me any attention. I never had anything of my own. She bought my uncle, who is only two years older than I am, everything, and if I wanted anything, she would just tell me to ask ... We'll call him Roger, I had to ask Roger if I could play with his things. It was always no. I couldn't touch anything. He did let me play his Atari with him. One time for Christmas, he got me two video games. One of them was "Where in the World is Carmen San Diego", and the other was...I really don't recall, but I think it was either "Space Harrier" or a game that reminded me of "The Never Ending Story." He actually got mad when he came home and saw me playing his game without him, so then he started locking his game system in the room, so my Christmas gifts were really his. It's like buying your wife a vacuum cleaner.

Forgive me if I reference my grandmother and not tell you which one I'm referencing. Just assume it's the one previously mentioned. At the moment, I'm speaking of my mother's mother. The one with the Foster children is my father's mother. So, my mother's mother was a nurse. Her husband worked for General Motors at the factory and was paid quite well. They both had a pretty good income and had a lot of nice things. Their house wasn't as nice as my other grandmother's, and didn't have as much expensive furniture, but they always had the latest electronic devices and nice cars. They always had one or two trained guard dogs that stayed outside, even during the winter. The dogs had the entire detached garage for themselves, and sometimes would be allowed into the basement. My little cousin, who was actually much bigger than I by size, used to live there, and my grandmother said that he would never feed the dogs because he was scared of them, so she didn't make him do it. Dogs sense fear and that would be a dangerous situation. We'll call him Delorean. Well, on the first day I moved back with her, they had two new German Shepherds. They always had German Shepherds, and if one died, they would replace it with another. So, my grandmother told me to feed the dogs. I went to the basement, filled their bowls with food, and went to the backyard to feed them as if I had done it many times before. These dogs never saw me before, and I never saw them, but they treated me as if we grew up together. They jumped on me and greeted me. I went back into the basement and filled their water bowls, and brought them their water. My grandmother was in pure shock. She told me she didn't think I would do it because my cousin Delorean was too scared to, and he was much bigger than I. Welp, that was now one of my chores, and I didn't mind. We had guard dogs because regardless of my grandparents making a lot of money, they decided to still live in "the hood", and they had a lot of nice things in the house. This was the East side of Buffalo on Moselle St near Genesee. There were several gangs in the same area, something like five if I recall correctly, so there was always violence when it was dark.

My grandmother would often remind me of how much money she spent on medical bills because of me, so this was probably the reason she never would buy me anything. To me, that wasn't my fault, and a child should never have that thrown in their face, especially if he or she has an illness they were born with. My grandmother had a few hardships in her life as well. I mentioned two of the ones that I know about. One, her son Dino being left for dead in the blizzard of '77, and the other, her daughter, my mother, disappearing in '79. I bring this up because she would take it personal if my sister and I didn't keep in regular contact with her. I admit, We were bad at keeping in contact with people, and it was largely due to the fact that we moved around a lot. The other thing is, we had our own trauma and found it hard to stay connected to people. I know for me personally, I didn't want to be hurt anymore, so it was more like "I'll see you when I see you." My grandmother would hold that against us and be mad at us for it. My grandmother and my father also didn't get along. Partially because she suspected that he was abusive towards my mother. She never said this to me, but I think she blamed him for her being for the streets, and the reason she always would tell me is because he was far too old for her and she could have had him locked up. Of course she blamed him for her decision to disappear. I also blame him for this, and it was for the first time in December of 2017 that I told him this during an incident where we got into an altercation. I will come back to this in a later chapter.

CHAPTER FIVE
MY HORRIBLE TEEN YEARS

I sat for maybe fifteen minutes trying to decide if I was going to tell certain stories about my teen years, as they involve other people. I'll be honest, I decided to tell the stories, as they heavily shaped my life. If I can't be honest and say the things that I'm uncomfortable with talking about, then what's the point of it all. I'm sure many things that I have mentioned have made my family members uncomfortable, but to be honest, we're all adults, and we're all past our 50s. I always tell my daughter, I don't care about your feelings if you're an adult, unless you have special needs. I only care about the feelings of children. The fact is, we were children when these things happened, so that's where my trepidation comes in. I decided to meet in the middle. I will only touch on the subjects, saying what needs to be said, and moving on. I will still change the names, as those directly involved and in my family will be familiar, but no one else will ever know who these people are. I don't even think anyone I know is in contact with anyone involved.

One of my biggest regrets involved a foster kid that lived with us. I was 14, she was 15. To make a long story short, she got pregnant and got an abortion. The case worker said that it wasn't either of our fault, and they should have known that placing two opposite sex teens in the same house could possibly lead to this. Me personally, and I'm sure for her also, we were lonely desperate teens, seeking attention, and we found it in each other. I recall everything I did after school up until the moment I found out she was pregnant. I got off the bus from school, and instead of transferring to the other bus from Kensington and Bailey, I decided to walk home. I had on my Syracuse Orangemen sweatshirt and some blue stonewashed jeans, and my white Nike sneakers with the blue snakeskin check on them. I get home, happy that day, and I walk into the kitchen from the back porch entrance, and my grandmother is there. Someone else was there too, but I don't remember who it was. She said "BJ, I got news for YOU. TEISHA'S PREGNANT!" I tried to act surprised and like I had no idea who the father could be, then she said "and she said it's you." She then began to badger me on how and when it happened, and how I could violate her house like that. I go upstairs, and my sister is in her room crying. This is one of the only times she ever showed any concern for me, but today, knowing what I know now and the things my sister and I have been through, I wonder if it was just her way to make it about herself. Teisha decided to get an abortion, and believe it or not, no restrictions were ever put on me. Now, one of the reasons I decided to tell this story is because it was the talk of the family, and one of my aunts, Claire, betrayed me in a way that I will never forget. You see, Aunt Claire started keeping Foster children herself. She kept one that was a girl, and would come over to my grandmother's to visit and hang out like part of the family, because she was. I learned my lesson, and I had absolutely zero relations with her, but one day I was confronted by someone. I don't remember who it was, but it was one of my aunts. I don't want to make up a name, because I truly don't remember.

Well, she told me that Aunt Claire came over to the house and was on the back porch, and that she saw me having sex with her Foster daughter in the kitchen. One thing I am not going to do is lie. I may keep certain stories that aren't relevant, nor needed in this memoir, but I will not lie about anything that I say here. I was so hurt by those accusations. I didn't know if aunt Claire was just straight up lying, or if she saw someone having sex with her Foster daughter in the kitchen. Her Foster daughter may have been about 16 years old. I think I know the truth though, and I won't say any names or indications of the person that I think it was, but I believe she did see something, but she didn't see me, and she knew it wasn't me, because thinking back, all she had to do was ask her Foster daughter who it was, and she would have got the answer. I know two male family members that I know for a fact had sex with her, but I didn't snitch. Well, I believe aunt Claire was trying to cover up for the person that it truly was just in case her Foster daughter ended up pregnant, and being that I had a history, it would be easy to pin it on me instead of the firestorm of what would happen to the person that it truly was. But guess what? No one believed me, and everyone was going around saying that I did, so you know what happens when you're accused of something that you didn't do, but you could have done? I did. A few months later, she came over and came down to the basement where I was watching television, and she seduced me into having sex with her. She told me herself the other two members of my family she had sex with so I had nothing to worry about.

    The other incident was major. It was big, and it traumatized me to the point that even today, I am careful and distrustful of women. I used to attend this after school function called RAVE. I forget what it actually stood for, but it was a program where we went after school that juniors and seniors were allowed to attend, and they actually gave you a paycheck. They had pottery classes and we learned how to make ceramic pottery. I met this girl. We'll call her CeCe. We showed interest in each other at the time, but we were both part of different social circles and already involved with other people. I ended up graduating and moving to California because I wanted to be with someone that I met when visiting California the previous year. I moved back from California after exactly one year because I was homesick, and I wanted to try to reignite a relationship I started with someone I was in love with all throughout high school. I was an assistant manager at the store I was working for and transferred to because I held the same position when I was in California. One day, I'm at Tops cashing my check. This is the same Tops that had the mass shooting. I saw CeCe there, and I was quite happy to see her. She stood in line with me and we chatted until I cashed my check. I had a brand new vehicle at the time, and it was flashy. It was a 1993 Ford Ranger. I guess I was doing well financially at the time as I worked two jobs and made enough money from each one to support my lifestyle, so one job was entirely extra money. Some people may have thought that I was a hustler, but no, I worked hard for my money. Anyways, CeCe walked me to my truck, and she was impressed. She asked me what I was getting into. I told her I was on my way home to relax before going to my second job later that night. Before I continue with this story, remember that I have no reason to lie, I was very attractive, had my own house that I was renting across the street from my grandmother on Minnesota Ave, and I had a nice amount of spending money. I actually had a girlfriend, and I was being a dog, because I ended up cheating on her. So, CeCe asked me where I lived, and when I said Minnesota Ave, she got excited and said "I live on Rounds Ave, just a couple of blocks past you." She asked if I was headed that direction, if I could give her a ride home. I agreed. During the conversation, I told her I was renting from a long time family friend across the street from my grandmother, and she was impressed. Not only was I good looking, had a brand new truck, had lots of disposable money, but I had my own place. She said to me that she wanted to see my place, and I said maybe one day. She insisted that I not take her home and that she sees it now. I indulged. We get there and we're sitting in the sun porch (many houses on that block had what we call sun porches), and she initiated the physical contact, and we ended up having sex. We exchanged phone numbers and I took her home. We ended up going out a few more times and we said we were boyfriend and girlfriend. I was fine with it, but I felt bad because I actually was already dating someone, but CeCe was an old crush, and I was going to leave my current girlfriend for her. Well, I never got a chance to. One day I came home from work and my roommate said to me that he got a call from a girl's mother, and she accused me of raping her daughter. My heart sank. One thing I did not have to do, was rape anyone. I was a player. I had so many girls that liked me, it was ridiculous. I mean, I was turning them away, there were so many. I was living my best life. There was no way that I would have the need to force myself onto someone. I called CeCe's mom and we spoke. I told her that we were dating and that we had gone out several times since then, and there was no possible way or reason I would have to rape her daughter. She then said "My daughter is 17, that's statutory." I got a call from the police and they asked me some questions. I looked up some laws, and found out it wasn't statutory unless she was 16 and I was older than 18 before we started dating. She was 17, almost 18, and I was five months into being 19. It was then determined that it wasn't statutory rape. Oh but wait, there's more. A few months go by and I'm at my second job doing a delivery. I'm at a 7-ELEVEn (pay attention, the "n" in the name is actually lower case) convenience store, and when I come outside, I hear someone call my name. I turn around, and I'm getting handcuffed and being told that I'm being arrested for rape. Ok, now I'm having an out of body experience. I tell the detective that I have money on me that belongs to my employer, and he takes me to the job, which is right up the street and gives them the money. I was in jail for a couple of days before I was allowed to make a phone call. I called my grandmother (father's side). I wasn't expecting anything to happen, but she actually bailed me out. It took a few days, but she got me out of there. While I was there, a couple of guys kept asking me questions about the details of what happened. My story was consistent. Well, I ended up telling my actual girlfriend what happened, and it was a good thing that I decided to tell her. I had toiled over whether I was going to tell her or not, but decided to be honest from that point on. Believe it or not, she was disappointed, but she stood by my side, and it was because of this that we ended up blowing the entire case apart.

Here's where there were several coincidences. I was a direct supervisor of my girlfriend's cousin. None of us knew it until I told my girlfriend her name. Her cousin (my employee) was dating the son of the detective that was assigned the case and arrested me. The detective was a long time family friend of CeCe's family. Do you see where this is going? My girlfriend decided to not tell her cousin that she was actually my girlfriend and called her cousin to see if she had any details about the case, in which she did. How, you might ask? Well, the detective's son would share these juicy details with her. He was being given this info by his dad, which was against department policy and against the law because it violated my rights. My cousin decided to help me. We'll call her Serina. Serina befriended CeCe. CeCe didn't know we were cousins. Well, my cousin called her and had her on speakerphone as I was recording. She brought up that she knew about the rape case, and CeCe admitted to my cousin that I didn't rape her and it was just her mother that was trippin' and coercing her to pursue this. One day after one of the court proceedings, my father straight up asked the girl "tell me the truth, did my son rape you?" He looked her in the eyes and she looked at him and said no. Other people heard this. Yes, he could have gotten me in trouble for intimidating the alleged "victim", but that was never brought up. I had a public defender. Yes, I used to have a lot of money, but I ended up losing both of my jobs because of this, so I was now poor. So, here's where it all comes together. I fired my public defender because I had proof that I was innocent, but he didn't want to present it. I didn't understand why. Maybe he wanted to grandstand and win in fashion, or maybe he was cutting a deal with the judge. I ended up with another public defender and they still weren't willing to present my proof. This was telling me that this was deeper than I thought and that something criminal was going on to where they may have been either paid off or intimidated. One day, my public defender and I had a mandatory meeting with the prosecution. They presented me with the option to take a class, and on top of that, write an apology letter to the alleged "victim" and they would knock it down to a class B misdemeanor with time served. I told them no, and my public defender asked me to at least take the classes while I thought about the rest of the deal. I didn't take the class, and during the next meeting, I said "I am not writing an apology letter for something I didn't do, and I'm not taking a misdemeanor for something that I didn't do. I would rather fight this in trial and do 10 years trying to prove my innocence, than to admit to something so horrible that I didn't do."

Now we're back in court. I don't know what this phase is called. It wasn't an arraignment though. That part already happened. I had all of my paperwork with me. I had all of my evidence, statements made, recordings, and all. I presented everything to the judge. My public defender wasn't speaking up for me, so I asked the judge if I could speak for myself because I wasn't being properly represented. He let me speak. I told him about the relationships between the detective, the detectives son with my employee, his relationship with the girl, and about all of the holes in the story, including how at first I was being prosecuted for statutory rape, but after they found out I didn't violate any statutory laws, how for some reason it was changed to forceful rape. I told the judge how I was being jumped on a regular basis by a gang that was affiliated with the detective. The two guys that were asking me details about what happened in the cell with me when I was first booked, I saw them talking to the detective after I was released, in my neighborhood. These same two guys were brutalizing me, and one time it was while my girlfriend was present, and we both fought them off and got away. I had a molotov cocktail thrown in my window, my windows broken to my truck, tires slashed, and more. I had people bumping into me in public places making threats, etc. The judge looked at all the evidence, and told me he was impressed and that I should be a lawyer, and he would give me information that I needed in order to pursue the field. He told me I was free to go and that I should probably leave town because of all the threats, and the case would be dropped. He didn't want to drop it on the spot because now he had some investigating to do, but he knew my life was in jeopardy, so he was allowing me to leave town. I moved back to California. Three years later, I looked into my case to make sure it was dropped. I searched on the internet for specifics and discovered that half of the Buffalo police department and half of the Philadelphia police department had been terminated and many of them prosecuted for extortion, along with many other illegal activities, including what happened to me. I was the victim of an extortion racket that the Buffalo police department was heavily involved in. The Judge kept his word and dropped my case and evidently took it a step further. With all the evidence that I had, I guess even he couldn't understand how this went as far as it did. I think the Judge was more impressed by how I conducted a full blown investigation to prove my innocence, which involved spies and inner family deception.

CHAPTER SIX
A LOST LOVE

I have to go back in time just a little. The year is 1988, the summer after 8th grade graduation. I'm at one of my uncles skating events. Upon entering, I see the most beautiful girl in the world. She is wearing a white ruffled button down blouse and a blue and black skirt. She's facing me and I'm just looking at her in awe, like one of those moments you see in movies. It actually reminds me of the Wonder Years when they first met. I can't remember their names. I tried talking to her and she was quite friendly, but kindly turned me down. Yes, I was saddened, but got over it. Summer is over and I'm attending orientation for the high school of my choice, and who do I see, two rows directly in front of me, but the girl I fell in love with at the skating rink. This was a pure coincidence, and I took it as a sign that it was meant to be. I was 14. I had not developed into my player ways as of yet, nor had I had the guidance of anyone to tell me how to interact with the female species. Sure, in grade school, I had plenty of girlfriends and girls that liked me. I had guys that hated me because the girls they were interested in were interested in me. I'm not saying all of them. There were the girls that liked the bad boys, and I wasn't one of those. I didn't bully people or put people down in order to make myself appear to be a better person or to feel better about myself. It was primarily the girls in my neighborhood or the ones that knew me from a distance. The ones that didn't see how I would get picked on in school. But all the girls one grade behind me, no problem. All of the girls from other schools, no problem. I really don't mean "all", but a good percentage of them. Hell, I even had the hearts of older girls and women. I was a junior when I took a senior to her prom, and it was someone that I always had a crush on that I didn't have a chance with, but she asked me. I say these things not to brag, but so that you understand that I realized I had power. I had my way. I learned that for every no, I would get 10 yeses. So understand my confusion when I was turned down by the girl at the skate rink. Our entire history can be summed up by the Michael Jackson song and video "The Way You Make Me Feel."

When Kyrah turned around and saw me, she smiled. I can tell she was actually happy to see me, but I did not want to end up in the friend zone. I honestly didn't even know what the friend zone was at this juncture in my life. All I knew was I wanted to be more than friends, and I would give up any player ways if I could have her. I would marry her and live happily ever after. There were no other females in history that made me feel this way. I had lusted over many, but I never loved until now. I looked forward to the one class that we had together. I recall sitting right behind her, and on one occasion, I saw a beauty mark on her face and I said "a flaw!" She was so tickled by that remark. The thing is, I really meant it. There were no flaws on her, yet the one blemish on her face is actually considered a beauty mark, and many models and movie stars paid money to have them added. Kyrah and I exchanged numbers and we actually became friends. I would go to her house to visit her and we would talk for a decent amount of time on her porch. She was proper, and I couldn't come in if her father wasn't home. Her parents and siblings loved me. I felt myself drifting into the friend zone, but I would always remind her that I wanted more than that with her. We both dated different people during these four years, and I did not understand her taste in guys. She dated a couple of guys that were hideous by the standards of most. No one could figure out why she chose these people. Most of the guys at the school were trying to date Kyrah, so there was healthy competition, but only a couple of us were at the top, and she didn't choose either one of us. She chose ugly ass Floyd. Yeah, she was into ugly guys. She couldn't be with someone that was as pretty as she was.

Senior year, I only had two classes that entire year as I already took all the necessary classes my junior year, and had I gone to an academic school, I would have graduated my junior year. Well, I completed my two examinations. Immediately after my second examination, I went to buy a bouquet of roses. I rushed back to the school because I knew Kyrah would still be there taking exams. I peeked into the gymnasium to see if they were finished with their exams, and there she was. I was nervous. All the years of failing to win her over, I had no reason to believe I would win her over with a Hail Mary bouquet of flowers. I had no idea how she would react. Would she be embarrassed? Would she embarrass me? Would she throw the roses away? I didn't care. This was true love, and I was not going to let my last ditch effort slip away. All the years I had to see her leave school without me by her side. Her father picking her up in his gray Jeep Eagle Premier and I would hope that she would turn around and see me staring at her from the window to wave at her. Here it was. This was make or break. It was either Kyrah, or the girls I had waiting in California, so either way, I made a decision.

I gave Kyrah the flowers. She had the biggest smile on her face and hugged me. It was as if she was saving the best for last and just wanted to make me wait all along. Maybe flowers are just that magical? I walked her across the street to her bus stop. We talked about what was next and when it was I could come to see her. Instead of no, I got positive affirmation this time. Then the moment I never expected...I will probably have this inscribed on my tombstone if I'm not cremated... "Kyrah kissed me...on the lips." I could not wait to tell my best friend Eric. He was not going to believe this. When we kissed, it was kind of a funny moment. I had on a baseball cap, and the brim of my hat hit her forehead, so I took it off, and she leaned in for another. After that, we hung out on her porch a couple times, and I was invited inside for the first time. I recall her younger brother smiling as he saw me coming in as if "yeah, my man...FINALLY!"

What ever happened between the two of us? I had troubles with my family and how they were treating me. A lot of unresolved issues came to surface. My grandmother on my father's side and I had a big falling out. There was an incident where she threw a knife at me. You might ask what I did to deserve that, but I'm telling you, I did nothing except witness something she didn't want anyone to witness. I didn't want to move in with my other grandmother because I was tired of hearing how she spent her life savings on my medical bills, and I just didn't feel welcomed over there. On top of that, I was reminded too much of my mother. I wasn't happy, and the hardest decision I ever had to make was to give up my chances with Kyrah, and move to California for a fresh start. I had very little family there, but at least they saw me. By that, I mean I wasn't invisible to them. My mind was made up. My mother's mother actually paid for my ticket to move. I caught the Greyhound. It took 2 days, 14 hours. Before I left, I told all of my family members I was moving, and that I would be at my grandmother's house if they wanted to say goodbye or give me a going away party or something. By that time, my grandmother and I were on better terms. Well, no one showed up. I don't know why I expected anyone to. Maybe it was because when Uncle El would go on short trips, they threw him big dinners, so I expected someone to at least pack me a lunch and give me $20 or something. But, NOTHING! No one at all. No one called or showed any signs of care whatsoever.

CHAPTER SEVEN
BUFFALO WON'T LEAVE ME

I'm going to use a real name here, as the person I'm going to mention deserves no anonymity. I'm living in California and only a few months go by. I got a call from my grandmother (mom's). She told me that I had a son that was 2½. I'm in shock. Who could have fathered my child and wouldn't tell me until that much later? Ok, so when I was living with her on Moselle St., girls would call the house for me. Sometimes my Uncle Roger would answer the phone. I found this out when I ran into one of the girls. I asked why she wasn't returning my calls, and she told me that she was calling, but my uncle would answer and tell her that I wasn't home, and he would convince them to stay on the phone and they would converse. Basically, he was either successfully stealing them, or he was trying to steal them. I do remember investigating. The phone would ring, and he would be in his room and answer on the first ring, but I had him figured out. I had the kitchen phone right by me, and the phone rang. I quickly picked it up but didn't say anything. He also picked the phone up and I would let him think he answered first. It was one of my lady friends by the name of Kim that I just met. Sure enough, he told her I wasn't home and they conversed. No need to get into the conversation as I don't recall exactly, but the gist of it was...you can figure it out. I had enough girls in my repertoire that I wasn't going to cry over it. I was just going to get revenge and try to steal one of his. One of his girlfriends used to always flirt with me, but that was too easy. I'm not going to name her. She was too nice, and maybe her flirts were just her being friendly, but I honestly felt as though I could steal her. Instead, I wanted to steal someone from him that I never met, but I used to hear him talk about all the time that he seemed to really like. Maybe he didn't, but this was my choice. I answered the phone one time, and a girl called and asked for him. I said he wasn't home but I could take the message for him. She said her name was Nugget. Yep, this was her. I kept her on the phone. It seems girls just liked to talk on the phone with strangers. I kicked my little bit of game at her and got her to go out with me. I picked her up, driving my grandmother's car (yes, my uncle's mother's car to pick up his girlfriend). We went to the Erie Basin Marina and made out, but we did not have sex. I honestly just wanted to steal her as revenge, and I'm glad it didn't go that far. I mean, most of our clothes came off, but that small Chevy Cavalier was just too small to be comfortable, plus other cars started coming around, so it kind of ruined the mood. Her panties never came off. Either way, that night, I accomplished what I set out to accomplish. I stole one of his girlfriends to let both he and I know that I could play the game too. I was never mad at my uncle. I had some fly females. Who wouldn't want them? Plus, I was used to people taking from me and never giving. Besides, girls usually liked the older boys, and Nugget was 2 years older than me, so I had the bigger win. Plus she was a lil freak.

Anyways, my grandmother forwarded me the mail that she received from the County ordering a DNA test and following orders for child support. I knew I never had sex with her, so I was confident that the child was not mine. What I did next, I took to the next level. In the midst of this, I communicated with Nugget and told her I wanted to visit and see "our son." I told her that I would have to stay with her because I didn't want anyone finding out that I was back in Buffalo. The only other person I told I was back, was my best friend, Eric. I really didn't care to see the kid. I knew he wasn't mine. I just wanted to see how far she was taking this. She knew damn well we didn't have sex, so since I was accused, once again, I may as well. I had pinned up unresolved sexual tension with her from not having sex with her at the Erie Basin Marina, so this was my chance to get it done. I arrived in Buffalo and made it to her house. I stayed the night, and accomplished what I set out to accomplish. I left and never called her again.

During my time there, Nugget showed me letters that my sister, Belle (not her real name) wrote to her on many occasions. I had already seen all these letters, as they were used by the County to make the decision to pursue child support from me and to order a DNA test. I will admit, the kid did look like me, but as much as I look like my uncle. He could have passed for any one of our kids.

So, why was my sister writing letters to Nugget? Good question, and I could never get a straight answer out of my sister, and this would come into play in another story. I told Belle and everyone in my family that I had never had sexual relations with that girl. That's on them if they didn't believe me. My sister was buying him birthday gifts, Christmas gifts, babysitting, etc. I couldn't understand this, but I was used to her betrayal, and little did I know, there would be more betrayal like it in the future. I'm going to tell you how dishonest she is. I asked her why she was writing letters to Nugget and she denied it. She didn't care that I could have proof. I asked her why she was saying such bad things about me in the letters, saying things like "I don't know why my brother isn't taking care of his responsibilities" and things in that manner. I couldn't understand how I was such a liar to her and how she would believe some random female over me, and I have never done anything to her to treat me this way. It was always her that lied and blamed me. She would tell people's personal business and tell them it was me that told, so I was known as the big mouth, but it wasn't me, it was her. It was her stealing the cake, and it was her doing all the stuff that she would blame me for. I stayed out of people's way and minded my own business. Needless to say, the DNA test was negative. I know this because I never heard from the County after that and they said I would only hear back from them if the test comes back positive.

Fast forward to about 2011. With the advent of social media, Facebook specifically, I got in contact with Nugget via a private message and brought up that entire incident. She accepted my friend request. I asked her if she was sorry about that and offered her the opportunity to apologize, because that actually did a lot of damage in my life, and there are still people to this day that believe I have a child that I abandoned. She refused to apologize, and I found it ironic that her Facebook page was filled with church gospel and forgiveness nonsense. What I did next, I wrote a long history of what happened between us and posted it on her public Facebook page. I'm sure several people read it, and she was humiliated. Needless to say, she blocked me, but we had a mutual friend that would share information with me. He also used to have relations with her, and he was also the father of my late little cousin, Demone.

Nugget was either part of an elaborate scheme, or she was that naive. She told me that her doctor told her that it was possible that semen could have traveled through my underwear, through her lace panties, and into her plumbing, and gotten her pregnant. For one, there was no semen, and even if there were, that would not happen. Here's what I think happened. I honestly believed at the time, that was my uncle's baby, and they had it set in their mind that because we were related, it was possible that I would be a DNA match. He does have a son that I have never seen. I could be way off base with age and date, but I have nothing else to go on, as when I tried to speak to both of them about it, I was met with resistance.

Let's get into how my sister betrayed me again in almost an identical manner...It's 2005, and my daughter is only a few months old. My daughter's mother was acting crazy and always starting things with me. I asked my sister to talk to her to try to figure out what the problem was, and to let her know that she has my back, and basically to stop coming at me in the manner that she was. Belle assured me that she would handle it and she would call to talk with her, and that she would call me back immediately after. Several days passed, and no call from my sister. I did talk to my daughter's mom though, and she told me she talked to my sister, and that my sister told her that she didn't understand why I was acting how I was acting and that I had another kid and I did the same thing to them. Let me say this, before I continue. I kicked my daughter's mom out the house. I did not abandon my daughter, and I had joint custody, and actually had her the majority of the time even though I worked a lot. I gained full custody when she was 7, so any misconceptions that I wasn't being a responsible parent, throw that out the window. Now back to the story. Basically my daughter's mom told her a bunch of stuff that wasn't true, my sister believed her and instead of having my back, talked crazy about me, and those things were repeated back to me, things that only Belle would say because she said them before to Nugget. This story is not about her so I'm not going to indulge her personal business, because I can tell you stories of things she has done to our other sisters and family friends. When I asked Belle about it, she denied telling my daughter's mom any of those things, but how would she even know about them to even mention? And why was my sister avoiding my calls and why did she not call me back like she promised she would? Well, it was because of this incident and a previous incident in which another of my sister's were involved in, that my daughter's mom now felt empowered to come at me hard. She now knew that my sisters did not have my back, and she had full reign to terrorize me with no consequence.

    The incident with my other sister is as follows. My daughter was around 1 years old. I took her and her mom with me to the Bay Area to visit my sister, niece, and brother-in-law. My niece wasn't there, but the others were. I don't know why, but my....I'll give her a name because I'm tired of referring to her as my daughter's mom. Sheray and I started arguing. It got ugly. Sheray started making accusations and saying a lot of false things. So many things that it was hard to believe that she was lying. She was so convincing. My sister and her husband are social workers, so they always like to bring their work home and use it on family. I told my sister that this isn't the time and that she just needed to trust me and to have my back. No, they both wanted to play neutral. I could not believe that they would think that I'm lying when I'm telling them that Sheray is lying about everything that she is saying, even though I could produce legal documentation to prove so. For instance, one of the things was I had to call the police because Sheray was acting violent and threatening me. My friend and co-worker was there and witnessed it. We eventually went to court because I had to have her put out of my house legally. The family court drew up custody orders and ordered that Sheray vacate my home by a certain date. I still have that paperwork. Sheray lied to my family and said it wasn't true. I told my sister that Sheray's own friends and family wrote statements against her in regards to things that she has done, such as slashing my tires and breaking my car windows. Sheray said that's not true. I reminded everyone that I had all this paperwork at home, but they chose to remain neutral instead of taking their FAMILY'S side. I can't recall everything, but there were about ten things that she lied about that I brought up specifically because I had the paperwork to prove it. She line item denied each thing, and honestly it seemed as though they believed her and not me. I left for a while to cool down. I came back and we agreed to not talk on the long one and a half hour ride home, and my sister and her husband informed her that was the best thing to do. Sheray actually listened and didn't say anything to me. See, if my family gets involved and says something, this proved she'd listen, but no, they don't have my back. I got up early the next day and gathered my paperwork, drove the 74 miles back to my sister's, and showed them. She could not believe that I was telling the truth and told me that she believed her because why would she lie like that knowing I had the paperwork? My response was, why would you not believe your brother when I say something, especially if I say I have the paperwork? You chose the stranger over me, and I have never lied to you, nor given you any reason to not trust me. She apologized. Another incident happened about 8 years later with my third sister. One that I haven't mentioned yet. Here's another disclaimer. The women in our family just have a habit of disrespecting the men unless they need you. The woman can get into it, and a week later, they're back on good terms. If they fall out with a man, it lasts for years. I had a falling out with Gina, and I'll get into specifics in a later chapter. Gina then went behind my back and made up lies and wrote a letter for Sheray, against me. She basically was trying to cause me to lose custody. She told her that I was living in a house with no electricity, no heat, no water, no gas. Sheray took that to CPS. CPS sent someone to my home, but I wasn't there, so then they sent someone back until they reached me. They waited until Sheray and I exchanged our daughter and I was alone. They inspected the home and saw that I had all the utilities on, and they were in my name. Even though they showed the report was false, this is just how the system is against men and how women help each other. I was informed that I was temporarily losing custody until our court date they set. About 3 months go by and we go to court and I end up with full custody again. Not only that, but Sheray lost her rights to decision making in regards to school, and medical. I promise, I will get into detail when I get to a topic directly related to this, but it's going to show how egregiously corrupt our system is against men. Right now you're thinking "you have to be doing something to cause people to always go against you', but I will tie everything together and you will see how things connect, and most of this dissension stems from one person spreading lies, and how money will make someone that's wrong, right. Another thing is, when people think you're a pushover, they will try to test you, and when you push back, you're the bad guy. They don't expect nice Benjamin to tell them no, or to not let them walk all over me. I'm so nice that people constantly try me, but I don't let them, so I'm the bad guy. I admit, I have a personality that a lot of people don't like. It's not a bad personality. I'm just not ignorant. I don't sit at the table and slam dominos and drink 40s while smoking weed and using obscenities. I read a lot and I keep to myself mostly, and for some reason, everyone comes to me in private and tells me their problems. I don't put up with nonsense, and if someone is wrong about something, I will correct them. I will not let you smoke in my car, even if you hold your arm out my window, I won't go to the store and get you a pack of cigarettes, even if you give me the money and let me keep the change, and I will not get you alcohol if I think you drink too much, though I will bring a 24 pack to the BBQ. I have ways and I don't fit in with a lot of people.

CHAPTER EIGHT
I'M GOIN' BACK TO CALI

So I told you about how I moved to California, then moved back to Buffalo a year later, and I moved back to California a year after that. This next chapter gets into my California experiences from the beginning and ties together some of the things I already told you about.

I have to skip back in time to 1992 when I first went to California to live, but not when I was visiting in 1991. I was on the Greyhound. I actually loved the trip, but to anyone that thinks it's cheaper to catch the bus, it isn't. The ticket is cheaper, but you make so many stops, you end up spending the difference on food and other things. Just plan in advance and get a plane ticket. Save yourself the trouble. I had a decent amount of money when I left Buffalo. My grandmother (mom's side) gave me some money, plus I saved a little. In Buffalo, there was this trick store that sold everything from stink bombs, to replica police uniforms, FBI shirts and badges, you name it. If you wanted to fool someone or play a prank on them, you went to this store downtown on Main Street. Well, I had a fake badge that was exactly like the real thing. The kind that you wear around your neck and it was encased in leather. I also had a black FBI t-shirt. I wore this on the bus underneath my jacket and black stonewashed jeans. I would sit in the back of the bus and open my jacket and act like I wasn't paying attention to purposely let someone see it. Mind you, I look young. I looked younger than I actually was, so no one was going to actually believe I was in the FBI. I lied and said I was. No one really questioned me, but I don't think they believed me, so it was left alone. Many people got off at stops in different cities along the way, but many were on the long journey to the west coast. I don't recall which city it was, but a lot of people got off, and many different people got on, including this lady that had an infant with her. The bus departed, and the baby cried incessantly. Yes, it was annoying, but if you don't like it, drive yourself or book a plane ticket. I understood that concept at 18. I observed this one man getting extremely agitated. He did seem a bit belligerent. Well, it's because he was. Before this happened, I had already switched seats from the back of the bus to the first third of the bus, but on the left side. The lady was sitting across the aisle from me and a couple of rows back. The belligerent man sat on my side of the bus, but three rows back from me. I sat in a manner that I could observe him without making it obvious. This was because he had a couple of outbursts to the lady regarding shutting her baby up. Several people on the bus were irritated by the baby, but we understood. Everyone was against the guy because he was taking it to the next level. I heard what sounded like him getting out of his seat. I heard the sound of a paper bag and a heavy breath. All in one motion, I got up and intercepted him as he was in the act of breaking his bottle and charging at the lady and her baby. I took him down. I actually did take a few karate classes, but my training mostly came from the fact that I learned how to fight at my school and I purposely chose that school because of its reputation of fighting. I was part of a fight club though we didn't call it one. We would fight other schools at games, and we practiced by fighting each other. I also learned how to fight from Kung-Fu flicks and practicing all of the moves. All my friends would practice with each other. Laugh if you will, but it works. Ok, so I intercepted this guy and took him down and had him in a submission position. The bus driver got on his radio, and he told the Sheriff that an FBI agent was on the bus and took the perpetrator down. Oh boy, what a time for someone to believe me. I was now scared because I knew that you could be arrested and prosecuted for impersonating a law enforcement officer. Me being "an FBI agent" (laughing emoji), the driver was instructed to drive to his next stop and they would meet him there. I held the guy down for about an hour by myself before I "deputized" (laughing emoji again) another male passenger to help. The two of us held this guy down for an additional half an hour to 45 minutes until we got to the next stop. We stood the guy up and I walked him off the bus as he was taken into custody by the Sheriffs that were awaiting him. I made no eye contact and I quickly went into the very large bus station and disappeared into the crowd. No officers questioned me, and I got back on the bus at the last moment that I could, and we left. My thinking is, the fewer lettered agencies involved, the easier the paperwork is, so the Sheriffs were probably more at ease than I was that I didn't want any further involvement. When I got on the bus, I was greeted with some "all rights" and hand claps. Oh, and a couple of "so you really are a Fed." At that point, who was I to deny it. Sad thing is, I could never be a law enforcement officer because of my blood disorder. I was in the process of coming to terms that I could not be any of the things I had aspirations of being. I went to a vocational school for four years to become an Air Traffic Communicator. If I were to actually become one, I knew I would have to lie on my application about my medical history. I had the book that my half sister's mom bought for me, I studied it, I took the test, and I scored in the top ten percentile. The test was like a really long IQ test. I made it past the first couple of phases to become hired, and all that was left was the interview process. I didn't follow through because during this time, many Air Traffic Communicators were being prosecuted for accidents within their zones. These controllers were working long hours, like 12 hour shifts, 6 days a week. I knew that my immune disorder would get in the way of the job and I didn't want to be the cause of planes crashing, so I gracefully bowed out. As you can see, my depression was compounded, because no matter what I did in life, my illness was going to become a problem.

Now I have arrived in San Francisco, CA. I get there and I'm wearing a t-shirt and an Orlando Magic Starter jacket. I was one of those people that believed California was all sunshine and rainbows. Boy was I wrong. It was COLD! I sat on my suitcase for two hours waiting for my sisters to come pick me up. I know it's politically incorrect and socially insensitive to say it, but at the time, I had never seen so many gay people in my life, and this Greyhound station was swarming with them, and I had many eyes on me. I was nervous and scared. All my FBI training (laughing emoji) had not prepared me for this. My sisters finally arrived in a 1986 Pontiac LeMans. We're going across the Bay Bridge at about 1 in the morning, and guess what? Her window actuator is broken with the window stuck in the down position. WHY??? Oh well, I was so happy to be in California. You don't understand. In the 90s, it was the place to be. People bragged about living in California. It wasn't run down and as dangerous as it is now. When I visited in 1991, it was in the middle of a freedom of expression movement. People were walking around naked. When I say naked, I'm not talking about just bras and panties. I'm talking about NOTHING on at all. Ok, some people wore backpacks, but that's it. They were getting on buses, riding bikes, breasts and balls out. Some of this still goes on in San Francisco on Sundays. Everyone is used to it, even the children. This freedom is one of the reasons I wanted to move there. Not because I could see naked chicks, but it was the culture. The idea behind it. The people were just different, as to where I was from, if you saw a girl with a skirt higher than her knees, she was looked at as a hoe. The raunchiest thing I ever saw going on in Buffalo was people dancing to the "Doin' the Butt" video by EU. Wearing biker shorts was their version of naked. Berkeley, CA., right along the edge of Oakland, and just across the Bay Bridge, was an entirely different world at the time. Nowadays, Berkeley has changed so much that most of that culture moved into San Francisco. I'm not saying that culture didn't exist in San Francisco at the time, it's just that San Francisco culture didn't really exist in the East Bay, except for Berkeley. Berkeley still has some of the essence of what it was like in the 90s, but it's just a watered down version of it. I mean, UC Berkeley still exists, so students will always keep places like Blondie's Pizza open, but all of the street artists, the flea market, and the overall festive atmosphere and troves of tourists, are all but gone. I used to catch BART just to go there and hang out. It was the thing to do. It's like how we used to all migrate to Lake Merritt on Sundays. It seemed like a festival, but it wasn't. We used to just go there and enjoy it and each other. Of course, the city decided to shut that down by passing "no cruising" laws and giving out citations to people for loitering, and Oakland is complaining about their image now. YOU MADE PEOPLE WANT TO PATRONIZE OTHER PLACES! Meanwhile, San Jose wanted to be more like San Francisco, which welcomed cruising and non-sanctioned gatherings. San Francisco had an Arts Commission. If I'm not mistaken, there were only three places like it in all of California, if not the entire United States. There was the Gold family that dressed as golden statues. Some of them were silver. They actually became rich off of their shtick, and they were all one entire family. There was the famous Bushman that dressed as a bush and would scare those passersby. He was there all the way from 1980, until 2019. Take a wild guess at what I blame for him stopping. Well, I honestly don't know. He is old, and COVID may have been a coincidence. Maybe he saw it as the right time to hang up his hat...or branch off into retirement... You know, leave into another season of prosperity...haha. His essence lives on with people like the Texas Bushman, in which I am a subscriber to his channel and enjoy watching his videos. San Francisco was a place where you could find anything just by walking the pier. People selling everything, drawing caricatures, beads, clothes, singing, food of all sorts from all cultures, and more. In 2012, I became one of those people. I was actually the first person that the Arts Commission licensed to sell my book as art. I was amazed that I was the first person that even applied. They allowed me on the basis of two arguments that I presented. The first was that the story I was telling was indeed art. The primary reason was because I actually designed my own book cover, so it was also technically visual art as well. I'm not going to pretend that I was selling a lot of books. I did ok, but I actually spent more than I was making. I had to commute from Sacramento to San Francisco everyday, and the cost of gas, plus parking, plus tolls, then factor in the cost of food... I was hemorrhaging money. It was a learning experience though. People just weren't interested in reading, and my book was catered to a niche audience, and it was a taboo subject that many people didn't want to admit they were interested in in front of their spouse and families. I did well with online sales after I did public appearances at things like conventions, popular YouTube channels, or radio stations. I think I actually gave away more books than I sold. My biggest market was the EU. I was actually invited to do an EU tour, which I had to turn down because I had my 7 y/o daughter to take care of at the time. It was just bad timing for me. Why isn't the United States as open to books about Aliens and UFO's and other conspiracies, as the EU?

Ok, so the Bay Area was a much easier and fun place to navigate without having to have a car, though I made it a point to buy one as soon as I could afford one. I paid $500 for a 1977 Chevrolet Impala station wagon that had nothing wrong with it. The engine alone was worth more than that. It was a 5.7 liter engine, the same that was used in the Camaro Iroc Z. But BART, which stands for Bay Area Rapid Transit, took you everywhere, and it was cheap. It ran all night, and so did many of the buses, which also took you everywhere, any time of the day or night.

I actually lived in San Leandro on 165th Ave, which was off of the main street, E 14th. It was considered dangerous, and it was. I literally walked by during two different drive-by shooting incidents and earned the moniker "Iron Man" after a third incident where I was shot at, at point blank range by a 45 caliber handgun. The undercover police were parked just up the street at the time it happened and couldn't believe that the guy actually had the gun aimed directly at me, yet they found the bullet lodged into the soil, stopped by a pipe, traveling in a completely different direction. If it weren't for the 2 dozen witnesses, they would have thought we were lying. How did I almost get shot you may ask? Well, I worked as an assistant manager at Blockbuster video, which was located in Oakland on MacArthur Blvd, between Dimond and Fruitvale. I caught the bus every day. There were several drug dealers on the street that would openly operate, and between sales, they often shot dice. I'm not, nor ever have been part of that lifestyle, but I can't walk past these people every day and not get to know some of them or at least be friendly with them. It was as simple as that. I walked by just as one of the several drive-bye's took place, ...twice.

One time, it was my day off and I would often hang out in front of the apartments just to talk to the girls, as there were many. The address was 1601 if you want to look it up. Well, I had a good friend that also wasn't a dope dealer and worked a regular job. We were out front chatting, as several of our friends that were drug dealers would do their business. Before you judge, this was just the culture of the neighborhood. There were no snitches, and no one treated anyone else any differently, and we were all like a family, regardless of career paths. Well, we were close to the top of the hill, and we noticed a shady character, well shady even by comparison to the shady characters that we were friends with, coming down the hill. He asked "who got the (he said some name for a drug)," and everyone knew not to indulge him. They audibly said "don't sell to him", so no one would sell to him. But one guy came to the window of his apartment. His apartment was right along the street side of the apartments in the grass area, which was convenient for him, and he said "I got you," and a few people repeated "NO, DON'T SELL TO HIM." He ignored everyone and pulled out his stash, and the shady character pulled out his 45 and robbed him. Everyone ran except for me. I'm about 15 feet away from them. The shady stranger finishes robbing the dealer, looks at me and walks towards me, points his gun towards me, fires, and runs away. The black undercover Chevy Caprice parked on the same side of the road was acting like he didn't see or hear anything. The D-boys that ran came right back out, and about three of them ran to the undercover car and called them out. "I know y'all saw that… We know you're undercover, we're not stupid. Y'all not gonna do nothing [sic]?" The officers came out of their car, embarrassed and called for back-up, took statements, and did an investigation, including statements. It was the funniest thing to see drug dealers giving statements, telling the cops they were selling drugs and how they almost got robbed. This was and still is crazy to me. These guys, which I called my friends, also saw me as a friend and put it all on the line because I almost got shot. I guess I did my fare share of looking out for them by alerting them that police were coming after I got off the bus. I even remember one time I was waiting for the bus to take me to work, and this new guy (they often had new guys rotating onto that block) that couldn't have been more than 14 pulled a gun on me and asked me what I was doing on his corner. Well, I always had people looking out for me, and as soon as this happened, several of the veterans of that block ran up on him and admonished him for not knowing who I was. They actually kicked him off the block. They told him "that's Iron Man, fool."

Here's where our relationship of respect started. When I first moved there, I was approached by several guys on the bus who mistook me for someone else. We all have at least one doppelgänger somewhere, and I happened to move to the same neighborhood that mine used to live in. I guess this guy did some real dirt, because it wasn't a friendly encounter. I can't recall the name they called me, but I eventually realized they were speaking to me, so I responded as someone would if their identity were mistaken. I was sitting, and they surrounded me by the rear side door of the bus. I informed them that I wasn't who they thought I was and said I just moved there from New York last week. I still carried around my bus ticket and my New York driver's license, so I told them I could prove it. They said "ok, prove it." I pulled out my wallet, pulled my license from my wallet, and then my bus ticket stubs. I kept those as keepsakes and just never took them out of my wallet. It's like when someone gets out of jail, they have to carry their paperwork so if anyone in the hood accuses you of snitching, you can show them you didn't. That was clearly enough for them to believe me, and it quickly went from a scary encounter, to a really funny moment. They even said to me that I seemed like a cool dude and would let people know that there's someone that looks like who they're looking for, but it isn't him. The next day, they introduced me to the entire hood, and from that moment on, we were friends, and I felt as though I owed them some allegiance for not doing whatever it is they planned on doing. As time went on, I would mentor some of them and get them off the streets, hence my good friend that I would talk to in front of the apartments. No one minded this, as many of them wanted to stop selling, and just wanted an income so that they could eat. I would help get them jobs. If I'm being honest, it was probably only a total of 3 or 4 people that I got off the streets, but everyone appreciated me for it, including the drug dealers, and even their boss was appreciative, as he had no shortage of people to replace them. I see it as we were all part of a "warfare to work" program.

During the same period of time that I had the encounter with the...gentlemen...on the bus, within the first couple of weeks of me moving to California, once again, same bus, same area, and this is a testament as to how much I looked like this guy that I was previously mistaken for, I was approached by a young lady that hit me and begun cursing me out. I was really confused. I did not know what I did to offend this girl so badly that she seemed to be taking her life out on me. The entirety of the bus was watching, as she made a scene from accosting me so badly. Evidently, I was sleeping with someone else. I know, I know, how'd we get there! I finally realized that she was also mistaking me for this same person that I was mistaken for just a week prior, and she even mentioned that she had all her friends looking for me and they were gonna (expletive) me up. I kept saying I'm not him. She's right in my face, going off on me even more for trying to make her look stupid by acting like we never dated. I then pulled out my license and my bus ticket stubs, which I knew to keep on me and ready to show. They literally became my hood passes. She calmed down enough to look at the license, which she couldn't help, because flashing a New York license in a hood of California, wasn't a thing. She looked at it, then my bus tickets, then was overcome with embarrassment and actually apologized. I recall the looks of some of the passengers as a couple of them shook their heads, and others looked at me with a funny smirk and those grandma eyes, looking down over the tops of their glasses frames like "boy, you finna have problems out here, welcome to Cali."

I know, with the stories I've told so far, California doesn't sound fun. Don't take that message from this. It was really fun, and I was enjoying my time. I made an honest living, the girls loved me, I was young, and I had things going for me. I even had the respect from the drug dealers, and the 9-5 folk alike, especially when they found out I was dating the baddest girl in the city. Her name was Nichole. I used to see her getting on the bus going to school. She was a senior and I was a year older than her. Everyone was too scared to talk to her, including myself. Then I used to start seeing her hanging out at the game room at the Bayfair Mall. I would go there just to play Mortal Kombat and NBA Jam. Finally, I gathered the nerve to talk to her. She had the prettiest hazel eyes and nice sized body proportions. Her school uniform is that which you see people dressing up as either for Halloween, or in an adult flick. It was like a Catholic school uniform. Well, she acted really snooty towards me, turned me down, and I walked away, not embarrassed, but mad. I went back to her and told her the truth. I said to her something to the effect of "you know, I see you all the time getting on the bus and always thought you were the most beautiful thing that I had ever seen. I was always too scared to talk to you, and when I thought I gathered the nerve to say something to you and would try to be where I thought you'd be, you wouldn't be there. I finally saw you at the same time as I had the nerve to talk to you, and you were rude. You didn't have to treat me that way. I don't even think you're pretty anymore after seeing how you are on the inside." I walked away and continued playing my game. Then just a couple minutes later, I saw a figure standing to my side, I looked, and it was Nichole, smiling. She apologized to me for how she treated me, introduced herself, and we exchanged numbers. It reminds me of that song by Mos Def/Yasim Bey, "Ms Fat Booty." We hung out with each other at the game room, then made plans to hang out later. We parted ways, but still stayed at the mall. The manager of the game room, a young Black guy with dreads approached me smiling. He said "I have to ask you, what were y'all talking about?" He and many many many many other guys have tried talking to her, and he has never seen anyone successful at it. He told me he saw the entire thing and how she came up to me. He just had to know my secret. I told him that I cursed her out and called her a stuck up bitch, which I actually did say to her. "AND THAT WORKED?" He asked as his eyes got big and jaw dropped. "Yeah, and she actually approached me after that." He said he saw the entire thing, but couldn't hear us. Awe man, he spread the word so quickly that I got Nichole's number. He saw me the next day, and I told him that I actually put in work that same night (don't act like you don't know what that means). He was so happy for me, yet jealous at the same time. Yes, he told all the guys, and Nichole didn't care, as she was in love with me and told people herself. Her mom even liked me and took Nichole to get a birth control patch put into her arm. Nichole lived at the apartments on E 14th, directly across from 165th Ave, and I would go to see her almost every day, immediately after her mom would leave for work, or go to her boyfriend's house. Her mom knew what was up, but didn't mind. It's crazy, because my girlfriend from Buffalo that I was cheating on, her dad knew the same thing, and I would come to pick his daughter up to take her to school just as he was leaving for work. No one was hiding anything, and they figured if it was going to be anyone, they didn't mind it being me. Both of their parents have actually said this to me, which leads me to this next story.

Bayfair mall, it may have been 1994. I'm just walking in the mall, minding my own business, and this older lady approaches me. By "older", I'm thinking about 40 or a little younger. Well, she approaches me, and she's clearly too old for me and she's by herself. I was working at the time doing surveys. She introduced herself to me, and I'm confused. Then she tells me she has a daughter about my age that would love me, and she wanted to introduce us. The lady asks me how much longer I would be at the mall. A couple of hours later, she brought her daughter there. She wanted me to take her daughter to the prom and that she would pay for the entire thing. She even said she would pay for my tuxedo and the hotel room. She wanted me to show her daughter a good time. She explained to me that her daughter was becoming sexually curious and she didn't like the guys that she was talking to, so if it was going to be someone, it should be me. She even said that she wanted me to get her daughter pregnant to ensure that I would always be around. We actually started making plans for the prom, but in all honesty, the mom scared me a bit from her straightforwardness. I also remember when this same thing happened before when I was working at Blockbuster Video. Something very similar happened, and this is the story....

February 14th, 1993. Yes, I remember the date. I cannot tell you how many girlfriends I had, nor can I tell you if I had any plans that day after work, but I did have to work. I'm using real names, as there is nothing bad in this story, and I'm hoping someone reads this that recognizes the names involved, as I would love to be back in contact with her, as friends of course... maybe. I'm at work and I'm behind the counter. At Blockbuster Video, the central location of where we performed customer service, we were surrounded on 3 sides, and the 4th side was actually the row of windows that face the parking lot. Basically, it wasn't hard for someone to sneak up on you. I was into whatever it is I was doing, and I could hear a soft voice behind me trying to get my attention. It was a short Black lady with shiny curly hair, and a younger girl standing next to her, looking very shy. She introduced herself as Marva, and her daughter Rashida. Marva was holding a relatively large combination of Teddy Bear, sitting on a wicker chair, which was also holding a small bouquet of roses, and one large rose, and a heart shaped box of chocolates. She said this was from her daughter to me for Valentine's Day. Yes, she actually spoke for her daughter mostly. She explained to me that they came often, and they loved my customer service and that I was always so friendly and helpful, and that her daughter had always had a crush on me. Rashida actually did eventually step in to speak and she introduced herself. She asked what I was doing later after work. I don't remember what my response was, as it was Valentine's Day, and I'm sure I had plenty of girls to take out, then again, I was always the type to ignore holidays and not put any thought into Valentine's Day. Marva interrupted my thoughts and insisted that I come over for dinner, watch a movie, and chat that night, and that I should just come straight over from work. They didn't live far, and it was only about a 20 to 30 minute walk, or a quick ride on the bus plus a 10 minute walk. She already had her name and number written on the card that accompanied the other gifts. I agreed to come over after work, we all smiled, and they left. I have to be honest with you. I had many girlfriends, and at this time, this was actually before the incident with the girl's mom at the mall. That didn't occur until just before Summer, so around May or June. Of course, I was the talk of the store at the time and I had to hear it from all of my co-workers.

I went to their house. I don't recall dinner, but we did eat and talk. We all got to know each other. They already decided that I was a part of their lives long before that day, and they already made their judgements about me. I don't think I was honest about having a girlfriend, and I probably was technically single at the time, but I was doing what an 18 y/o was supposed to do at the time...you know, live my life and have fun. So, it's February, so that means it gets dark early. Marva and Rashida insisted that I stay the night. I was honestly shocked at this point even though we were getting along so well. I was making excuses to not, but they were insistent. I can't really say they were excuses, because I didn't have clothes to change into, clean underclothes for the next day, toothbrush, or anything. Guess what? They had a new toothbrush for me and told me I can just leave in the morning. I stayed the night. I slept on the couch, and the two of them slept in their rooms. I actually think Rashida slept in the room with her mom where her mom could keep an eye on her just in case teenagers decided to be teenagers.

Rashida and I got along quite well, and I would go to visit her often. It was quite some time before we took the next step of actually becoming boyfriend and girlfriend. My apprehension was that she seemed to be too close to her mother. They were like conjoined twins that look nothing alike. Rashida is short with very long thick pretty hair. Marva was much lighter skinned and shared none of the same features. I didn't know if Rashida and I took so long to make it official because I wasn't used to someone having such a close relationship with their mother, or if it was another reason. But we kissed just outside of her door. Rashida said to me "You know I have to tell my mother we kissed." I didn't like that if I'm honest. The first thing I thought was, is she going to tell her mom about everything we do, or everything I may try to do with her? That scared me off. That was the quickest relationship I had ever been in, and I started coming around less often as I didn't know if this was something I was willing to pursue. This entire relationship of us being friends, me spending the night, sleeping on the couch, hanging out on the steps, lasted until I got homesick and moved back to Buffalo. I moved without telling her, but came back a year later. One day I gathered the nerve to go back to her house after moving back. She was quite upset with me and did not want to pursue a romantic relationship with me, and we just remained friends. She did slowly come around to being open to it, but I just hurt her so much that she just couldn't. I did eventually tell her about the trouble that I had gotten myself into while I was in Buffalo, and she was sorry for me that I did, and told me that would have never happened had I never left to begin with. She was right, and though it wasn't her fault, it was just the circumstances of how I grew up that I had poor communication skills of keeping in touch with people, or even saying bye. Thanks to social media, I did find her on Facebook in 2010 or 11. We didn't communicate much on it at all, and she was never really on it. We did exchange numbers though and we did talk, but I was bad with consistency. Fast forward to 2022, I found out where they were living and during home time from my job, as I worked on the road, I went to the house to surprise them. I found out that Marva had just passed away a couple of months before, and that Rashida moved to Los Angeles. The guy that was there said he'd contact her for me and give her my number. The lady inside the house is the one that told me about what happened. I felt, and still feel so badly for Rashida because I know that she and her mom, even this much time later, were inseparable. Last I talked to them was around 2014 and they were still as tight as can be, so I had no reason to believe that 8 years later, anything would have changed. Well, Rashida never contacted me, as I got the feeling that the boy didn't contact her and she had no idea I was looking for her. We were both living in the Los Angeles area at the time, so it would have been perfect if we were able to get together, even just to hang out or catch up. I did find her new Facebook page, but that has very little activity on it, and she has not read any of my messages I left her since finding the page.

I'm not going to detail all of my relationships that I've had as far as girlfriends go, as that book would be the size of a Bible, but I think it's important to bring up the girl that made me want to move to California in the first place. Lameka. I did mention her in my last book, and I won't get into much more detail than I did in that book. I'll just say, many people in other States have the same mindset, in California, if you tell them you're from New York, everything is in NYC. The same goes with New Yorkers. They think that if you live in California, that it's Los Angeles, and that Los Angeles, Oakland, and San Francisco , are all within a five minute walk of each other. Well, Lameka lived in Rialto, and I lived in Oakland and San Leandro during this time. In short, it was a long distance relationship, but our two families were close, which is how I met her in the first place. But whenever she was in town, she would contact me. Sometimes her aunt would contact me before Lameka would even know she was coming, and we'd meet up and make the best of our time. I did actually buy her a ring and we got engaged. It just never worked out. It's been about a year and a half since we've spoken because our personalities just clash in our older ages and we're just so much different. I'm not with this new idea of how men are supposed to be simps and do everything for someone that's not willing to do anything for me. Maybe one day I'll contact her and attempt to let it go and continue on as friends, but as of right now, I'm just not there yet. I do admit, our falling out was dumb and could have been avoided, but we both have our pride. I'm thinking that she's learning a lesson right now as well.

Going back to 1993 in California, working at Blockbuster, this was my first encounter of racial profiling by the police, and I've seen people sue and win ridiculous amounts of money for similar circumstances, but I was young and didn't even think about retribution. I closed the store, being the closing manager that night. The store closes at midnight, and the earliest we get out is around 1:00 a.m.. I still don't have a car at this point, and I made sure to close the store to catch the last bus that goes down Fruitvale and takes me to E 14th (now International Blvd). I'm sitting at the bus stop, and I get swarmed by three police cars with guns drawn on me. I'm light skinned, hightop fade haircut, wearing a long sleeved light blue button down collar shirt with a blue/yellow Blockbuster badge on it, and khaki pants. I'm asked questions about where I was, my name, etc.., I'm searched for weapons and drugs, made to get on the ground. I'm roughed up a bit. Not hard punches or anything, but I felt them stepping on my back, and the way I was thrown to the ground was totally uncalled for. I was told that I fit the description of someone that robbed an old lady for her purse. A squad car pulled up, and I could see the elderly White lady and hear her obviously upset and telling them that it wasn't me and that I did not fit the description. I can still hear it in my head "That's not what I told you. I told you he was wearing a red shirt, black pants, he was tall and dark skinned, and he had long dreadlocks." I can tell that she felt badly for me. During this encounter, I saw my bus coming. I let them know that it was the last bus and it was a long trip from MacArthur to E 14th St. The lady already told them that it wasn't me. The punk ass police kept me and purposely made me miss my bus. I asked them if they could at least give me a ride to E 14th, and they were angry with me for reasons I could not understand. The only racism I had experienced before then was being told that I was one of the good ones. I didn't even know it was racism at the time, but realized in my 20s that it was a snake tongued compliment. But I had to walk all the way to E 14th St, which at that time of night, was very dangerous.

I had no way of even blending in. I had "victim" written all over me, and the punk ass Oakland police were probably hoping something would happen to me on the way. Come to think of it, I probably should have gone back into the store and slept there. I would have risked losing my job, but I'd be alive at least. Well, I made it to E 14th St, but guess what happened! A car came speeding down the street and they started shooting at me. I ran behind the cement barrier, avoiding the barrage of bullets. It wasn't long after that that the 82L came and I was so excited to be on that bus. The next day at work, my manager, Danny, told me that I should have just stayed at the store.

This time working at the store, I also experienced my first bout of double standards and sexual harassment allegations. There was a girl working there that ended up dating the senior assistant manager's little brother. Before I knew they would end up dating, she would flirt with me. One time she told me that I had a nice butt. I, in return, told her she had pretty lips. I got called into the office the next day and scolded by my two senior managers. Evidently, they weren't told about how the girl initiated it by complimenting my butt. They called her and asked her about it and she admitted it, but she didn't get in trouble, and I still ended up with a sexual harassment allegation on paper. Wow, a man has to be careful. Crazy thing is, my senior manager's brother and I got along quite well, and he was super cool. I couldn't see how he could date her after knowing what she had done and accused me of. I even told him I didn't know they were dating. He knew she was no good and that I had no reason to lie or even try to talk to his girl or sexually harass her. He saw my girlfriend Nichole (from Bayfair Mall) who would catch the hour and a half bus trip every day to hang out with me at work. His girl couldn't hang with mine. I'm just sayin'.

I admittedly had to come back to this chapter to add this.

You'll see a bit of that as this is a memoir. I sometimes remember things later after being reminded, so forgive me if it doesn't seem to fit into the last thing you read. The United States is fairly large, and running into someone in your own city that you know is not uncommon, but running into that specific person you haven't seen in a long time is rare. Imagine moving across the country from New York to California, and hearing someone calling your name as you're walking down the street on your way to the mall. I hear a group of people calling me "BJ....BJ.....BJ....(short for Benjamin, not Benjamin Junior, as I'm not really a Junior)." I turn around, and I immediately recognize them. This time, someone spotted me and it was really me this time, as they weren't confusing me for my doppelgänger. They were members of a church that I used to attend. I dated quite a few members from their family, and they all knew it. It was like they were taking turns to date me. It was like a game for them. "I bet he likes me next" or, "I bet he likes me more than you", or maybe it was "I bet I can steal him from you." It turns out that they moved from Buffalo to San Leandro right after I made the move. This was hilarious to me. Last I heard, they eventually moved back to Buffalo. California became too expensive after a while. But running into them in San Leandro of all places was crazy. It reminded me of when I was catching a Greyhound across the country and I ran into a neighbor at an odd station in another State. Probably lower on the totem pole is when I moved to Antioch, CA., I used to go to the barbershop when I was feeling too lazy to cut my own hair. I would see this guy that looked just like Phife Dawg. He was a member of an iconic rap group called "A Tribe Called Quest." We became barbershop friends, and one of the reasons I would go to the barbershop was because of the camaraderie. I didn't learn until years later that he was actually Phife Dawg and he moved to Antioch. In fact, it wasn't until not long before he passed away that I learned it was him. This wasn't the only time I was friends with someone and I didn't know that they were famous. This next story should probably go in the next chapter, but I think it makes for a good segue. It was 2001. I used to live on Madison Street in Oakland. Madison is just a couple of blocks over from Lake Merritt. Let me first say this. It wasn't odd being friends with celebrities. I would go to the barbershop on Clay Street and all the football and basketball players would be there at one point or another, so the story I'm about to tell you is a bit different. So, I had knee surgery in 2001 and had to take some time off from work. I also gained a lot of weight. I had a new car that I could not drive and I could barely walk. There was a pizza shop right up the street at the corner on 14th Street. Across from there was a Taco Bell, and across from there was McDonald's. That's all I had to eat for several months, so I had some weight to lose. I remember my best friend and roommate's aunt got on me about how much weight I gained. Coincidentally, I just learned yesterday from my old friend that his aunt passed away a few days ago. Crazy story, but they used to take care of Don Johnson's dog. So, I used to go to the lake to walk around it and get my steps in to lose this weight. I made good money, but I'm not very attractive when I'm overweight, so I took it seriously. I actually had a girlfriend at the time, so I wasn't really looking for anyone, and believe it or not, I met her not long after my surgery while I was overweight. So, on the other side of the lake where downtown is separated and things get bad once you get away from the lake, is a luxury condominium building. Many if not most of the professional athletes that got traded to a Bay Area team, would live there. It's 1200 Lakeshore Ave. So after a few days of my routine of walking the lake, I would see this young lady in the same general area across the street at the lake. She would always look depressed. She was cute, but so was my girlfriend, and I had no intentions of cheating on her. I was just a nice guy, and I consider myself an empath. I couldn't walk by her anymore without speaking to her and finding out what was wrong, so the next time I saw her, I went out of my way to say hi to her. She would say hi, look down and go about her business. I would do the same. This happened for maybe a week. She wore the same basic style outfit every day. A Grey sweatsuit with white sneakers, a navy blue sweatsuit with white sneakers, etc... She did look familiar, but she really didn't look much different from the average cute girl in Oakland. I'm not saying she's average. I'm saying she blended in well with the other pretty girls, and she was trying to look plain. So a few days went by and it's the same "hi" response, then finally, she opened up a little more to me and didn't just give me the routine "hi" and looked down at her feet or at the lake. I honestly don't remember exactly what she said, but it was probably something like "How are you? Keep it up!" I do remember suggesting she walk the lake with me, and to my surprise, she said she'll walk a little of it with me. She told me that if she stops walking, for me to keep walking, because she didn't want her boyfriend to think she was cheating on him. I knew immediately that she was in a bad relationship and she was probably dating a baller. You put 1 and 1 together... 1200 Lakeshore, pretty girl always out front...Dating a controlling baller.

    I asked her name, and she told me her name. I will tell you her real name at the end of the story. I have to build a little suspense. I told her my name and I informed her that I have a girlfriend and that I was faithful. I told her I just wanted to be friends and hopefully cheer her up because she was always looking so depressed. Side note, if you think you know who I'm talking about, send me an email and tell me you figured it out. Be honest. There are no prizes involved. Sometimes we would go to the bird sanctuary and watch the birds and kids play. This entire relationship with her lasted maybe two months, but we became close. We never exchanged pager numbers, we never made plans to meet up anywhere, we were like the fellas at the barbershop. "I'll see you next time it's time to get chopped and trimmed" type deal. One day, I didn't see her. I felt something was wrong, but I couldn't be sure. Hey, sometimes people switch up their routine. Several days would go by without seeing her, then a couple of weeks later, Jonathan and I were at a club/pool hall on 12th Street. It was a popular spot for the Ethiopians to frequent. We played a couple of games of pool, had a drink. I'm a light drinker and don't drink much at all to be honest, and we're just sitting down, chillin' on the couch style seating. Jonathan points out that we're sitting right across from Andre Rison. Another face I put a name to that I saw often. Not even two minutes later, Jonathan points across the room in an entirely different section which was empty except for one person and says... "Look, there's Left Eye." I looked, and Lisa and I locked eyes on each other. That was the moment I knew that I was friends with Lisa...as in Lisa "Left Eye" Lopes, from TLC. Look y'all, I'm bad with faces. I see so many people and have worked with so many people, everyone just looks familiar. Plus, I've never been the groupie type. This was 2001, and in the 90s, I knew everyone and had everyone's pager number that was famous in the Bay Area. Famous people would recognize me before I recognized them. I couldn't tell you the actor's name on the big screen to save my life. That's how bad I was and am with faces. I get tunnel vision in public, and I'm not being funny or exaggerating. So Lisa and I locked eyes. She looked so disappointed that we saw each other and she couldn't speak to me. I think she was even more disappointed that she knew I figured out who she was at that moment, as she saw Jonathan point her out to me as I looked up. She saw me before I saw her. I think she observed me in my natural habitat, hanging with my best friend, not talking to any other girls. She must have found solace in having a male friend that not only wasn't trying to get in her pants, but just enjoyed being around her and didn't know she was famous. She did tell me her real first name. I never asked her last name, and she only knew me as "BJ." She never told me what she did for a living, as I assumed she was just living off of her baller boyfriend. She used to tell me that her boyfriend was abusive and wouldn't let her talk to anyone. She told me that she couldn't even speak to any of his friends or hang around them when they went out, and here I was, witnessing it first hand. At the time, I told her I had lots of friends and could handle her boyfriend for her. I told her she needed to get away from him and not let money be the reason she was staying, and that she could make her own money. I remember telling her I get the feeling from her that she has a lot of potential and I know for a fact that she could make it on her own, and that she didn't need a baller boyfriend. I even suggested that she meet my best friend and that he was a really good guy, and that he was single. She wasn't interested in dating anyone, and she was confused about the relationship she was in.

That night was the last time I saw Lisa and we could only speak with our eyes. I feel as though we read each other's minds. Call it hubris, but I honestly feel as though if we had met under different circumstances, that we could have been more than friends. I definitely could be wrong. Sometimes friends are just friends and things are better that way. We had a sweet relationship, and I honestly wouldn't have changed it for the world. I knew Lisa. I didn't know Lisa Lopes. I never met Left Eye. Lisa was one of my closest friends ever, just over a 2 or 3 month period. Fast forward to April 25th, 2002...I'm back working at the auto factory in Fremont, not far from where I used to go to Hammer's dance studio. I was a Team Leader and would have to chase defects down the line to repair them, which the vast majority of the time meant "tapping a bolt." That's when someone puts a bolt in at the wrong angle and it doesn't go in correctly, so I have to take the electric drill and create a new hole and fit a new bolt into the hole. Because of this, we had to wear bump caps and eye protection. Eye protection wasn't foolproof. A metal shaving ended up piercing my left eye and I had to be sent to the ophthalmologist to have the metal pulled out. Lisa passed away between 4 and 6 hours before the metal shaving lodged into my eye, and I gained solace in believing it was her saying goodbye to me. I may have been her only friend since her fame, that was friends with Lisa, not the person that everyone else knew, including her family. I sometimes wonder if she ever wrote about me in a journal. I would love to meet the other members of TLC so that I could share my story with them.

CHAPTER NINE
THE INDUSTRY

The first time I was actually interested in getting into the music industry was when I moved to California. I didn't have a lot of hopes and aspirations in Buffalo and there were very few artists in Buffalo. I remember Joe Public and they were pretty successful. There's a rapper named Tracey Lee that was born in Buffalo and spent much of his youth there, but then moved somewhere else, and then to Philadelphia. He never laid any claims to Buffalo. Rick James is from Orchard Park, which is a suburb of Buffalo. He was a friend of the family. I remember he used to come over to my grandmother's house on Minnesota Ave. I always thought he was scary looking. My family went to his funeral, but I was in California and couldn't make it. Now there's Griselda, which made a big splash into the music industry and is credited for bringing real street rap back to the industry, and now New York City is laying claim to Buffalo as its own. I'm willing to bet Tracey Lee started mentioning he's actually from Buffalo after Griselda hit the scene. The first rap I ever wrote was when I was maybe 10 years old. I wrote it with my sister, Belle. There was a guy who lived a few doors down from us that had a brother not much older than he, and two younger twin sisters. His name was Ed, but he went by the name "Music Man." He became a truck driver and a cab driver and was murdered while driving his cab. Belle and I were in the downstairs bathroom when we wrote the rhyme to battle against Music Man. Here are the lyrics... "So you say your name is Music Man, you go around rappin' the best you can. You sound like little boys rhymin' up the street, if you really want something to say, just repeat...Little boys sound much better than you. They make you look and sound so through. You know I'm right, don't say I'm wrong, I finished my rap so you can start your song." He was quite surprised by the witty little battle rap lyrics coming from such young kids. He didn't even have a comeback for us as we recited the lyrics together from memory. I grew up listening to WBLK, which in the 80s played all the hits. It didn't matter the genre. You could hear anything from Dolly Parton and Kenny Rogers, to New Edition, to Boy George, to Lionel Richie, to LL Cool J, and whatever was a hit, all on the same station, within the same hour or radio segment. I remember that Lionel Richie was the only secular singer my grandmother would listen to. She would blast his music loudly. I found out it was because we were related to him. I never met him, but my cousins would go to California every Summer and he was one of the people they would visit, at least this is what I was told. I was sad that they would never take my sister and I, and during the 3 year stint I lived in Buffalo, my cousin told me that her parents tried to take us there, but my grandmother wouldn't let us go. Maybe she knew Lionel Richie would try to adopt us after hearing our story like he did Nicole Richie. The group that got me interested in rap was Beastie Boys. When I heard them, I was excited and had to hear more. They just sounded like they were having so much fun and were really just being themselves. No need for me to go down their track list. Their entire "License to Ill" album was amazing and had no skippers, which meant you could just let it play and rock out. I thank my grade school friend, Kyle, for dubbing the tape for me in the 4th grade, which I took home and painted it multicolor with my Aunt Sonya's fingernail polish. She came home and saw me playing with her nail polish and wasn't even mad at me. She laughed and just let me finish doing what I was doing. I was at the same desk that my aunt that I hated, made me memorize the Bible. After the Beastie Boys, it was LL Cool J, then Rakim and Big Daddy Kane. I liked Run DMC, but I wasn't that big on them. My uncle El was a big Run DMC fan and I didn't want to copy him. Run DMC and Knight Rider belonged to him. I also had a disdain for Adidas because my grandmother would spend my money on buying Uncle El every colorway of Adidas there was.

Tied for my biggest musical memory out of Buffalo, was with my uncle, Roger. We had a full day of fun planned. It was a Friday, and it was the first day that Boyz N the Hood hit the theaters. We went to see the movie, and that very same day, Ice Cube and the Lynch Mob were performing at the Connecticut Street Armory, which we had first come/standing room only tickets to. Yo-yo was also performing, which was Ice Cube's artist. We got to the Connecticut Street Armory super early, like maybe 3 or 4 hours before the show was set to start. We wanted to ensure that we were at the front, right next to the stage. We were there so early, they hadn't even begun setting up and doing sound check yet. We were standing outside the doors at the top of the steps when we saw a white limousine pull up. A young Black guy hopped out of the driver's seat. He didn't look like a limo driver. My uncle said to me that he thinks he's Sir Jinx, who was part of the Lynch Mob and also had a big role in the movie we just saw. He opened the trunk of the limo and started to take cases of pop (we called it pop in Buffalo, but it's also soda or soda pop elsewhere) from out of the trunk and stack them onto the ground. Uncle Roger and I ran down to the limo and asked if we could help. We were honestly just being helpful, at the same time, it would help us to gain favor with the Lynch Mob. Maybe we thought we'd become honorary members or something. We helped unload the limo and carry everything inside. We thought it was strange that not only was Sir Jinx driving the limo, but he was also doing manual labor. This let us know that not everything in the industry is as it appears. They put in real work and tried to save on budgets as much as they could.

Ok, so the show is almost about to start, but the doors weren't open yet, but my uncle and I were on the inside while the crowd was lining up outside. Our efforts in helping Sir Jinx paid off. I also remember while we were there waiting while they were setting up the stage, and almost time to start letting people in, Ice Cube was highly upset at Yo-Yo for not being there. He was right next to us, but on the stage asking where she was. He was saying how he was tired of her not being on time for shows. Ice Cube is one of the people that I wish I had the opportunity to see and talk to again as an adult. I have a screenplay I would love to forward to him that I believe only he could pull off. One day I will get that chance. I do have to complete it, but it's already written in my head, and much of it is already written. It is completely unique and no one has made a movie based on this premise. If I were to meet him again, I would lead with the story of him performing the day his first movie released, in my hometown. I met two other celebrities in Buffalo, but that was later in life. I do remember Uncle Roger dated a Canadian rapper named "Michie Mee." She didn't do well and sold maybe 3 albums. I'm really not kidding. I remember years ago once the internet became a thing, and it was around the time of Napster, I looked her up on Soundscan and it said a total of 3 albums sold.

As for the other two famous people I met in buffalo, the story is this, I used to do Lyft and Uber as a side gig when my daughter and I moved to Buffalo for a 3 year stint. I picked up Angela Kinsey from the Buffalo Airport, and the very next day, I picked up Kenya Barris from the same airport. This was either the biggest coincidence, or they were in town for the same event or a meeting. Buffalo isn't known for celebrities visiting, and I picked two of them up. I had a very interesting conversation with Kenya. I knew he was someone I saw on television, but I couldn't put my finger on where it was I knew him from. I recognized Angela Kinsey immediately though, as I had to ban my daughter from watching The Office because she would binge watch it. That wasn't the problem. The problem was, after she binge watched it, she would binge watch it again, then again. Then I remembered who the guy was. I ended up watching "Black-ish" for the first time, and that's when I realized who it was I was conversing with. He said to me "I see why you have a 5 star rating with so many rides." It was because I went above and beyond for him, but not because I knew he was famous, but because that's what I did for most of my passengers. If they needed to be let off somewhere other than the app indicated, as long as it was fairly close, I did them that favor. I also made suggestions on where to eat and where to stay away from.

Ok, back to musical memories from Buffalo. This goes back to the RAVE program I mentioned earlier. I dated a young lady that was part of a group that did En Vogue covers. That's the extent of that story. "What's so special about that?" you may ask. Well, it's because when I moved to California, I ended up meeting En Vogue and seeing them often, as I worked directly with them, and it wasn't long after I dated the girl that did nothing but En Vogue covers. So I went from the copy, to interacting with the real deal. I'll get to those stories later, because oh boy do they get really interesting.

I can't recall the exact year, but it was somewhere around the height of MC Hammer's reign. My sister, we'll call her "Shawna," was dating one of Hammer's lead dancers. I believe his name is Randy. Shawna knew I was interested in getting into the music industry, and figured she would help me by having me meet up with Randy while they were rehearsing at Hammer's dance studio in Fremont, CA. His main office was just around the front of the same building. I caught the BART to the studio and met up with Randy and he introduced me to a few people. This is when I met a female dancer. I'll call her Jameila. I didn't introduce myself to her. She instead introduced herself to me. This was because I caught her attention. How this happened was, there was an ice cream truck that was outside, and Jameila's daughter was there, and she was maybe 2 at the time, maybe 3. I bought her a Tweety Bird ice cream popsicle. Jameila smiled and thanked me. We then began to talk, and we exchanged phone numbers. Like I stated previously, I was "Mr Steal Your Girl" long before Trey Songz. I didn't have a car at the time, so this was definitely before 1996. I honestly believe it may have been around 1992, but I digress. She was driving either a Geo Tracker that was a combination of turquoise and fuchsia, or it may have been a Suzuki Sidekick. We hung out a couple of times and we even hung out at the house that Hammer was either renting or owned, that he had his out of town dancers staying at. I don't recall why we never really ended up dating, because we got along pretty well. I actually did learn why just a couple of years ago after reuniting with another more famous dancer of his, and she put us in touch with each other after I told her the story. It was a member of a group called "Oaktown's 357" that I met in the dance studio. I saw her as a friend suggestion on Facebook and we had a mutual friend that is a Sheriff in Texas, and he also has a famous YouTube channel where he races his Dodge Demon against others. I sent her a message because she looked familiar and her name was familiar. I asked where she knew our mutual friend from. That's when I learned she was a member of the rap/dance group. I told her the story of how I briefly dated someone else she used to perform with, and when I gave her the details, she immediately knew exactly who I was talking about, and she gave me her name, because I mixed her name up. I was close, but I had it wrong. Hey, it's been 30 years. I sent Jameila a message, expecting a friendly reunion, and now I knew why we never dated. It wasn't because she was mean back then like she was being now. It was because she was dating another one of Hammer's dancers at the time, and she was either in denial, or she truly didn't remember me. She told me that her boyfriend lived at the house with her and that she never picked me up in her car. She did say that she didn't understand how I had so many details right, such as her daughter, the color of her car, the house she lived in, etc., but we couldn't have dated because she had a boyfriend and she'd never cheat on him. She was actually quite nasty to me, but I remained nice and said we never kissed or were intimate, but she had her facts wrong and she just didn't remember. We agreed to disagree, and our mutual friend apologized to me and said she doesn't know what's wrong with Jameila and that she would talk to her. She did say she obviously believes my story, otherwise I wouldn't have had the facts straight, especially the details about her car. This is because there's no way I would know the car she drove to such detail and the description of her house, inside and out, unless she picked me up and took me there. I only hung with Randy at the studio. Anyways, you're probably wondering if I met Hammer. Yes, and this is when I discovered he wasn't some soft and friendly candy rapper. He was not who I expected him to be. There were a few occasions that he kicked me and a few other people out of the studio. This wasn't because he was intentionally being an asshole. It's because he said they were working on a unique routine and he didn't want it leaked. It was kind of too late. I already saw all of the routines they were working on and even practiced with them, but I understood. Hammer even extended me an olive branch and let me go to the front where his record label office was located. He truly just didn't want his secret routine leaked, or maybe we were a distraction. Whatever the reason, I understood and didn't take it personally. One of my favorite stories I used to tell people is how I noticed he was spending a lot on his staff, long before his financial troubles. Like I said, he was paying for the housing of all of his out of town dancers, and I learned more recently that he was also paying for the housing for his local dancers. He didn't provide them with money or food, and they were sleeping on the floor and were living poor, because they were, but they all had cell phones, which Hammer paid for. He paid for their transportation to and from shows and practices also. He had a van and a driver that would make the rounds. I never thought he'd go broke from that though. It had to be someone stealing from him, because yes, cell phone bills at that time were a couple thousand dollars a month, but if you add that up, it's maybe $20 to $40 thousand per month he was paying in cell phone bills. I only personally saw two of the houses he was renting for his staff, and they were both in nice areas. One in Oakland, and the other in Fremont. Those two combined were maybe $4 thousand per month, if that. The housing market wasn't crazy back then like it is now.

My next intro into the music industry was when I started doing a type of internship for Thomas McElroy and Denzel Foster. They were the founders and producers of En Vogue, which ties into the story of me dating the girl in the cover group.

It's 1995 and I now live on 10th Ave in Oakland. I worked at Trader Joe's in Emeryville and drove a 1977 Chevrolet Impala station wagon. I loved that car, but I didn't take good care of it. I don't know why, but I just never got the oil changed and the engine ended up seizing on me. No one ever taught me about maintaining cars, and my 1993 Ford Ranger before that, I didn't have long enough to ever have to go get maintenance on it other than once. I remember getting into it with the guy at the shop because he gave me a price, but then charged me almost double. This was because my truck was a 4 cylinder, so he quoted me for 4 spark plugs. My truck had 2 spark plugs per cylinder, and I felt as though he should stick to his quote. My station wagon was an 8 to 9 passenger vehicle. It had a bench seat in the front, a bench seat in the middle, and a bench seat facing the rear of the car. The rear tailgate had a window that rolled down electronically, and the gate would swing open, or flip down, and the seats could be folded into the floor. It is by far, the most versatile and practical vehicle I ever owned. I remember we went 9 people deep to Reno so that two of my roommates could get married. One of my roommates, I'll name her Tamala. Tamala's mother worked in the music industry and would put on shows together with her partner, Leila Steinberg. Tamala knew I wanted more experience in the music industry, so she got me an internship at the record label she was working for. She was an assistant for Leila. This worked out for Tamala also because she didn't have a car and we could carpool together. If the name sounds familiar, or maybe if it isn't familiar to you at all, Leila is the one that discovered Tupac and was his manager. Atron Gregory later was his road manager, and he and Leila worked together to manage Tupac. For some odd reason, the history books and Google search seems to leave Leila out of it, but if you do just a little digging, you'll see that it was Leila that discovered him and made him famous. A small coincidence, I have a niece and nephew that are relatives of Shock G from Digital Underground, and it was their dad that introduced me to Little Dee, whom I will mention later. There's a reason why I mention anyone here. I don't just name drop, though this section is partially about name dropping. It's more so detailing my experiences and memories in the music industry.

So like Tamala, I'm a personal assistant for Leila Steinberg, who aside from her management role for a few artists and her being the creator of Mic Sessions, which is how she met Pac, was the President of Alien Records. Alien Records was a subsidiary of Y? Entertainment. Greenhouse Records was the mainstream subsidiary of Y? Entertainment. Alien records was the Hip-Hop/R&B side. The owners of the label were Thomas McElroy and Denzel Foster, as I previously mentioned. I did everything for this company. Everything from fetching bagels and coffee, keeping things tidy, being Leila's personal driver, and an all around "gopher." Go for this... go for that...After a while, I ended up doing some ghostwriting and chaperoning. We had one act that went by the name of "Premiere." They were the group that Tommy and Denny invested the most time and money into. They were considered the Filipino En Vogue, and no one minded having that moniker. They had one of the highest tech music videos of the time for "Something About You." That video shoot was long and intense, and this is when I first met the girl's parents. Two of them were sisters, and one was a cousin I believe. I might have that wrong, but they were all related. I remember meeting the parents of the two sisters. Please don't ask me which was which. There was GiGi, the youngest and the one that received the most attention and had the biggest fanbase, then there was Leslie, and then Alicia. I believe it was Leslie and Alicia that were sisters. Their parents never let them go anywhere unless they themselves were there with them. They had to be at all the shows, video shoots, and any events they held, such as autograph signings. It was during the video shoot for the aforementioned song, that I got to know their parents, and I recall them telling everyone that they were fine with not being there as long as I was there to chaperone them. I was honored that their parents trusted me to that extent. That wasn't the only success that I had during the shooting of that video. I also made a couple of key suggestions for the video that they ended up using. I wasn't loud about it as to try to gain attention or glory. I quietly went to the director and told him what I saw, and what my suggestion was. He smiled, got that look in his face, and changed it to the way that I suggested. The director then wanted me around and asked my opinion on other things for the video and even asked if I would be around for the next video shoot. I was on cloud 9. I got along very well with all the groups. Premiere loved having me around, as I was still young and they were able to have fun with their parents not around and I wasn't so strict, but kept them safe and still would go with them to the local store or wherever. I was fun but not intrusive, yet I did my job. It was a delicate balance that I pulled off. There was another group by the name of No ID. I was super cool with all of them, and we'd talk outside of music and we often would hang out.

Ok, so you're probably wondering if I knew Tupac. Yes, and no. We weren't friends, we weren't enemies, and I didn't even know him because of Leila. We actually just ran in a couple of the same circles and would often be at some of the same house parties, and we had Leila in common. He knew I worked for Leila, so he kept his distance because he probably didn't want me snitching on him to her about what it was he was doing and where he was at or who he was with. I don't even think Leila knows I knew him outside of her. We never ever ever talked about him outside of quick casual conversation. He stayed at a large luxury apartment complex where she lived in the same complex, and Mac Mall also lived in that complex. I won't name the location, but it was very nice with a very nice view of the Bay. I'm not going to tell any Tupac stories as he is not here with us and I'm not going to get into conspiracy theories, as there are things that I know, but I just cannot discuss...EVER. This is out of respect for friends and family, and generally because I want to live. The only thing I will say is, I was driving my car, listening to KMEL when they announced that Pac had been shot in Vegas. I was driving up MacArthur Blvd just past Fruitvale (right near where I was harassed by the police), and yes, Fruitvale is the street in which the Fruitvale Station incident occurred with the BART police murdering Oscar Grant. Once I heard the announcement on the radio, the first person I thought of was Leila, as she and Pac were extremely close. Pac wrote a book of poems, and yes, they were dedicated to Leila. He had a great appreciation for her because of everything she has done for him. It was mere moments after the KMEL announcement that Leila paged me 911. I knew immediately what it was about and why she was paging me. I went to the nearest payphone and called her. She was at a nail salon and asked that I come get her to take her to the airport so that she could fly out to Vegas. I stopped what I was doing and I picked her up. On the way to the airport, she redirected me to take her to the label, which was located right across from the Oakland Coliseum. The building where the record label was located had a sign on the top that said "Unisys", so I called it the Unisys building. Leila and I showed up, and there were about 4 others, including Tamala that showed up to the empty office as Leila went into her office and talked to Afeni, Pac's mom. She was on speakerphone, but then Leila had us all leave and close the doors so that she could speak to Afeni in private. That's all I'm going to share about Pac. If you ever see me in person, do not ask me anything else, as this is one of the things that will have me leave the chat.

We still continued to work for the label, and Leila, along with Tamala's mom (I never knew her first name) would still throw shows for grade schools, high schools, and junior colleges on

Thursdays. En Vogue were regular performers, Mac Mall would make appearances, along with several artists from a label called "Cell Block Records." After Pac's death, Leila would have one of her daughters read poems from his book of poetry. This was before it was actually a book. This was actually just a collection of poems that he wrote and gave to Leila. It became a book much later. I Coincidentally ran into Leila in 2023 in Lodi, CA. This was odd because Lodi is a town that you pass by. Leila lives in the Los Angeles area, and I live in the Bay Area. We both happened to be charging our cars at the Tesla charging station at a truck stop/gas station there. I didn't see her at the charging station, but inside the store. I was standing in line, and a guy, maybe about an inch taller than me, thin muscular build and bald head, almond shaped yellow eyes, darker skin yelled "Leila, we're next, hurry up!" Of course when I heard the name, I thought of the Leila I knew, but in no way did I think it was her. Then she walks to the line. I honestly think she saw me and was avoiding me. Her oldest daughter was there and she was standing in a manner, smiling, halfway between the entrance, the mystery man in line ahead of me, and where Leila was, hiding in one of the aisles. I think Leila told them she recognized me and was trying to avoid me, but they weren't playing her game with her. I just got that feeling. Her daughter and the guy were both looking at me, smiling, then here comes Leila with the "damn, I'm busted" look and smile on her face. I said "Leila?" She said "yeah" I said "Leila Steingberg?" She said "that's me!" We hugged, chatted, went outside to the charging stations, took a picture together, and went our way after charging our cars. She said she was on her way to a celebration in Rosa, which is short for Rosarito, Mexico. All I can say is, the gentlemen she was with spoke with a Jamaican accent, but he looked awfully familiar. AWFULLY familiar, and I'll leave it at that. He didn't join us in the photo op and Leila insisted we take the picture with her phone and she would text it to me, which she did. She was careful to angle it so that her male acquaintance was not seen. I probably said too much already, but it's stressful not being able to say what it is you really want to say. I respect my friends too much.

I did witness quite a few things during this run. People, celebrities or not, are human. They feel just like we do. They stress, have financial problems, have growing pains, lost friends and loved ones, etc... I don't feel too bad for what I'm about to divulge, and this is because for one, I'm not telling you anything that wasn't made public already. I'm only telling you this from my perspective because I was there for some of it. Here's just one of the stories involving the group as a whole. One day, we're doing an outside show in Richmond, CA. This was at Richmond High School. It was nice out and everyone showed up that was supposed to show up, except for Ray J. I'll tell his short story really quickly. At this time, no one even knew that Brandy had a brother. When people realized she had a brother, he was known as Brandy's little brother. He didn't have a name. For whatever reason, Mrs. Johnson, Tamala, and Leila decided to book him, as his team was trying to get him some exposure. This wasn't odd in the 90s. Just a few years before that, I met Usher on MacArthur Blvd across the street from Blockbuster at a mom & pop record shop. We played Street Fighter together. Ok, so Ray J decided not to show up. I heard the phone call. He literally said that he was too big of a name to be doing little high school shows, so though he was in town, he just decided not to show up. Guess what? NOBODY CARED...AT... ALL. The show went on. Mac Mall was there, En Vogue was there, Holly Robinson-Peete was there, along with many other local artists. It was a packed basketball court. I sat right next to Holly Robinson-Peete and her best friend from En Vogue, Terry Ellis. We were sitting on the bleachers outside. I thought I had a good enough rapport to speak to them, all of us being people and all. I threw in my 2 cents on the petty conversation that they were having. Yes, they were talking to each other, not me, but we're outside and I figured they knew who I was, being I'm at every event, helping set up and making sure everything goes as planned, and being the gopher for whatever Leila, Tamala, and Mrs. Johnson said do, or for the talent if they needed anything. They both looked at me, and I can't recall which one of them said it, but she said "who is he?", then went on to ignore me. I didn't have many interactions with Holly Robinson, but I figured Terry Ellis would be more friendly. I never knew her to act nasty, except for what I heard they did to Dawn Robinson. They were all there if I recall correctly, but don't quote me on that, but they didn't sit with each other and you could cut the tension with a knife. I knew what was going on in the inner circle. I used to go to the studio where they recorded on Arlington Ave. Come to think of it, it may have been either 57th, 58th or even 59th Ave. in Oakland. It was so long ago and I haven't been there in so long. It's one of those side streets off of Martin Luther King Blvd. though. It was a big brick building that looked run down and abandoned, but it wasn't. It had lots of expensive equipment in there and one of the world's most renowned groups recorded their albums there. I knew the engineer, Michael personally. I introduced him to my sister, Belle. Just a friendly reminder that I changed my sister's name for her protection.

Let me tell you the story of Belle moving to California from Buffalo, New York. I honestly can't remember the year as I have nothing to relate it to in order for me to recall exactly, but it was around 1997. En Vogue and Premiere both had albums released that year and we had a really big album release party. I believe it may have been a joint party, but it could have just been one of the groups and members from the other group were there. You have to give my memory room for error, but the main story is still there.

Everyone was there. I'm going to have to go backwards a bit, maybe about a year, and I'm going to have to jump back and forth in time a couple of more times in this story as I'd rather make connections with events rather than a chronological story. My family in Buffalo was bad at keeping in contact with me. I admittedly was bad too, but it was still me that always initiated contact. My aunt, you know, the one I didn't like, would contact me every now and then and I would fuss at my sister for giving her my number, because I would have to keep changing it. So, I would call and brag about all the celebrities I knew and worked with. No one believed me. For whatever reason, they always believed me to be a liar. One day, Tommy and Denny held a meeting in which we all at the label had to attend. It seemed they had their plates full and needed help with writing and producing. I was called into this meeting because it was recently brought to their attention that I was an excellent writer and producer. Not even Leila knew that I was musically inclined until Tamala told her and she asked to hear one of my songs, which I obliged, and I was about to be the next artist signed to Alien Records. They were more so impressed that I wasn't trying to push a demo tape down their throats like everyone else was doing, and I was just there to work, learn, and make connections. They were also impressed at how I helped with videos and how I handled things with the talent, so this made me feel good that I was finally called in on a huge meeting...one of the meetings that I was usually on the other side of the huge double doors for. They asked if I was willing to help and if I knew of other people that could come in and help them knock some of these projects out. Well of course I did, so I told them about my uncle, Arnold. They told me to use the company phone and call him, and to let him know they would fly him out, all expenses paid, and he could be involved with some projects. I told them that Arnold was a professional songwriter, producer, and played bass, guitar, and keyboards, and he himself had been signed to recording deals. I called my grandmother's number, which was the central hub for contacting anyone in the family. My cousin Serina answered the phone. I told her I was looking for Arnold and to pass him the good news that I had landed him the biggest musical opportunity of his life. She sounded like she didn't believe me but said she'd pass the message along to him. I told her of the urgency and that all expenses would be paid. I to this day, don't know if she actually gave him the message. I called back a few days later to see if she had passed the message along to him. She said that she did, but he wasn't interested and he was only focused on his construction business, painting houses and doing renovations. Oh well, we moved on without him. Mind you, a lot of the family wasn't speaking to me because of my relationship with my grandmother, and others weren't speaking to me because I turned down being the heir to all those millions of dollars and lost them the opportunity to extort it from me maybe. It could be any of those reasons, but it also may have been that Uncle Arnold had too much pride to catch his big break from his little nephew. It was always him that took me to shows, but now it was me that had the bigger connections and opportunities. Fast forward to 2004, I talked to Arnold and asked him about it, and he honestly looked as though he never even got the message, but then stumbled on his words and said he was busy working at the time. I think he didn't get the message. My family was clicked up and feuding with each other, and Serina and Arnold probably weren't getting along. Okay, so back to my sister, Belle. It was not long after that phone call to Serina that she decided to move her and her son out here. This was when I introduced her to Michael, and she was Michael's date to the album release party. Belle contacted the family in Buffalo and informed them that her brother BJ wasn't lying and that I actually did know the people I said I knew, and that she even attended the album release party, and was now dating a big time studio engineer. Suddenly, people wanted to keep in contact with me and even wanted to come out to visit me.

Now let's go back in time just a few months. I was also working at the college bookstore. I was a Peralta student, but even before then, my niece's dad got me a job at the bookstore he was the manager of. I wanted to use the experience and connections I had gained, so I put together a talent search to be held at Laney College. I did everything the legit way. I got the licensing and permission to use the campus and their equipment. I made flyers, passed them around and hung them up throughout. I even got Leila, Tommy and Denny to agree to give the winner a chance to sign to the label. Several people showed up to the search and I was interested in a couple of acts, but no one really blew me away. It was either the next day or the day after the talent search that a guy came down there looking for me. His name is Damian. He handed me a tape and said he managed an artist, but she couldn't make the talent search and he asked me if I could listen to her tape. I'll tell you now that Damian and his artists are both friends of mine on Facebook to this day, so anything bad I say, we all got over it and there is no bad blood between us.

I listened to the demo, and I was blown away. She still has one of the top five voices I have ever heard in my entire life. She ranks up there with Whitney and Mariah. I had a book that I studied inside and out that taught about recording contracts, management, production contracts, advances, etc. I believe it was called "All You Need To Know About the Music Industry." That book is almost obsolete today, but I knew my stuff because of it. I told him I could get her a deal, but she had to sign my contract. I told Damian that I understood he was her manager, but as my talent search said, I was looking for an act to manage and produce, which meant I would have to take over the helm as Kenya's manager. I did tell him he could co-manage her, but outside of regular business, such as making sure she performed her obligations to me and the label. He agreed. I drafted a contract. It was a simple and to the point contract that would give me 15% of all monies earned. The industry standard for new artists was 20%, so I was being quite fair. Also, this contract was management, production, and as a writer, all combined, which was a big discount for her. This would leave Kenya enough to pay Damian out of her pockets, as normally she would have to pay for all of that separately, adding up to about 60%, leaving her with 40%. Days, then weeks went by, and they never returned the signed contract to me. One day, I got a call from Leila, and she called the bookstore directly. She asked for me, and my boss knew it was important. He knew who she was and he was excited that she called looking for me. I was like a little celebrity there. This is exactly verbatim what she said to me. "BJ, did homechick sign your contract?" I responded no. "Well she's here at the label trying to talk to us directly. I told her we don't talk to the talent and they need to have their managers talk to us and that she needs to sign your contract before we sign her and before she can step foot at the label." I contacted Damian and he wasn't happy. I'm not sure if this was a move he orchestrated, but either way, it wasn't going to fly. She never signed my contract, and the word was put out that she does bad business, and no labels or anyone that was reputable, wanted to work with her. She was blackballed. Before any of this happened, Damian wanted to confirm that my connections were real, so he asked if he could meet Leila. I talked to Leila, and she set up the meeting. Leila was excited to sign Kenya. She really wanted her on the label, and they all thought she'd be the next biggest thing even though she was lying about her age. I think she was trying to pass herself off as 24, but she was really 30 or something. So Damian and I get to the label and when we walk into Leila's office, she's actually listening to my music. I was honestly shocked. She was really into my music. It was a song I wrote and produced called "Black Plague", and it was along the lines of Nas and Lauryn Hill's "If I Ruled the World." Damian started fanboying out and tried to get Leila to listen to his music. She immediately stopped him <u>and</u> asked "Is this you I'm listening to in the tape player? Okay, because that's the only rapper we're signing right now." That was the first time I heard that I was being signed. Tommy and Denny spoke to me more and we had a good rapport. I don't know how to explain it. I wasn't the gopher anymore. I was the talent, producer, writer, co-director, manager, etc... My high on cloud 9 would be short lived. You see, the label was having financial problems. I don't recall, but it was either Tommy or Denny that had a $20k/mo mortgage, which was ridiculous for the time period. They had been working hard to pull in outside investors and was close to a deal, but it fell through. They began selling off the acts. I couldn't tell you the financials, but No ID was sold. I remember them specifically because I was really friends with them. No ID is of no relation to the Chicago producer by the same moniker. Things would just not happen for me. This wouldn't be the only time I was so close to making something big happen, only for outside forces to pull my opportunity away. I remember years ago trying to find information on Y? Entertainment, Alien Records, etc., and finding it. Now if you look up the name of the companies, some other companies come up, but they're no relation to the ones I worked for. The only hint of them ever existing is if you look up the group "Premiere" and see the credits for their hit single and video "Something About You."

Now that I've detailed some of the experiences that I've had with the record label, I will now get into a couple of stories involving specific people that I've come across during this time. Dawn Robinson, the Black Sheep of En Vogue. As I've stated, I was around them at times when they did appearances at the little events we did for the schools and the lure of being around En Vogue in person wore off, especially when four ladies are behaving just as the ladies in my family would behave, you know, arguments and all. You learn that they're people just like everyone else. We've heard through the media and members of the group of all the spats going on between them. The stories of the other members giving Dawn the wrong address for the video shoot I have to believe is true. Well, I didn't witness that specific thing, it's just that I know it had to be based on things, specifically one I will mention shortly. It didn't seem like the other members liked her very much, and I would soon experience first hand exactly why. Oh boy is this story going to get interesting. It is laced with coincidences you wouldn't believe.

DISCLAIMER

Before reading this next segment, please know that what I'm about to tell you was in the 90s and how I felt back then. Dawn and I weren't friends and I didn't know her like that. We had interactions because we worked with the same people though. I have since connected with her and I understand her better now. The things I say about her are not reflections of her personality, but just the way I felt at the time. I would be a hypocrite, because I have done the same things that I accused her of. I push people away and I have disregarded their feelings. I have invalidated others myself. Anyone can take a segment of someone else's life and make them to be the bad guy, and I have done this with Dawn. After seeing how she is as a person today, it brought me nearly to tears to the point that I had to apologize to her. She forgave me, though she didn't know what I was apologizing for, but she will have known before you, my audience, read this. I will not omit anything, though I have changed my tone about a couple of things, and what I say about her during her time with Lucy Pearl, I was not there. I was still angry because of what happened with Tassiana in Berkeley. I can only hope she still forgives me for judging her so wrongly after she reads this. I still have to keep my story about her because it's something that affected my life and caused me trauma. It's 12:48 in the morning, just past midnight as I write this addendum because I couldn't sleep. I just felt so bad. Dawn, I love you lady! I love your spirit. Less than an hour ago, I wrote in a comment on her YouTube channel, "Hold On to Your Love" means more than something romantic, and I truly believe that. She held on to her love after all she has gone through. Please forgive me again.

My friend Jonathan and I went to a Jamaican club in San Francisco. I met a young lady by the name of Tassiana. I'm not sure of the spelling, but that is her real name and that's the enunciation. We got along right away and quickly made plans to go out together. I believe it was our first and only date, but I could be wrong. I for some reason hung out with her a few times, but only remember the specifics of one particular date. We agreed to go to Berkeley, as Berkeley was a very nice place to go, hang out, and have fun getting to know each other. There was a large diversity of people around, lots of different places to eat, lots of street vendors, and generally no way to get bored. During the car drive there, I told her about my musical excursions and about some of the people I have worked directly with, one of them being En Vogue. Let's just say it's a small world? I got into details of experiencing some of the chatter behind the scenes and how Dawn was being treated. Tassiana seemed intrigued. We decided to eat at a salad place and low and behold, who do we see... "Dawn?" Tassiana said in excitement. "Tassiana?" Dawn said back. Yep, you guessed it, Dawn of En Vogue, at the salad bar. Tassiana said something to the effect of "I take it you know my friend already." Dawn looked confused, or at least tried to look confused, or maybe she suffers from the same tunnel vision of faces that I suffer from and people that I work directly with, only look familiar to me. Dawn told her that she has no idea who I am. I told her who I worked for and that I knew her from the label and that we threw many shows that she performed at or attended as a special guest. Dawn's response was that she has never stepped foot in that label in her life and never saw me before. Dawn was right, she didn't know me from the label, but I told Tassiana that only because I didn't feel like elaborating on the shows we used to put together. It was just easier to simplify it and relate everything through the label, as that was the basis of how I met many people. As you can imagine, it was a very awkward moment. Come to think of it, it could have been a pure coincidence, or maybe Tassiana and Dawn orchestrated the whole thing after Tassiana possibly told Dawn about me previously. I tried to explain using truth and facts, Dawn was denying it, Tassiana thought I was a big fat liar. Needless to say, we never went out again. Dawn and Tassiana knew each other because when Dawn first moved to California from New London, Connecticut, she moved in with Tassiana and her mom, and became like a sister and a daughter. I wanted so badly to tell her then and there that I overheard Holly Robinson-Peete telling Terry Ellis that she so desperately wished they would hurry up and kick Dawn out of the group so that she (Holly) could replace her. I will say, Terry Ellis shut Holly down on that notion, and I started to think that the group really wasn't against Dawn and they just had things to work out, or maybe it was Holly Robinson causing dissension in order to take her place. Who knows?

Anything is possible. Hey, at least the last names would be partially the same if Holly Robinson were to replace her, but personally, no one could replace Dawn. Regardless of her personality, we just don't know, and she shined and deserved so much better in retrospect. It being so long ago, I wanted to give Dawn the opportunity to tell her side of the story. I sent her a message on Facebook Messenger. She has yet to respond, and it may be because she has notifications turned off and doesn't check her messages. I am doing my due diligence. I did comment on a couple of her Facebook posts and she replied to me in one of them. It had nothing to do with me trying to contact her about my story about her. I did read through her posts, and she seems to be a new person. I think the industry just had her acting like someone else, or maybe she has just grown over the years. She and I have so much in common, so I'm hoping to extend an olive branch to her. I have no romantic feelings for her, and chances with her sister have long since passed and there's just no interest from me. I invited her to read what I wrote about her and will be publishing my writings about her either way. If she writes a rebuttal to what I wrote, I would be happy to add it without omitting any of her words, and leaving it up to the audience to decide. Hey, I may even give everyone a chance to rebuttal my writings and include an entire chapter full of rebuttals. That's something to consider. My only problem with it though, is I honestly don't care to contact anyone and really don't care what they have to say. I already heard all they have to say and may just include what they've said to me via texts. They can all sue me. They won't win because I am telling the 100% truth and I have receipts.

 I'm going to jump ahead several years to the next biggest coincidence, but it's directly connected to the story I just told you. This was around 2007 maybe. I befriended someone by the name of Dre Allen. We may have met on MySpace, but we exchanged numbers for music business. When we talked on the phone, we became pretty good friends and would just converse about everything. He would call me when he was frustrated with his wife and they'd get into an argument. I'd listen and give him advice from an unmarried man's perspective if called for. When we talked about music for the first time, he told me about his musical career and "The Dre Allen Project." Mind you, I have lots of friends that have different projects going on, so this was no different. He also told me about a reality show he and his wife were filming, documenting their daily struggles and how poor they were. He said they would sleep in a trailer on a dirty mattress and no food to eat, infested with rats and roaches. I immediately recalled the time I lived on Woodlawn Ave in Buffalo, so I could relate. You know, to this day, I have never watched an episode of that reality show. I looked on YouTube and did see a 30 minute pilot episode, so I will have watched it by the time you read this. So one day Dre calls me and I can hear him and his wife arguing and yelling. It was bad. There was screaming, and I could hear a ruckus going on in the background. I think he not only needed a friend to talk to, but maybe also a witness in case something violent happened. I recall him saying something to the effect of "I had to call you before I killed this bitch." That's not verbatim, but that was the sentiment of what was said. He never mentioned her name before this conversation. He always referred to her as "my wife." Her name was "my wife" as far as I was concerned. He says her real name this time. "Dawn......." I told him that she sounds like and is acting exactly like the Dawn that I knew from working in the industry. He then told me his wife is Dawn from En Vogue. Oh boy.... "Dre, that's the Dawn I'm talking about!" I then went on to tell him how she caused Tassiana and I to break up. He could not believe it and he went from angry to sad because I told him that I really really liked Tassiana and I was serious about her. His voice went from enraged to somber when he called out to his wife to question her about why she did what she did to break us up. "Dawn, my friend on the phone said he knows you and that you lied to your sister about knowing him and made him look like a liar, so she broke up with him. Do you remember that?". Then I gave him the details of the salad bar. I could hear Dawn in the background "Oh yeah, sorry!" The trouble that she caused, and all she could say was "Sorry" You know, maybe she knew I witnessed some of her nastiness in the group and wanted to shut out anyone that was around at the time. You know, an assassination of character rather than actually killing me. Oddly enough, this seemed like the thing that ended their argument, and I did get the sense that she felt badly about it. I wonder if she even remembers this happening, or would she deny it like she did me with Tassiana in Berkeley.

Going back in time a little, and this is a real loose approximation, but it may have been around 1998 or 1999. My brother-in-law lost his father. We'll call him George. George was good friends with one of the members of Tony Toni Tone, D'Wayne Wiggins. I had never met him at this time, but became fairly acquainted with him after a video shoot my associates and I did at his coffee shop/Speakeasy, "The Java House." So, I told George that I was going to an event and that Tony Toni Tone was supposed to be there, and he told me he grew up with D'Wayne Wiggins, and D'Wayne was close with George's dad, so if I saw him, to let D'Wayne know that George's dad passed away. I told him that I would definitely tell him when I saw him. So I got to the venue and it was a packed house. It was a popular location and was primarily a grown folk club on Fridays and Saturdays. It was called "Geoffrey's Inner Circle". I only saw one member of the group, and it was Raphael Saadiq. This was my first and only interaction with him, and I equate his personality to the crackhead from the Five Heartbeats, Eddie, but a real version of him. I'm not saying Ray was on drugs, but his real life persona that night was spot on with Eddie. I have never been a groupie in my life, and I was honestly never really a fan of Tony Toni Tone. I liked a couple of their songs, but I couldn't quote any lyrics outside of the hook or chorus of a couple of their songs, so I felt weird approaching Raphael Saadiq. I didn't know which member he was, but I recognized his face as one of the members of the group. When I approached him, I told him who I was and that my brother in law wanted me to deliver news that his father passed away. Ray (for short) asked me a quiz such as "Did he go to bla bla bla high school?" I responded that he may have and it sounds like it might be right". Ray gave me the groupie treatment and said "I never went there, wrong person", and proceeded forward, kind of nudging past me as if I were a peon. I was confused by this behavior and what he wasn't understanding about what I was saying. This guy was an asshole and he reminded me of Dawn at the salad bar. Low and behold, he and Dawn Robinson later formed a group together called "Lucy Pearl". Their personalities were so similar that they often clashed and got into arguments over a range of things. Needless to say, the group would break up as quickly as they formed, and it was no coincidence that the two of them would end up together in a group and not get along. Dawn Robinson and Raphael Saadiq are two people that I just did not like and didn't care to ever be around again. D'Wayne Wiggins on the other hand was a totally warm and welcoming person. I first met him when, like I said, we did a video shoot where one of the scenes was moved over to his shop after our original venue canceled our use of their spot. It was for a video by a female rapper named "Silk-E," not to be confused with "Silk-E Fyne." She won a contest on MTV, and the prize was 2 video shoots. I of course wound up being part of the crew and even turned down a part in one of the videos. I did get one of my best friends at the time,

Patrick Pulliam, a spot in the video. If you look up "Silk-E" and see her videos on YouTube, you'll see him with the long dreadlocks. That was my spot that I gave up because I only wanted to be behind the scenes.

I slowly got out of the music industry after realizing what sacrifices you had to make in order to actually make it. I spent more money in the music industry than I ever made. I started my own production company, and time after time, the artists were trying to get something for nothing. They want you to produce and executive produce their music and albums at no cost to them, but they don't want to sign your contracts, then they wonder why they never made it in the industry. I have come across some very talented artists that I know would have made it had they only allowed me to properly represent them, but first they had to sign my contract, which was never a rip-off. I always asked for less than the industry standard. I never went above 15%, plus I was paying for everything.

This next time period is between 2003 and 2008. I had a very big house that I had built from the ground up. 4109 Sq ft., 6 bedrooms, 4 1/2 baths. I had one of the bedrooms turned into a recording studio. I eventually ran across a guy that was a decent producer and engineer, so I hired him to run my studio. He would work on my projects for free. In exchange, I gave him a place to stay, which was the bedroom directly across from the studio, only separated by his private bathroom. He also had many connections in the music industry, just not of the same caliber as I had, but he had quite a bit of work, and he made good money off of sessions. I never asked him for a dime for the money he made using my equipment, my studio, or anything, but he still found a way to burn me. I tell you, It seems like everyone in the industry was out to get over on whoever they could. He had the nerve to tell people that it was his studio, so when artists came over, they would think the house was his, the studio was his, the equipment was his, and I was sometimes met with disrespect by the people he had over there. For instance, someone would be smoking in the studio and even have an open drink sitting right on my expensive and non waterproof equipment. I would tell them they can't smoke in there and they can't drink in there either. "This is Lee's shit and he said it was cool." No, this is all my shit, and you're not even supposed to be here when he's not here. Get out." Another incident that happened was an artist that he worked with often was there, and he was a very talented rapper that had a distinct voice and rap style. He promised me a verse on one of my artists songs, but he kept putting me off. Finally, he was there, by himself, and I asked him for a verse. This dude actually talked about charging me and he had to make sure the song he was on was on the caliber of what he thought was a good song. I told him, "I'm letting you record in my studio, using my electricity, my house, my utilities, my equipment, all in which for I paid for myself, yes Lee helped build it, but that was part of the agreement, but this isn't his, and you have the nerve to try to charge me, and you're recording your entire album, in my studio, for free?" He then told me, according to Lee, it was his studio. I had to set them both straight on that, and I had to have Lee explain to me that how is it his studio just because he helped build the recording booth!? That wasn't the only time one of my tenants claimed my house as their own. This is off topic, but I'll keep this short. I had a tenant that I allowed to live there, and he told his girlfriend it was his house. I came home from work one day and she was there alone. I asked her who she was because my tenant wasn't there and she was roaming around like no one else lived there. I wasn't going to kick her out or anything, I just wanted to know who she was. She had a nasty attitude with me and said "I'm Harold's girlfriend and this is our house, who are you?" "Um, I own this house," I replied. She wanted to argue with me as to who was the owner of the house. Harold was at work and I left him a text message that his girl was disrespecting me and had to go. I told her she had to leave, and if she really thought this was her and her man's house, then she can have him address me or call the police. Of course she decided to leave, and that was the last I saw of her. Harold apologized to me and said it wouldn't happen again. I told him I don't mind him telling girls it's his crib, just don't have them disrespecting the other tenants.

I know, you're reading the title of this book and wonder where things start to get dark. Don't worry, that's coming, and the story of this house and tenants disrespecting me is somewhat of a segue into the darkside, but I still have some stories to tell of the music industry before I get to that, but it's coming. At this point, I've only told maybe less than half the story. I still have to jump back in time to 1996-2005.

After my experiences with Alien Records, I ended up meeting someone by the name "Lil Dee." My niece's father introduced me to him. He was from St Louis. My niece's father was cousins with Shock G. His name is Jason. Jason gave me the address of the studio that Lil Dee would be at, and I met him there. Lil Dee was a very cool dude, and he was Road managing a group by the name of M.O.B. (Mind Over Body) and was overseeing the recording of their album "Unexpected Lockdown." This group is from St Louis and they were recording in Oakland because the owner of the studio is also from St Louis and was giving them a good deal. His name is Lev Berlak. Lev also managed a very popular Bay Area artist by the name of Richie Rich. Lev had a dry personality most of the time with me and didn't seem to like me very much, but sometimes he was very cool with me. One time though, he actually stood up for me. There was an investor there that was a very well known street gangster and drug lord. I will not disclose his name, but let's just say it was something along the lines of "The Mayor", but it wasn't the Mayor. It was a higher office than that though. "The Mayor" was there and so was M.O.B., Lev, Kayo, and myself. I'm not sure if Jimmie the Clip was there. But someone stole "The Mayor's" weed, and he immediately blamed me. He actually pulled out a silver and gold 50 caliber Desert Eagle and pointed it at my head and demanded his weed back. I insisted that I did not steal his weed and had nothing to do with it. I was the only one in the studio that didn't even smoke, but maybe he thought I was more of an entrepreneur and not a smoker, therefore I took advantage of an opportunity. Alfie defended me and told him that there's no way I would have stolen his weed, and Lev saw the seriousness of the situation and also said that there's no way I would have done it. Lev even offered to pay him for the weed. They went into the room where the reel to reel machine was kept and came back out, and we all forgot about the incident. The very next day, I was back in the studio, as I was now in charge of making sure M.O.B. did what they were there to do and to chauffeur them anywhere they needed to go. Lev was rich, so if he indeed paid for the weed, it was no skin off his back. This man was one of the first people with the new Lexus GS 400 and paid cash for it. I got along with these St Louis dudes so well. It was like I grew up with them. They were so hospitable and friendly. There was Kayo, Jimmy, and Alphie. Kayo wasn't in the group, but was there to help write and to do a couple of features. Alphie and I grew the closest and Alphie would have me come to St Louis to hang out and also help write. He probably would be upset with me saying so, but the cat was let out of the bag a long time ago. I have written for several artists as a ghostwriter, and I will never expose them, but let's just say I should have 3 Grammy's on my mantle, but I don't. If I could go back in time and change one thing, I probably would have insisted on my name in the credits. But when you're working for big wigs, it can be intimidating, and I was just trying to leverage my way into bigger and better things, and helping to write a few songs wasn't a big deal for me. The owner of the label was Prim Rogers. Prim and I got along quite well on the business level, and he, having no experience in the music industry, looked to me for guidance, which I gladly gave. He had several artists he signed, one of them being a group called "Out Of Order." If that name sounds slightly familiar as a musical act, it's because one of its members was also a small-time producer and produced their own tracks in a production team called "9mm Productions." His name is Sham, or Shamar Daugherty. He would venture off and form a new production team with a talented musician and producer by the name of Lonzo. The name of the team would be known as "The Trak Starz." They discovered Chingy and recorded his first album and their first solo project outside of PD Waxx Records, went triple platinum, won 3 Grammys, and the rest is history. Sham was another person that I got along with like best friends from the beginning. Sham was so cool and still is. I remember he had to keep another member of his group in line because he just didn't like me. He didn't like the fact that Prim placed me in charge of them while in California, and that Prim announced to a few people that he was naming me as President of PD Waxx Records. St Louis is known for being close knit, and helping or promoting someone else from another city or state was almost unheard of. Well, Like what happened with Alien Records, the same thing happened with PD Waxx records, and groups began to get sold off. I remember going to St Louis and going with him to his dad's house where he had his simple equipment to make beats. His dad and I also grew close over the years since the introduction of Facebook. Sadly, he passed away a few years ago. I recall not speaking to him in a while, as he used to always message me or comment on my posts, then I just noticed it had been a while, so after doing some digging, that's when I got the news. Here's another little coincidence...Just early this morning, a little after 12 midnight, I was going down my friend's list on Facebook looking for a good candidate to write my forward for this book. I came across the name "John Lear." John sent me a friend request several years ago, not long after I published my first book. I'm not promoting that book because it has my name that I've used my entire life in it. John was also interested and a leader on the topic of what that book was about, and if I'm honest, I think we have a mutual friend by the name of Laurie McDonald. She's an award winning hypnotherapist in Sacramento. She's a public figure and has appeared on countless television and radio programs using her real name, so she doesn't mind the mention. Laurie has helped me in my career by acting as an agent for me. She and her husband, Wayne, have helped me so much in life, and they were there for me when I had nowhere else to turn to. Ok, I digress again. Back to John Lear. I came across his name in my friends list and it struck me that I hadn't talked to him in a very long time. He would comment on a post or message me every now and then. If his name sounds familiar, he is the son of the famous founder of Learjet, Bill Lear. So when I say I had friends in high places, you can take that literally. Admittedly, John and I didn't know each other that well outside of UFOlogy and our books on the subject and having mutual friends, but he knew me well enough to write a forward, plus his name might grab some attention. I hadn't decided on him, but when I saw his name, I did think he might be a good candidate, but I knew that I would ultimately ask Laurie to do me the honors, which I haven't as of yet asked. The thing is, when I came across his name, his profile was grayed out due to deactivation. I clicked on it, and yep, it was deactivated. I Googled him and learned of his death, then I started to remember that he wasn't doing too well at one point in time, and that was around the time I had last heard from him. I have several friends with profiles that are grayed out, so now I'm thinking I should check on them.

Another person is Kristinia DeBarge. We were friends for a brief period of time due to "family" ties. She is the daughter of James DeBarge, of the famous singing family, "The DeBarge's." Well, her profile is grayed out and I never thought to call her phone, as that just seems awkward because we were merely acquaintances. I think I may have sent her a text a long time ago to check if she'd reply. I never got a response, but she's still alive. How are we related? We're not. Let me explain... A lifelong friend of the family by the name of Monica Peyton had two children. Both of them by El DeBarge. Monica used to live in my house. We had a tumultuous relationship. I honestly think I could write an entire book on things that have transpired between the two of us and things that I know. I'll try to give the abridged version as I don't want a 500 page book. I came home from work very early one day, and when I walked into the house, Monica and My daughter's mom were having a conversation in the mid-stairwell section leading upstairs. I had a very large foyer. The ceiling of the foyer exceeded the downstairs ceiling and stretched all the way to the ceiling of the second floor, so sound carried quite well and I was surprised they didn't hear me come into the house, but they were so caught up in stabbing me in the back, that they didn't hear me coming in the front. I could hear Monica telling her ways she could get me for child support even though my daughter and her mom lived in my house, I paid for everything plus gave her an extra $250/mo, which was a lot at the time, and I gave her exclusive use of an almost brand new car. I couldn't believe Monica would stab me in the back like this. There was also another incident when my other tenant told me she was trying to get him to team up with her to try to get me either for money or something else. He wasn't sure what she meant, but he said she was trying to form an alliance with him against me. Keep in mind, I was giving Monica a place to stay at such a discounted rate, it was practically free, on top of that, I was letting her use my vehicle for transportation, which she broke a window even after I told her to keep the seat belt plugged in or it'll swing and hit the window, and I made her pay for the window. This was probably one of the things that caused her to betray me. She thought she could just run over me. Another thing is, I came home one day, and her two sons are jumping up and down on my dishwasher door, and she's just letting them, and I said something to her about it. She had the nerve to have an attitude. There were just so many things going on that I finally had enough. I had already kicked my other tenant out because they weren't getting along. Monica was in the wrong, but she was a friend since 1991 and a family friend since the early 8os. To end this section about Monica, she stabbed me in the back so many times, I contacted the DeBarge's and told Bunny DeBarge that Monica's youngest son is indeed not El's son. Bunny said she's not surprised and that she already suspected. In fact, Monica told me who she thinks the father is, and that is so shocking of who the real dad is, I refuse to give up the goods...At least not for free, and honestly, it's not my story to tell, but his father is super famous...or was...RIP. Put it this way, if you Google her name and do some intermediate digging, you will see who her sons are, and you'll come across a video or two, and in those videos, you will see a younger exact clone of his real dad and immediately know who he is. Monica was famous for sleeping with celebrities. Another one of those celebrities was Tupac, and no, that's not the father of her youngest son, so I'll save you the trouble of speculation, but he was up there in fame, if not more famous.

Before I get onto the next chapters of this memoir, I would like to include a couple of quick stories of a couple heroes that I met that were as real as they were in their music. By that I mean, how they seemed on their records, is exactly how they were in real life. I remember hanging out with Redman a couple of times. He was doing a special appearance in a clothing store called "AJ's Clothing" on Lakeside in Oakland. I was a gopher, and Redman literally ate an entire bucket of KFC, drank Moet, and smoked weed. When he ran out, I went and got more. When the appearance first started, there was a long line waiting to see him and it was getting dark. The problem is, he wasn't there. We knew he was in town, but Redman was at home in Oakland and one of his reps lived in the Oakland hills. We looked up the street and could see a tall lanky figure walking up the street in a goofy manner, and it was Reggie Noble, with a big cheese smile on his face. He was by himself and evidently just got off of a bus, likely from seeing a female. I remember I hooked him up with the girl that worked at the store, which I was friends with. I can't lie, I actually liked the girl and we were really good friends, but I have a belief that you let the female choose. Her name is Aisha. She has a younger sister named Jolene that was attending veterinarian school. I actually grew fond of Jolene and would visit her often. Aisha chose both of us, so hey... This very same female was trouble. Not on purpose, but she was so fine and so beautiful that she would have people acting out of character and risking it all to get with her. I remember being at Ahn's Burgers with her and Keak Da Sneak tried to talk to her in front of me, totally disrespecting me. He's a little dude and probably had the complex that comes along with it. He had people with him, but I still told him not to disrespect me like that. He said, "Let her decide." I left it at that, and she turned him down.

    This wasn't the only time that I've almost gotten into an altercation with a celebrity over a female. One other time, years later in 2001, I went to a club in Sacramento and met a young lady named Gayle. I was in my "going to the club solo" phase, because just a week later, I met a young lady named Roxanne. They heard of each other as I would find out later, but they didn't really know each other. Well, Gayle and I didn't last long, and it pretty much ended when she met Gerald Wallace who was just drafted to the Sacramento Kings. How could I compete with that, right? Well let me go back in time. Roxanne and I were talking, but we didn't go fast like Gayle and I did. Well, I noticed things with her also seemed different, like she was hiding something. She was also talking to Gerald Wallace. This is how Roxanne and Gayle knew of each other because they found out their NBA player was talking to both of them, but they were both also talking to me. The only reason I found out about Gayle talking to him is when I went to pick her up and her brother came outside and snitched on her. This was after Gerald Wallace found out I was talking to Roxanne. Roxanne called me one day because she went with Gerald Wallace to some event out of town. It may have been a celebrity basketball game or dunk contest or something, but it was an event that involved NBA players. She was crying because he left her stranded out of town and she called me in hopes that I would send for her to come back. This is when he found out about me, and there were 3-way calls involved and everyone found out about each other. Gerald Wallace was upset that this "nobody" was seeing his girls. Like, how could the same dude that works a 9 to 5, compete with him? So this struck a nerve with him. Gayle and I got into an argument and she gave Gerald Wallace my phone number and he called me, threatening me. Pride wouldn't let me back down. We picked a place to meet for a little showdown, R. Kelly and Mr. Biggs style. I called a few of my people to follow me out there and stay hidden for a setup and to see what the situation was. I wasn't so stupid to go trying to fight some 6'7" guy alone. I have to admit, I really liked Roxanne, and I was upset that this young ass Gerald Wallace guy stole two of my girls. One, I think the both of us could let it slide, but TWO? This had to be resolved.

He never showed up, or maybe he did and noticed I wasn't alone, and I didn't stick around for too long after our agreed meeting time. I was internally happy that I didn't see him and I could call Gayle and tell him her man is a punk. This was another time that I could have been dead or in jail over a female.

I remember Das Efx, one of my favorite rap groups of all time, had a performance in San Francisco, and I took that day off of work to make sure I was there to see them perform. In one of their songs called "40 and a Blunt", they say "So if we're in your town at a club near you, if you got the bomb, muthaf**** bring it through, how we do?" So guess what I did? I brought them some of that good Ole Cali bomb. I don't smoke, but as a budding entertainment rep, I felt obligated to make them feel comfortable. They shared a tour bus with Blacksheep. After the show, we're all on the bus playing video games. I whipped out the bomb and they were ecstatic. They told me they just did a show in Canada and brought back some of the weed from there. I forget what it was called, but it was red. They kept it inside a singular cigar shaped canister. They rolled it up and had me hit it. I obliged and said it was weak. This coming from someone that doesn't smoke. They all looked at me with grins on their faces like they knew something that I didn't know. A few minutes later, I was geekin' and they were cracking up! It was like wine. It went down smoothly and hit you hard later, quite the opposite of Cali bomb. They had their crew with them called the Resless Click. These were some super cool dudes. After the video game and weed session on the tour bus, the Resless Click and I went out to get food for everyone. Scoob, aka The Books in Reverse, wanted a chicken sandwich from Carl's Jr. Scoob asked me if I could get Dawn Robinson to do a song with them and I said I would try, but this was just before she broke Tassiana and I up.

One last musical story I have worth mentioning is when my friend Aisha and I went to the Rocafella concert in San Francisco.

She's the same one that worked at the clothing store that I introduced to Redman. The show was either at Maritime Hall or the Fillmore. I honestly can't recall because I've been to so many shows. They had a lot of people there with them, including artists that I never heard of. Dame Dash was there and it wasn't long after Aaliyah passed away. I will tell you this, Jay-Z was not pleasant to be around. He was not approachable, even by members of his own team. He seemed to have an attitude with everyone and would snap. We were in the room "backstage," and Jay-Z was not happy with the accommodations. I'll be honest, I wouldn't be happy with them either, but not to the point where I was snapping at everyone. The room was small and there was a picnic table with a bowl of punch and red Dixie cups. There was also a bowl with chips and a charcuterie layout I believe. You could not expect millionaires to eat and drink from that. Hell, I worked at a factory and I didn't want to touch that stuff. It was in the open for everyone to breathe over and touch with their dirty hands. I recall Dame Dash cracking jokes and Jay-Z not being happy with him. Crazy thing is, I saw Dame telling stories of how Jay acted on tour, and I swear, he described the exact same thing that I witnessed first hand of him cracking jokes at Jay-Z, and Jay-Z having absolutely no sense of humor and having an attitude with Dame over it.

CHAPTER NINE – BONUS
GIFT OF GAB, TIM PARKER

The year was around 1996 or 1997. I lived on 39th Street in Oakland California. I had two other roommates living there. One of them was a guy by the name of Timothy Parker. He was very quiet and reserved. Just like many other people, he was into music. I never took him very seriously only because almost everybody I met was a rapper. One of his friends would come over sometimes and they would go to Tim's room and they were quiet, nothing funny. They were in there coming up with musical concepts. I recall one time Tim came to my room and asked me what I thought about one of his songs. He started rapping the song to me and it was at this moment that I knew he was unlike any other local talents. The song that he rapped to me was A to G. This guy was nothing like anyone I have ever heard and I knew he was special. It made me think back to the time he and chief Excel laughed when I asked if he needed help writing. You see, I wrote for several people during that time period up until then so it wasn't uncommon for someone to enlist my help because I myself was a very good writer. You would be surprised by the people that I wrote for. But Tim needed no help from anyone. His craftsmanship and genius is beyond any rapper I have ever heard in my life dead or alive. This includes Eminem, The Notorious BIG, Nas, and whoever you would put in your top 10. I'm not saying this just because I knew him, but two of his albums are my two top favorite albums of any genre of all time. One of them is his second titled Blazing Arrow. The other album which I consider tied with "Blazing Arrow" this is posthumous album titled "Finding Inspiration Somehow." Gift of Gab knew how to create songs without using much profanity. You'd be hard-pressed to find many instances where he drops the F-bomb or anything as such. I've been to a couple of shows, well actually several of his shows and he has a segment to where he will freestyle from the top of his head and his freestyles were better than anything that Eminem could write. I used to listen to Blazing Arrow back to back. I would rewind songs over and over again. After we both moved out of the house on 39th street, we didn't really have much communication, but we did keep in contact. Every now and then I would call him and he would call me or text me just to chat. My other favorite album of his, Finding Inspiration Somehow, he recorded while he knew he was on his deathbed. I didn't learn that he had kidney disease until maybe 2016. He told me that he would still do shows and he would schedule dialysis on the road during these shows. I knew that had to be difficult.

I recall going to several "small" shows of his. He was known as an underground artist, but anyone who knew anything about underground rap, knew who Gift of Gab was. His shows were always packed. Pretty much standing room only. It was a special treat to see any Quannum Projects artist performing. Anytime one had a show, you knew they brought along other Quannum Projects artists to guest appear. Blackalicious did make some mainstream waves too. I recall him doing a cell phone commercial (sorry, no free advertising), and if my memory serves me correct, I think he did one for a beverage company. When I realized he was bigger than underground was when he was a performer at a "Rock the Bells" concert in the San Jose area at the outdoor arena called the Shoreline Amphitheater. He was amongst the greats that day such as Rakim, Nas, The Pharcyde, Method Man & Redman, The Immortal Technique, A Tribe Called Quest, De LA Soul, and many more. I brought my niece with me to that concert. Yes, Elana. I took her to two different concerts and I don't remember which one I took her to first. Thinking back now, I may have only taken her to one concert. It's difficult for me to remember as I have taken many people to many concerts and I do recall taking Elana to her first concert. Ready for another coincidence? My niece met him once and she told me that Tim (Gift of Gab) tried to get with her. She turned him down though. She wouldn't have been happy though. She was a lot younger than he was and he was always on the road. Tim was a little older than I am, and I'm a lot older than my niece. She was born in 1987 or 1988. Tim was born in 1970. She may have been 15 or 16 when they met. Of course he probably didn't know her age at the time and I did get upset with him for trying to get with my niece. He obviously didn't know she was my niece, so I had to back up a bit. I only lashed out at him in a message on MySpace but then sent another message to him asking him to forgive my ignorance. I was very protective of my niece, but not overbearing. I didn't get involved in who she chose to date, but I will come down on any of her boyfriend's with the full force of fury if they ever crossed her.

 I moved back to California in February of 2021, and it was in June when a long time friend of mine contacted me either through text message or Messenger on Facebook and asked me if I heard the news about my friend, Gift of Gab. He had passed away due to kidney failure. I had just spoken to him that April and we talked about a lot of things. He told me that he just got a kidney transplant in March after waiting for so many years for one. He said he was recovering and that he lived by Lake Merritt not far from the Grand Lake Theater and that someone was tending to him. It was either his aunt or his sister. Maybe both of them. He told me he had plans to retire soon and wanted to buy a house in Arizona. I told him I wanted to come visit him and asked if there was anything I could do for him, being that he was still recovering and I was often in the area. He didn't want me to see him in a weakened condition. I could hear it in his voice. He turned down my offer and said we'd hang out after he recovered. He did tell me that it was a hard recovery and that he wasn't doing too well at the moment, but I didn't take it as he was dying. I found solace in knowing that I spoke to him fairly recently. Mind you, a couple of years could go by and we wouldn't hear from each other. I was sad. I usually don't mourn death in the way most people do. I don't cry or anything like that, but I will think of you and hope your family is fine. I know the person that passed away is just fine. Maybe in a parallel universe and survived, or probably in their heaven that they imagined or believed in while they were alive. The way I mourn him is by honoring him. I will play his albums for several hours. In fact, his posthumous album is the only music I listened to when I went out for my runs after work. It would play one and a half times, and when it got to a specific song on the second playback, I knew exactly how many miles I had run. I went from 225 lbs down to 177 lbs, mostly while listening to his aptly titled "Finding Inspiration Somehow" album. It truly gave me inspiration. His music is full of positive affirmation and should be played around the world. He should be taught in schools and churches. I kid you not, even if you're not into rap, you would find yourself enjoying these two albums. All of his albums were awesome, but those are the ones I go back to the most. I like to go onto YouTube and comment on the videos of people reacting to his music and sharing my experiences of him with them. Timothy Jerome Parker, Gift of Gab, Rest In Power my brother, one of my favorite Gods to ever grace us by walking amongst us mortals. Rock on in your new life and continue looking out for me. I did experience a miracle after his passing, and I'll keep it at that.

CHAPTER TEN
I WON'T FORGET WHAT YOU DID

I think I gave you a good mixture of good and bad. I tried to give you a few things to show you the basis of what shaped me into who I am today. I'm going to step it up a notch, and these stories are going to focus on both the good and the bad, but more so into the things that made me more cynical in my thinking and dealing with people. I'm not going to talk so much about my personal romantic relationships , though a couple of them have to be mentioned by default. We have to go back to the 90s again. I was living close to downtown Oakland on 10th Ave. My old boss was one of my roommates and I would occasionally work for him as a temp whenever he needed me at the bookstore. I was also working at Trader Joes. Everyone was always really cool and we always got along. Every now and then, a couple of the fellas would argue, but it wouldn't last long and within no time, they'd be back to smoking weed, playing cards, dominos, drinking, or just generally hanging out in our large living room of the upstairs corner apartment where we had an excellent view of the local area. Everyone was always invited everywhere. BBQ's, parties, clubs, etc... When two of our roommates got married, we all hopped in my station wagon and drove to Reno for the affair. The two that got married were Tamala (not her real name) and Tommy, also not his real name. Tommy had a younger brother that did nothing better than getting into trouble and making enemies. He and his girl were tight and often would have violent fights with each other but would be right back together as quickly as the fight started. I mean, they came to blows. Tommy's brother, Harry, would do anything illegal to get money. He would scam anyone that would fall for it. I was a bit wet behind the ears when it came to certain scams. He ran one on me where he needed me to cash his paycheck for him by depositing it into my account and I would give him the money. I didn't know it was a scam because I had no reason to believe Harry would run a scam on someone he was so close to. Well, the check was no good and I was out of I think $1500. Keep that in mind for a later story involving his brother Tommy. This was the second and last time anyone would scam me. The first time, I was with my girlfriend, Daphne. It was a slide of hand, wad of money scam. She tried to warn me, but I didn't listen. I'm going to skip several years in order to finish the story of Harry, then go back in time to Tommy. I let the scam slide. Harry told me he thought that there would be no problem with me cashing the check. I didn't believe him, but I didn't want any negativity in the household. He didn't live there at the time, but came over freely, and there was a small stint where he and his girl did live there. One day, we got word that one of Harry's victims caught up with him and tried to kill him. Harry was in the hospital, suffering from several gunshots from a .22 caliber pistol. He was shot several times in the face, head, chess, arm, and leg. I was on the list of people that were allowed to visit him. Keep in mind that this was after the scam, and I truly forgave him, and we were actually pretty cool after that. If you weren't on the list of people the hospital had, you not only weren't allowed to see him, but you were actually told that he passed away. This is when I learned that this was done for all gunshot victims that are targeted. I really want you to think about what I just said. I can't say a lot, but I can say things, if you catch what I'm throwing. When Harry was released from the hospital, he was supposed to disappear and move out of the area where no one would recognize him. He had a lot of enemies, and Harry was one wild boy. Someone you don't want to mess with. He was unrestrained and unchecked, but he was no different than a lot of people in Oakland. Well, one day after things already happened and I already moved out of the apartment, I ran into Harry's girl and she told me that someone got him. I had already gotten word of his murder, but I didn't know what to believe, being that I knew what people were told about his first murder. My suspicions of him faking his death were further perpetuated by the fact that his girl pulled out Polaroid photos of him. It looked staged, and who carries photos of their long time dead husband around like that? I got the feeling that they suspected I was after him or something, but I was never the type to be vengeful to the extent of murder. I would always just let Karma deal with the situation.

Now let's go back to when I was still living in the apartment. I had been there for a couple of years. When I first moved in, it was agreed that I would pay cash because I wasn't on the lease. I had brought up several times that I thought it was time for that to change. I never liked carrying cash. People get robbed and money gets lost. I had gone to enough BBQ'a, events, clubs, parties, etc., and I had deep ties with everyone no different than anyone else. All of our family's were intertwined somehow. My boss at the bookstore lived there and he was my niece's father. His brother was engaged to my girlfriend's aunt, and still married to this day. In fact, they're the ones that played matchmaker when I was 17 and she was 14. Tommy's wife was my co-worker at the label.

Everyone and everyone's family knew each other. There are other people, but there's no need to mention them as of yet. Tommy and I also grew close. We went many places together and he was one of the only people with a car phone. We would go and meet girls and we were both dating an older sister/younger sister pair that lived right around the corner. Yes, he was cheating, and I held that secret. Tommy's girlfriend/wife wasn't exactly faithful herself. Did I know this for a fact? No. I do know that she came onto me quite heavily on several occasions and was known for showing her lady lumps when coming out of the shower. We would all secretly talk about it behind Tommy's back, and I believe a couple of the fellas might have had relations with her. What's one of the things that she said to me you may ask? I recall her getting out of the shower one time and having on nothing but a white t-shirt, still wet, so you know what could be seen. She was thick and well endowed. We were talking about a girl that I just dropped off and how I stole her from my friend's brother. She saw that the girl scratched my back up, and my roommate was telling me that she would be mad if she were in my shoes. I told her I didn't mind it because it was worth it. Tamala told me that hers (you know what) is good too and that it "snaps back" so no one would be able to tell if she did anything. I knew what she was hinting towards, but guess what? As tempted as I was to see how far this could go, I didn't indulge. This was out of respect for Tommy. There was another occasion where another roommate's sister was visiting. We were on the couch together and I was rubbing her feet. Things were a little freaky, I admit, but we were both adults. Tamala walked in the living room on us, and we could tell she was a little surprised, and a little jealous. I'm not quoting Tamala, but she gave us a look like she wanted next and made a statement to the same effect.

Tamala and I spent a lot of time together. We worked together at the label. We were roommates, we carpooled together, and when she got her little Nissan 350zx, sometimes she'd drive, and sometimes I'd drive my car, but we usually rode together. I never really thought anything of it, and I'm going to get back to the "paying rent in cash" story, but I had to give you a little backstory. I could definitely see how Tommy would start getting a little jealous, and I could see how he would think that I would tell Tamala some of his secrets of infidelity, but I never would and never did. I had been to Tamala's mother's house with her. I honestly saw her as a big sister. Tamala's mother used to flirt with me and I honestly think she brought me over there for her mom.

We're all in the living room. I recall it being three of the fellas not including Tommy and myself, and Tamala. I wrote a check. The other two fellas had no problem with it. It was only $350. Tommy had a problem with it, and it had been discussed that it wasn't a big deal to write a check because they were going to add me to the lease. The holdup was they didn't know how long I'd be there for, so they didn't want to go through the trouble of adding me if all I was going to do was turn around and leave. They were also concerned that rent would go up being that it was an opportunity to do so because of a change in the lease. But it wasn't a new lease. You're just adding a name to it and removing the name of the person that moved out years ago. Things got loud. I wasn't yelling, but Tommy escalated things. He had a little man complex. He's 5'3" on 4" stilts. He was no physical threat. His young son was almost the same size as him. Because of this, he carried a gun wherever he went. I was 5'8" and all of 160 lbs. This punk went upstairs to his room and came back down with his gun. It was at that point where everyone knew they were living with a tiny monster. A termite with a gun. He's one of the few people that if I ever see to this day, he owes me a fair one. It's needless to say that I moved out, and their rent went up anyway because it was no longer being split between more people. No one else moved in behind me, and it wasn't too long after that when others started moving out. Others saw him for what he was and just quietly made plans to get out of there. I don't understand the need to pull a gun on someone over a rent dispute. It's not like I was behind in rent. I just wanted to pay by check instead of always having to travel through that dangerous area with all that cash in my pocket, or to even have to make the extra trip to the bank or ATM to get the money. I think maybe I'm too nice outwardly, yet I don't let people push me, so this makes them want to kill me. I remember in late 2005, my daughter's mother called me and started an argument with me. I had one of those Nokia flip phones. When she hung up, I could still hear talking. It was she and Amber. She obviously had me on a 3-way call and was trying to get me to act out of character so that Amber could witness it and record it. I guess I didn't give her what she wanted because she resorted to asking Amber why I wanted to spend so much time with my daughter. She tried to accuse me of being a pedophile and this angered me. I started recording the conversation. She even went on to disclose to Amber different plots she had to "get rid of" me. She did actually use the word "kill". I gave this recording to the police department, and they didn't do anything about it. I told them that if she ends up dead, it's self defense. They took note and told me not to do anything stupid. I told them that I did my due diligence by reporting a plot from my daughter's mom to have me killed, and they did nothing, so if anything happens to anyone, it was self defense. They agreed and left. Why do police wait until something happens before they're interested? Then my evidence would be suppressed and I'd be in prison for murder.

I remember sitting in the living room of that apartment and a couple of the fellas and I were watching "America's Most Wanted." One of the fellas just happened to be someone that was featured on that show that was wanted for robbing a jewelry store near downtown Oakland. They detailed how he ran across rooftops and evaded them, and here he was, right next to us giving details of the adventure. I don't know if he was actually wanted at the time, but we didn't snitch, and I actually just met him, so it wasn't my business to tell. People watched the ATM machines and followed people and robbed them. It's because of this that we all came to the conclusion that Tommy suspected Tamala and I were messing around, which was untrue. Believe me, had I known this is how it was going to turn out, I would have. I can't lie, as you've read previously, if you accuse me enough times of doing something that I didn't do, I will eventually do it.

Around the same time period at the same apartment. My niece's dad and I hung tight. I was tight with everyone. There was not a member of that household that I didn't hang with personally on a regular basis. I'm not talking about just around the house. We went on excursions together. I'll name him Jody. Jody and I were super close. Even though he had a child with my sister, Shawna, he knew he could trust me. Even when they were dating, I never told his business. Jody had lots of girlfriends, and we would hook each other up with girls. It was mostly me introducing him. He knew I was a chick magnet. He was used to being that person, and I recall him saying one day at the bookstore, "How is it that you are getting all the girls? I'm the one with the better job, better car... I don't get it?" Honestly, all it was is, he was a little more reserved than I. He had a somewhat unapproachable stigma about him because he was the store manager and wore a tie. He was messing with a few of the female employees. I would only mess with the temp workers and the students...and oh boy, there were a lot of them.

During this time period, there was this pyramid/Ponzi scheme going on, and everyone with a pulse eventually got in on it. I knew this would blow up in people's faces, so I steered clear of it, that is until Jody's mother insisted on me joining her pyramid. Let me explain what the pyramid scheme was. You drew a pyramid on a piece of paper that you kept with you like it was real money. You divided each level into blocks. The bottom blocks were the new recruits. They had to pay to get on. So five people on the bottom would pay $20, $50, $100, $500, or whatever the cost was. There were cheap pyramids, and there were expensive ones. Let's go with the cheaper one. Five people paying $20 would pay the person on the top. The people in the middle blocks had to pay nothing, but they had to recruit people to get under them so that they could move up. Eventually, this went on until the person at the bottom made their way to the top and they were the ones receiving money from the new recruits. The person at the top would then get bumped to the bottom and start over. Well, Jody's mother insisted I join hers. I didn't want to join any at all, but I did because she started getting crazy about it. I didn't expect to ever make it to the top. I was on a $50 entry pyramid, and $50 was a lot back then. She took the money from several of us and ended her pyramid. The rule was you always reentered the pyramid and gave the entry fee, and if you wanted to quit, you had to do so after paying the entry fee, which doubled as the quit fee. The premise is, you made enough to pay your way out. I know people that were in $20k pyramids. Lives were lost behind this and the government got involved. Employers were firing people if they discovered you were part of this scheme. Back to Jody's mom, and I'm going to share some sensitive information, but as I stated, things are going to get dark. Jody's mom got sick. It turns out she was a drug addict. She used to be heavyset, but she quickly started to lose weight. I don't know when she started using, but she wasn't always a user. Jody would bring me to her apartment in San Francisco in the Alemany district, which was dangerous and drug infested. Jody and his brother knew of how she got me for money, and I don't recall, but Jody probably even gave me my money back. I just don't remember, but he's just that type of person. Well, he told me that his mom wanted him to bring me to see her. I really didn't like her, but didn't verbalize it or show any indication of it. It's for a couple of reasons and not just her pyramid scheme. She just turned into a different person. I didn't know that she was an addict at this time when Jody told me that he wanted me to come with him to see his mom, but this is when I found out. On the way, he told me that his mom is dying of full blown AIDS and that she contracted it from sharing a needle. My heart sank, and all of my disdain for her went away, and I now understood why she started acting the way she did. Jody told me that he went there a lot to make sure she was taking her medications. When we got there, she apologized to me and explained herself. She was really sick and bed-ridden, and it was obvious that she didn't have much time left on this earth. We talked, hugged, and I let things go. I understand. What kind of person would I be to forgive Harry, but not Jody's mom?

Fast forward to about 2011, I recall telling my niece, Elana, that her grandma didn't die of cancer, but it was AIDS. Jody told me to keep her real cause of death a secret from Elana. I honestly don't even know if my sister, Shawna, even knew the real cause of death. I didn't just hear it through rumors. I heard it from the horse's mouth. I saw her medication, which was specifically for people with AIDS. I saw her actual prescription. I saw the sores. I recall, because I honestly didn't want to touch her. I couldn't wait to get back home so that I could shower. I recall being over there and her boyfriend coming over with drugs, not realizing Jody and I were there. Jody and I had gone there several times together. Jody and I were thick like thieves, and no matter how uncomfortable the situation, we were there for each other. So, when I told Elana that her grandmother died from AIDS, it didn't come easy. I was contemplating it for months, and it had been around 15 years since her death, and Elana wasn't a kid anymore. There was no need to keep lying to her, and she and I were close. I took her and her friend to Puerto Vallarta, Mexico as a chaperone to make sure they were safe. I paid her to edit a book I wrote, and it wasn't chump change. It was $800. I took her on a shopping spree on her birthday and paid for the dinner of everyone that went with us to her birthday dinner at the expensive seafood restaurant in San Francisco. I had to get gangster and legal with a modeling agency who had photoshopped and scathing images of her floating around on the internet. I did so much for her. Hell, I took her to her first concert. We were close, but she betrayed me in the end. At this time, I just didn't feel comfortable with her believing the lie. She did not believe me and insisted that I was wrong and that she knew the truth. Elana, if you're reading this now, just ask your dad the truth. Look him in the eyes. I think telling her this was one of the reasons we grew distant during that time. Elana had some spoiled brat mightier than thou qualities about her and could act quite nasty. Her mom and aunt have both said this, and she and her aunt were on bad terms for quite some time and could not stand being around each other. Reminds me of Dawn and Ray in Lucy Pearl if I'm honest. I know, you want to know if things are bad between us, and I will get to that, but now isn't the time. You'll have to read further in order to get to that. I'm just laying down a trail before I show you the river.

CHAPTER ELEVEN
A DEGREE DOESN'T MEAN INTELLIGENT

I'm in 1992 on this story. As I said in the beginning, I have an autoimmune disorder called cyclic neutropenia. When I first moved to California, my very first sick cycle, I got extremely sick. One of the reasons, and there were a few, that I moved to California is because my doctor told me the weather there should be much better for my illness, and that I should find that I would get sick far less often. I was young, and the way he explained it made perfect sense to me, but as I have told my daughter on several occasions after we observed doctors getting it wrong, having a college education doesn't make you more intelligent than someone that hasn't even graduated high school. It may make them more disciplined. That doctor or lawyer may even happen to be smarter, but it's not because of their degree. A dumb doctor will know more about medicine or whatever specialized field of medicine they studied and/or practice, than a genius mathematician. One thing people never seem to realize or even think about is, university education wasn't always around. I will get into that in a bit, proving that someone doesn't have to have a formal education in order to make great contributions to society or even be respected. Some of the most brilliant people that I have ever met were along the lines of barbers, janitors, chefs, musicians, dancers, or any type of artists. I have even encountered several homeless people that probably would have been someone we read about had they been born in another century, but once again, I digress. I got so sick, I had a 107° temperature. My body was so used to getting high temperatures that I didn't have the same reaction as someone else would had it been them. I had septic poisoning. My doctor was so excited to see me because she had done her thesis on my condition. Keep in mind, there are only a handful of people with my condition. She acted as though she just met Michael Jackson, how giddy she was. She told me she ran across my name and that she did her thesis on cyclic neutropenia. Her name is Dr Martha Ann Berberich. I bring this story up because out of all the doctors that I ever encountered, other than the doctor from Germany and the doctor from Japan, she is the only one that was at least somewhat versed in my condition, and out of the three, she was the only one that was already aware of it and specifically studied my condition as part of her formal education. How does this tie into my point about having an education not making you more intelligent? Well, I cannot tell you how many doctors that I've come across that tried to put me on a medication that only works on neutropenia as a side effect of chemotherapy or an infection that can cause someone to become neutropenic. Cyclic neutropenia isn't the side result of what I have. For me, an infection is the result of cyclic neutropenia. My bone marrow is not producing neutrophils. In this case, giving me Neupogen (a shot used to treat neutropenia) does not cause my bone marrow to produce neutrophils faster. It only causes bone aches. As I stated, $0 \times 100 = 0$. For someone that just has neutropenia, their bone marrow is still producing neutrophils, so for them, Neupogen helps, because $50 \times 100 = 5000$. Would you believe that I have had the hardest time explaining that to more than a few doctors? It wasn't in their manual, so that deviation was hard for them to compute. Even my current hematologist didn't know the difference between congenital neutropenia, and cyclic neutropenia. When my daughter, who also suffers from the illness, was in the hospital, they wanted to try the shots on her, even after I explained to them that it would not work. I finally agreed to let them give her the shots, and a few days later, they said "see, here are her charts. It worked, just like I told you." I had to explain to them that our counts go up within 3 to 10 days on their own anyways, and even without the shots, her white blood count would have improved anyways. They would ask "well why did you bring her in then?" and my response is, because she has an infection and needs treatment for the infection. I don't know if they were just trying to make money and thought I was that stupid, or if they were genuinely that stupid themselves to not understand the difference between cyclic neutropenia and being neutropenic, even after reading about it. Whenever I or my daughter go to the hospital for reasons due to cyclic neutropenia, even if it's a hematologist, after short conversation and realizing they think I'm coming to them for answers, I have to explain to them that I'm old and that I've had my condition since birth, and that I'm actually the expert on the illness, not them, and reading about it after looking it up on the internet or reading their books, isn't going to make them more knowledgeable on it than I am. I know, it sounds like hubris, but it's necessary for them to understand that my hubris outweighs theirs. It is me that has to look out for the best interest of my daughter and for myself.

The following is a compilation of searches I did from the internet in regards to civilizations, inventions, and advancements before colleges and universities ever existed.

'Ancient Mesopotamians: They developed early mathematical systems, such as the Babylonian numerals and the sexagesimal system, which influenced later scientific thought.

Ancient Egyptians: Known for their advancements in architecture, medicine, and astronomy. They developed techniques for mummification, built the pyramids, and observed celestial phenomena.

Ancient Greeks: Notable figures like Pythagoras, who formulated mathematical principles, and Aristotle, who made significant contributions to philosophy, natural history, and scientific inquiry.

Ancient Chinese: Made advancements in various fields, including astronomy, medicine, and technology. Figures like Confucius and Laozi also contributed to philosophical thought.

Ancient Indians: Made significant contributions to mathematics, including the invention of the decimal system and the concept of zero. Scholars like Aryabhata and Brahmagupta also made important discoveries in astronomy.

Islamic Golden Age: During the medieval period, scholars in the Islamic world made significant advancements in mathematics, astronomy, medicine, and philosophy. Figures like Al-Khwarizmi, Ibn al-Haytham, and Avicenna made enduring contributions to science and scholarship.'

These individuals made remarkable advancements in their respective fields through observation, experimentation, and innovation, often without the formal education or institutional support that we associate with modern science...

Archimedes: A Greek mathematician, physicist, engineer, and inventor who made fundamental contributions to mathematics, including geometry and calculus. He discovered principles of buoyancy and developed innovative machines.

Hippocrates: Often referred to as the "Father of Medicine," Hippocrates was an ancient Greek physician who revolutionized the field of medicine by emphasizing observation, clinical documentation, and the natural causes of diseases.

Aristarchus of Samos: An ancient Greek astronomer and mathematician who proposed the heliocentric model of the solar system, placing the Sun at the center and suggesting that Earth and other planets orbit around it.

Euclid: A Greek mathematician known as the "Father of Geometry" for his work "Elements," which laid the foundation for Euclidean geometry and influenced mathematical thought for centuries.

Zhang Heng: An ancient Chinese astronomer, mathematician, inventor, and polymath who invented the first seismoscope for detecting earthquakes and made significant contributions to astronomy, mathematics, and cartography.

Ibn al-Haytham (Alhazen): A Persian polymath who made groundbreaking contributions to optics, mathematics, and the scientific method. He wrote extensively on optics, including the principles of reflection and refraction, and developed the concept of experimentation and empiricism.

The following individuals demonstrate that formal college education is not always a prerequisite for making significant contributions to science or other fields. Many achieved success through self-study, practical experience, and relentless pursuit of their interests and passions...

Michael Faraday (1791-1867): Widely regarded as one of the greatest experimental physicists of the 19th century, Faraday made groundbreaking discoveries in electromag-

netism and electrochemistry. He received only a basic formal education and was largely self-taught.

Thomas Edison (1847-1931): An American inventor and businessman who developed many devices that greatly influenced life around the world, including the phonograph and the electric light bulb. Edison had only a few months of formal schooling and was primarily self-educated.

Wilbur and Orville Wright (1867-1912, 1871-1948): The Wright brothers were American aviation pioneers who are credited with inventing and building the world's first successful airplane. They had no formal college education but gained their knowledge through self-study and hands-on experimentation.

Marie Curie (1867-1934): A physicist and chemist who conducted pioneering research on radioactivity. Curie was largely self-taught and pursued her education informally due to restrictions placed on women's education in her native Poland.

Edwin Hubble (1889-1953): An American astronomer who played a crucial role in establishing the field of extragalactic astronomy. Hubble made groundbreaking discoveries about the nature of the universe, including the expansion of the universe. He attended the University of Chicago but did not complete a degree in astronomy.

All of the above is information I extracted from the internet, copied and pasted from general searches. There are no individuals that I can give credit to, as none of the above are from sources from individuals, but are from AI inquiries. No plagiarism is intended. I did already know about each of these individuals, but of course, I did not have extensive knowledge and details about each individual. It may seem like I veered off course, but I had to bring it up in order for you to get a deeper understanding of who I am and how I view the world, specifically people I either encounter or see through other means such as television, social media, YouTube, etc... I am somewhat eccentric. I started college but decided not to finish. It was because my instructors didn't seem very intelligent to me. They were smart, but not intelligent. They could easily write things on the board and explain to us how to do it, but if I asked them something that wasn't in their textbooks, I would almost always throw them for a loop. "Who came up with that formula, and can you walk me through how each symbol was placed in the order it was, and why?" was something my math instructor was not prepared to answer. It seemed like everything was a canned response. Try calling Uber in regards to a problem and getting a response that isn't robotic or something that you couldn't have read on their app or website. Yeah, this was how I viewed them, even way back in the 90s.

I recently made appointments for therapy. I went to 2 different screenings to evaluate what my needs were. I made it clear that I do not need a psychiatrist and that I just want to see what therapy has to offer, being that I don't talk to anyone. There was an evaluation that she wanted me to fill out that asked questions such as "how often in the past two weeks did you feel like you were worthless and had no interests in doing things or hobbies" and "how often in the week do you not have the energy to get out of bed?" The answer choices were A-E and were options such as "never, several times, every day, half the week, always." To me, they jumped from one extreme to another. Also, there was no way to fill in my own answers. I tried explaining to the intake therapist that I could not answer those questions and end up with a truthful evaluation. No matter what I said, she did not understand me, and it was because she was not there to listen. She put up a wall to talk, not listen, and took me not doing the questionnaire as a challenge rather than something to discuss. She had the nerve to say "all of the other clients have no problems answering these questions. They're simple." I had to tell her, the problem is, they are simple and one size fits all questionnaires . It offers no room for nuance, and also, that I was happy that I'm not like any of her other clients because I think most people are stupid, or they even think that because they're an expert in a field, they're more intelligent than I am. She tried to backtrack and change her words, but it was too late. She said that I would have to bend. I refused to do the questionnaire. I told her to pay attention to what's going on in the world, and ask herself does 'she' want to be like most people, and why should I want to be like them? I went in there humble with no intentions of being difficult or challenging, but because when that happens, people look down on you, make assumptions, and they take advantage of you. This is one of the reasons why I told them, the moment they try to send me to a psychiatrist because their computer misevaluated me, I'm walking out, which brings me to this...

A couple days after my second intake evaluation, I looked online for the Kaiser intake questionnaire and answered them anonymously. It got me totally wrong. Let me tell you why. Now understand, I do realize I do need therapy and that I do have symptoms of depression, but when I answered the questions, I answered them based on how I was feeling due to my illness. No, I did not have the energy to get out of bed. This is because my body was fighting an infection. No, I had no will to do things that interest me. This was due to cyclic neutropenia. Basically, 75% of the questions at that time were due to neutropenia, and also, when I'm neutropenic, even before my body realizes it, my mind realizes it and I get depressed. Had I answered the questionnaire a week later, my answers would have been different. I tried to explain to her that the questionnaire gave no room for explanation and didn't give instructions for how to answer them, and not to answer the questions based on an illness. She would not listen. So the online questionnaire diagnosed me as having "moderate extreme depression," which is moderately extremely wrong. The first evaluation I had from someone else a couple of weeks prior, I had the same difficulty with. I had no idea that she was punching in the answers on the computer and was going to let the computer diagnose me. Her evaluation said that I had no depression at all, though I was not sick at the time, I was depressed, but I was not able to tell her the things that were bothering me. I only had 15 minutes and started out with the small things. She told the 2nd evaluator that I refused to fill out the evaluation. That was not true. It was that I was ambushed with it and they didn't understand that I have nuances. It was that first evaluation that gave me trepidation towards doing another evaluation, being how wrong it got me. So, just a few days ago, I had an appointment to have my blood pressure checked to see if the medication I was prescribed was helping. This was just a couple days after my 2nd evaluation. The assistant came in with a whiteboard of questions and handed me a green dry-erase marker, and asked me to fill out the questionnaire while she stepped away. She stepped out, I read the questions, and it was the same damn evaluation that my therapist was trying to get me to fill out. Do these people think I'm dangerous? Are they trying to get me to say something on paper so they can put it into their books or as evidence or contact the police? Is it because I said I wouldn't mind if certain people were dead, but I have no intentions on causing their deaths? Guess what, if we're all honest, we all have those thoughts, even if it's just the person that didn't go on during the green light. It is not common for you to have to fill out a psychological survey when getting your blood pressure checked. I have had many checks done. A couple done at Kaiser just within the past month alone, and before my therapy intake, they never asked me to fill out an evaluation before getting my blood pressure checked. When the young lady came back in, I handed her the board back, along with the marker and told her I am not filling that out as that's for therapy and it does not pertain to why I was there to be seen. If they want to evaluate me, they can talk to me and evaluate me. I have no problem with that, and I told them that. Either they just could not see going outside of their paradigm of their routine because they're mindless automatons, or they just wanted to win a battle. "If I can't get him to fill this simple questionnaire out, he wins. I can't lose. I have never lost to someone lower than me." Either way, I am not willing to bend, and I possibly would have been willing to after a couple of sessions, but now I see it as a challenge myself, plus now I'm paranoid as to why this is so important to them when I'm willing to tell them everything I'm thinking. It's supposed to be client/doctor privilege , but they want me to fill out an online survey that can be hacked.

CHAPTER TWELVE
NARCISSISTIC

Going back to when I first moved to California, I don't want to sound unappreciative because I was, but my two sisters that lived here are only my half sisters. We only share a father. Their mother would try to act like my mother and I let it be known that I wasn't open to that. We would go places and she would introduce me as her son. I would never embarrass her by calling her out on it in front of those people that she said it to, but I ended up telling her afterwards that she is not my mother and I didn't appreciate her telling people that. It was for a couple of reasons. For one, it diminishes my story of not having a mother. People are going to think I'm a liar, and what if we ran into someone we both knew, or if I ran into someone that she introduced me to as her son and I didn't remember them and ended up telling them I didn't have a mother? I understood what she was trying to do, and I realized that I hurt her feelings, but I also must consider my own feelings and that she didn't consider my feelings when she decided to tell people that without first discussing it with me and asking how I would feel about it. Ever since then, she acted differently towards me, whether it be on purpose, or an unintentional feeling she harbored. This would come into question later in life, and I would know which side of the fence she was on, which is why I kept myself guarded. You know of course that women will discuss these things amongst each other, and I know she brought it up to her daughters, who were in their early 20s at the time. It would be a miracle if the three of them ever agreed on anything at all. I also think that this topic would probably be one of the times that the two daughters would have agreed with me. I didn't have the easiest of times transitioning back to California. I remember Shawna and I getting into a big argument, and I honestly think she carried that with her throughout the years. Gina and I never really got into it. She was more empathetic to my situation and did more for me than anyone else out of the three of them, then again, I would find out why ten years later.

Gina was narcissistic. She controlled people with money. She would do people favors and then expect for them to forever be in her debt. If you wronged her, she would write you off as an enemy that she hated and wouldn't care if you were to die. She would not go anywhere you were and avoid you at all costs. There was an instance where a cousin of hers "stole" a computer from her. I won't say whether it was true or not because I learned that Gina is not the most honest of people and will lie about you in order to rally the troops behind her. Well, her feud with David went on for at least 10 years before they started speaking again. That seems to be a magic number for her, but that's only if you apologize for wronging her. Even after you apologize, she will still hold this long grudge. She's not much unlike me, except, I will be happy to accept your apology, forgive you, and move on. I will hold a grudge against you until I'm dead though, depending on what it is you did to me. There are people I haven't spoken to in 10, 20, or even 30 years because of something they did. Like I said, I will always give you the opportunity to make things right. Go back to when I talked about Nugget. She refused to apologize even though I told her that's all I wanted, and she refused. Pride is the devil if the devil is real. Nugget altered my life and caused a lot of dissension between several family members and myself. To this day, people think I abandoned a son that DNA and common sense proved wasn't mine.

Shawna and I weren't all bad though. Yes, there were instances where she should have had my back and she didn't. I let that slide, but I will never forget. One thing I will never forget though is in 2007, I worked at an auto factory in Fremont, CA,. It was June. I showed up for my shift. I didn't even make it past the turnstiles to enter the facility. I was exhausted, not from lack of sleep, but my body was exhausted because of my immune deficiency and I had an ongoing infection. There was a chair in the lobby area just past the entrance. I saw it and grabbed it and sat down for a moment. I had no idea that I looked as bad as I did. Many people use the chair to sit on for a moment when they're either waiting on someone or if they're early and just don't want to enter yet. One of the managers of the area saw me sitting there and came to me and told me that I didn't look too good. It's not normal for an area manager to volunteer for you to go to medical, especially being that people called in a lot and we were short workers. He said I was pale white and actually insisted that I go. I owned a vanpool and I knew if I were to go to medical, that I would end up having to either go home or spend the night in the hospital. I went to the medical department and my temperature was 105°. I had swollen glands and had the chills. My bones were aching, and I had no appetite. They sent me to the hospital in a cab and I was there from early that day, well, early for my shift which was around 2:00 p.m., all the way to the end of 2nd shift and some time after. Believe it or not, the same manager that I had gotten into several disputes with, mainly because I was also a union rep, called to check on me. I told him they were trying to keep me overnight, but if I were to stay, I wouldn't have a ride home the next day. He came to pick me up and drove me all the way home, which was maybe an extra 30 miles out of his way. I always appreciated him for that and had a deeper respect for him, as he had a deeper understanding and respect for me. He had no idea that I was suffering from such an illness but still came to work everyday.

At the hospital, before my manager came to get me, the doctor came to me and confirmed what I already knew was true. He said I was suffering from septic poisoning and that my organs were beginning to shut down. He gave me a 50/50 chance of making it through the night and immediately put me on antibiotics and fluids. He told me I should call my family because of how serious the situation was. It wasn't my first rodeo though, so I really wasn't too worried, but no one ever told me before that my organs had begun shutting down. I called my sister, Shawna. I told her that I was in serious condition and that the doctor said I should call someone close to me to be by my side. She told me, and I quote, "I just started this job and I cannot call in sick, so I can't come see you." That let me know right then and there where we stood. Personally, I don't care what my situation was, if someone in my family were to tell me they were given a 50/50 chance to live, I would make sure I was by their side, especially if you were my brother or sister. This would be a reoccurring theme throughout the years. The very next month in July, my very next sick cycle, so 21 days later, I would end up in the emergency room for the same thing. I evidently had an infection that had not yet left my body. Crazy thing is, I am going through the exact same thing right now as I write this.

As I stated, Gina was a light switch. She was either on, or off. There was no dim setting. When I was sick and didn't know why, she came all the way to Modesto to pick me up and take me to the doctors and helped me fill out all of my paperwork in order to be treated. This was even after the time she did me so dirty, it was I that should have never forgiven her. This is about to get crazy. If you have anyone in your family that has done the following to you, stay away from them. Don't even waste your time trying to make things right. If they're ready to make things right with you, let them, but don't go chasing apologies. Stick to the lies and deception you're used to.

I was engaged and fully committed to a young lady I had been dating for three years at this point. We'll call her Kay. I had worked so hard at my job to straighten out my credit and to save the money necessary to put down as a deposit for a house. Kay and I went to Shasta because that was the best bang for the buck as far as sq. ft. per dollar goes. Kay really didn't mind either as she had many relatives in Shasta County. We even went to visit them while we were there house hunting. We found a house and I went through the process to secure a loan. We were headed towards the dream life and Kay saw a way out of living the meager life she had been living, several people in a very small house in a really bad, crime ridden neighborhood. We found the nicest piece of property for $100k. It was actually two houses, 2500 sq. ft. each, on a very large plot of land. If I recall correctly, it was 5 acres. The houses were joined by a walkway. The day had come for us to go sign the paperwork in Shasta, and Kay and I got ready. I was living in Antioch at the time, and Kay would spend weekends with me. We were literally ready to walk out of the door, and being the type of person I am, always putting others in front of myself, I looked at Kay and said to her that I wanted to call my sister and tell her I was buying property and that it was two houses and she could go half in with me. The reason for this is, Gina was living in a 2 bedroom, 1 bath home with her two children, her mom, her best friend, and her friend's three kids. That's eight people. They could all stay in the other property if they were willing to move that far. I called Gina and she was excited, but told me she didn't want to move that far. She asked me to hold off on signing the paperwork for that house, and I reluctantly agreed, but was excited that she was excited and wanted to go in on a house with me. Gina called me back and said that she had been searching for houses a little closer and found some in a city called "Manteca." I had never heard of it, but she sent me pictures, and the homes were huge and a fraction of the cost of houses in the Bay Area that were ¼ the size. We agreed on a house that was about $350k and made an appointment to go see a model home, as we would have to have it built from the ground up. On our way there, she informed me that she found other houses just 20 miles further that were even bigger for the same money. We found a house that had 6 bedrooms, 4½ baths, and one of the other rooms could be converted into a bedroom just by adding a sliding door. It was 4109 sq. ft. and came out to $377k. We could definitely handle that mortgage between the two of us, and with the number of people moving in, including my fiancé, we had all the bills covered. We went through all the phases of having the home built, signing new paperwork along each way, and saw the empty lot, then a lot with 2x4s outlining the property, then we saw the skeleton of the structure go up. We eventually saw the walls and floors added. There was one more phase after we signed off on the "rough and ready" installation and the installation of the extra add-ons of the house, and that was the final completion before handing us the keys. That included cleaning and painting, and the installation of all the doors, windows, appliances, etc... Kay and I couldn't wait. It had been several months, and we were supposed to have already had a house and moved into it on our own. Kay didn't have the credit or the finances to be on the paperwork, but she didn't mind. Once we were married, it was ours together anyways.

We had an appointment set to sign off for the house. There was one major problem. I hadn't heard from Gina in a few weeks and she wasn't returning any of my calls or texts. I grew anxious being that I had put down a $25k non-refundable deposit on the house and she also put that amount down. The day before the signing came and I still hadn't heard from her. I knew she was avoiding me as this was not something that you'd forget about, especially since she was so excited about it through the process over the past several months, going out there even when there was no appointment just to look at it and take pictures. I ended up going to the final phase signing for the house on my own, nervous. I couldn't afford that house on my own and I didn't want to lose the money that I put down on it. I made good money, but that's not how I wanted to live, and I didn't want Kay to have to burden herself with helping me pay the mortgage. I met up with the realtor and informed her that I had not heard from my sister. The realtor gave me an extra couple of weeks to straighten things out, but informed me that I would either have to secure a loan on my own, or forfeit my deposit. Either way, she didn't care, but I believe she wanted to see me in that house.

I talked to several people in our family trying to find Gina. You would think that someone would have contacted me and told me that they knew what was going on, as I am a blood member, but no, narcissists control everyone around them. I finally got someone to tell me what was going on. Our uncle Junior contacted her and told her that she needs to contact me. Uncle Junior was the Patriarch of the family. He was very respected, and his word was mostly final. No one argued with him except for his wife. This is odd, because he was once on drugs and doing bad in the streets, stealing and overdosing. No one cared about him until he got himself cleaned up, got a great job as an elevator engineer and was also a union rep, and got married and had property and nice cars. Then suddenly, he was everyone's favorite uncle, dad, and brother. They didn't bother with him before his success.

Gina still didn't contact me, but I was told that the family was getting together for a trip to the Monterey Bay Aquarium. I wasn't initially invited because Gina was going to be there. Gina's mom and my sister Shawna figured Gina was dead wrong for what she was doing and that it was important for she and I to meet up so that I could know what was going on. They expressed that they felt responsible for knowing what was going on and I didn't and that I would lose out on all of my money I put down on the house because of their loyalty to their daughter and sister. Mind you, my full blood sister, Belle, had no part in this, knew what was going on, and didn't tell me, so when I get to the story about her, you'll know why I responded the way I did to her. I remember the day and what I was wearing. I had on my sky blue velour sweatsuit, white Adidas (irony), a navy blue/sky blue cartoon printed t-shirt, and a fitted baseball cap that brought the entire ensemble together. Gina wasn't aware that I would be joining them until it was too late. They promised not to tell her until I got there. They wanted this to be resolved and assured me that they all tried to convince her that what she was doing was wrong and you don't do family like that. They admitted she was wrong. Remember I said that.

I went to Monterey Bay Aquarium. I went without Kay, as I didn't want there to be an issue and she had been quiet about the entire situation. But I knew her. She could blow up at any moment, and she had my back. I didn't want her to get into it with my sister over this, as Gina was also messing up her life and plans. Remember, Kay and I put our lives on hold for Gina by not signing for the property we originally intended on buying. When Gina saw me, I swear I could literally see her spirit leave her body as her face melted and a gasp of air left her body. I approached her and she knew it was time to fill me in on why she was not responding to me. It was obvious that she changed her mind, but I had to know why. I had spent so much time trying to find someone else to get onto the loan paperwork with me, and out of maybe 30 people I asked, no one was willing to, including Belle. I didn't need anyone to have good credit, as I would be the primary, though the interest rate would have gone up a bit because I didn't have the excellent credit that Gina had, but the other person just needed fair credit and a history of income. I looked for every avenue that I could in order to keep the house, but I just couldn't secure a loan on my own.

Gina and I sat down and talked not far from the manta ray pond. I told her of the troubles I was having securing the loan and that I didn't want to lose my deposit because I worked so hard to save the money. I also reminded her that she signed the contract and she was legally obligated at this point and she better have a good excuse for leaving me hanging like this. The irony being, she excommunicated David for much less. She let out a gasp and began telling me what was going on. Regardless of what she had going on, I deserved for her to let me know when she first knew she changed her mind. Gina said she went to a nightclub and met a guy. They had a whirlwind romance and she got pregnant immediately. They decided to buy a house together, but she explained to Jerome, her new man, that they would need to do it expeditiously, being that her credit report would soon depict a home loan for the property that she and I were buying together, so they found a home and purchased it in the amount of time that I stopped hearing from her, to well before we finally spoke again. I was disappointed, and she was steadily trying to find a way to make it a good reason for what she did to me, but there was no reason that could be explained that would ever be good enough for doing this to Kay and I. I told her that I exhausted every possibility, and I had a week to secure a loan, or lose the deposit. She offered no solution or remedy, but at least I left knowing what happened. I was heartbroken. I thought I was finally moving along in life, making progress as a young adult, accomplishing the American Dream. I thought I was done having my heart broken by my own flesh and blood, but this would just be another time out of many more times to come that someone would stick their filthy hands into my chess and rip my artery out again. Gina called me while I was at work and I returned her call while I was on lunch break. She told me that she would pay me back my deposit. At this point, I wanted the house and I was just being difficult because I was exhausted from the initial process of buying a house. I told her that I didn't agree with her and I just wanted her to sign on the loan with me. She basically said she didn't know what to tell me. Three days went by and I called her back letting her know that I changed my mind and that I would accept my deposit back. The response I got from her, and the way she said it, made the one chamber of my heart I had left, sink into my lungs, sucking all of the air out of them. "Well I don't have it. I don't know what to tell you. Jerome and I spent it on the house we bought together and we had to get a loan from his brother to put on top of that." I can't tell you how long I was silent for. She had just told me that she would pay me back, and this guy had enough money to pay me back. I was just a couple days away before time to secure a loan or forfeit my deposit. Out of despair, I told her mom and sister that I was just going to have to use my last resort and take her to court, which meant she would probably lose the house that she just bought if I won, which I definitely would have won. Gina contacted me back and agreed to stay on the loan with me. We signed that paperwork, but she of course never moved in. It was Kay, her son, and I, alone in that giant house, which was known as a McMansion. Please don't ask me the origin of that word. I think this was the beginning of my light being slowly dimmed by life, yet I never had a thought about harming anyone. I just continued searching for happiness, and I still had Kay.

You would think that would be the end of the story between the two of us and the house, but then again, whenever you have someone else on the paperwork of a home, it is never the end. I had that house from 2003 until 2009. I paid the property taxes. I paid the insurance. I paid the mortgage. I paid for upgrades such as a water softener, which in Modesto, is needed. I paid for the upgrades to the landscaping, which included turning all of the areas that had grass, into brick and gravel. I planted the tree and shrubs, and basically everything that involves homeownership. Gina paid for NOTHING. The value of the house continued to skyrocket over the months. I bet she was certainly paying attention to that, which is the only thing she paid in regards to that house. From the time I moved into it, until when I moved out in 2009, the value jumped to $840k. I didn't list it on time to take advantage of it. The month I listed it happened to be the very month the housing market crashed. Literally two weeks after it was listed, it was announced that the market officially crashed, so people stopped coming to the open houses. Just a couple of months before, my neighbor a few doors down sold his for $840k. We paid the same amount and they were the same models. He had more upgrades such as marble countertops and things as such. I had the advantage of having a corner home. We were both on the same block of a cul-de-sac. After the market crash, I held on for another year or so before I let it go into foreclosure.

I did take out a couple of loans against the mortgage. One was a refinance in which I took some money out for upgrades, in which I actually did upgrade the house and is how I was able to do all of the landscaping, which included a wraparound cement patio. I would argue that my house was worth more than my neighbor's that I mentioned. I took out a total of $100k on the house. Guess who was paying attention to the market and wanted me to pay her $50k? You guessed it, my wonderful sister, Gina. Why? Because at the time, her name was still on the mortgage. I had to explain to her what a loan is. I didn't make $100k on the house. The value went up and I just took out a loan, half of which went straight into the house. She let her stupid ass baby daddy talk her into telling me that she deserved half that money. That's crazy because these were the very people that were stiffing me on my deposit. These were the same people that stiffed me on having to pay a mortgage that was 3 1/2 times the amount I was going to pay had my fiancé and I bought the house in Shasta before Gina talked me out of it. If you add up all the extra expenses I accrued due to her bailing on me, Gina cost me about $86k alone in extra mortgage I had to pay, not including other expenses. She cost me over $100k in extra expenses and had the nerve to think I owed her $50k for the amount in value the house went up just because I had to force her to sign for the final phase of purchasing the house. I told her of the extra added expenses and said if she was going to insist I owed her that amount, that I would happily let a judge decide and hear my countersuit. She said it was all Jerome's idea so she would consult with him and get back to me. She did rather quickly and decided to drop the issue because she evidently didn't want the smoke. Well, she didn't totally drop it as I would find out approximately 9 years later, so I will just fast forward in time to tell you what she did, which will be a good segue to another time I was betrayed by blood. Before I do, I will tell you what fueled her rampage. It was 2012 and I was having a difficult time in life and was weighing options. I was a single father and doing my best to take care of my daughter, being that her mom was not fit to do so. I won't get into it at the moment and will get into detail later, but Sheray had supervised visitation.

So I called Gina and told her I was having a difficult time. I knew that Gina also needed help with her daughter, who is exactly a year and a half older than my daughter, and they got along like best friends. Gina used to have to drive all the way from Sacramento to the Bay Area to pick up and drop off her mom, and sometimes her mom would drive herself, but she was getting old and sometimes couldn't even make the trip. She was babysitting so Gina could go to work. I wasn't working at the moment but I still had plenty of money from a settlement. My hard time wasn't really financial as much as it was me knowing the finances would run dry and I was investing a ton of money into publishing a book. I was also towards the end of a disability case which my attorney thought I was sure to win. I lost, but it was a corrupt system. I have the disability, but they didn't want to award it to me because of my age and they didn't have enough data on the immune disorder. Of course they wouldn't. There's only 236 known cases in the United States, so there's almost no data at all, but let's see how the people on this panel would get along having no immune system. Gina saw the advantage of my daughter and I moving in. She had an in-home nanny and company for her daughter. I did all of the cooking and cleaning, and I basically was raising her daughter while keeping her juvenile delinquent son in line. I'm not taking a crack at him, and I think he outgrew his ways, but I'm just stating the facts. Gina saw a money opportunity if I had won my case. I lost my case and that's when her attitude towards us living there changed. We had been there two years at this time and she started becoming abusive towards my daughter. She knew that Sheray and I had an agreement that we would not physically discipline Anjolie, but I noticed a difference in behavior from my daughter, but she wouldn't tell me what was wrong. Finally, she told me after she had enough. Anjolie told me that Gina slapped her in the restaurant for something that wasn't her fault, and didn't slap her own daughter for the same thing, and this wasn't the only time this had happened. I did not care whose house I was living in, I will go to war over my daughter. I confronted Gina and she gave excuses. I said to her, I don't care, if you do it again, I will defend my daughter by all means necessary. You see, Gina thought that just because she was paying for my daughter's gymnastics, that she had the right to override my wishes. That's her thinking that just because she's paying, she can control us. Do I blame her for thinking this? Not when everyone else in the family allows it. They ALL talk about it and know it's a problem, but because Gina "pays" for things, they allow it. Another example of how controlling she is, and this isn't an anomaly, we could all be going out to dinner and deciding on a restaurant. There might be 9 or 10 of us that agree on the Spaghetti Factory, but if Gina would rather go to the Cheesecake Factory, guess where we're going. It doesn't matter if she's out-voted 9 to 1. She will argue with everyone until they give in. Yes, she usually paid for the dinner, but I would usually pay for myself and my daughter because I knew what the true cost would be otherwise. I learned not to be indebted to her. Even when we were living with her, I was earning our keep. She didn't have to worry about anything. She wouldn't have to pay her mom, go through the troubles of a 200+ mile round trip, or not be able to go places unplanned. If she wanted to go on a date, she only had to let me know. On top of our arrangement, and here's the kicker, she had her friend living there with her. She was living there even before me. She had her own bedroom and bathroom. Leona was nice and we got along, so I don't have any complaints about her, but why would my own flesh and blood sister throw in my face that I was living there for free, though I really wasn't. It was Leona that was living there for free and not contributing anything whatsoever to the household. She didn't even cook, I mean ever. She would only eat Top Ramen noodles. I never saw her make anything that a 7 y/o child couldn't make. She would barely even clean. All she did was sit around the house and watch television. She did start going to school and she did get a part time job at the stadium.

It was the incidents between Gina and hitting my daughter that we stopped speaking. I even took it a step further because Gina threw down the gauntlet. She thought that she was going to be able to treat my daughter the way she was treating her and I would just take it and smile. I found out she was still mistreating her, so I got in her face about it, literally. I told her that if I were to hit her, how would she feel, and what if I treated Keahna the same way she was treating my daughter? There was one time where Keahna told her I either hit her or yelled at her. I can't remember which it was, but it was false. I never laid a hand on my niece, and if I yelled at her, it was no different than any other time, which was more so fussing at her, not yelling. Because of this, I told Gina that our arrangement was now off. I would no longer be her nanny. I would not have dinner waiting for her when she got home from work, I was not going to babysit for her any longer, and Anjolie and I would be out soon. Until then, it was just going to have to be an uncomfortable situation unless she apologized. She didn't want to apologize, so we really didn't speak much. She would turn to Uncle Junior to try to set me straight. I was always respectful to him. I was respectful to him before he was doing well, unlike ANYONE ELSE, including his own offspring. One day, Gina handed me her phone and he was on the other end. He actually threatened me in a round-about way. He must have mistook me as a punk or something, I guess it's because I let him assault me because he thought I was messing with his wife, slide. I let it slide because everyone convinced me to let it slide and I was in shock at the moment it happened. His accusations came out of left field and what he didn't know was, his wife was like an aunt to me, but she was extra nice to me because she told me she wanted me to date her daughter, not because we had anything going on. Natasha was too young at the time, but she was "grooming" us I guess. She told me that she wouldn't mind us dating. I used to go over there a lot, not for Natasha, and not for her, but because it felt like the family I never had and they were so welcoming, but I digress. Uncle Junior told me he wasn't going to allow me to threaten his niece like that. I told him in a firm way, that for one, I didn't threaten her. I told her the same thing about my daughter, that you're telling me about his niece. I then told him that in no way shape or form was I worried about him or his threats and that I don't need him to allow me to do anything. I could hear the surprise in his voice that he wasn't expecting for me to stand up to him. He hadn't seen me in a while and maybe didn't know that I was in great shape and was running several miles a day and lifting weights. Gina had a graduation party for her son and I was still living there. I stayed for the occasion. Gina figured that getting uncle Junior to threaten me didn't work, that she'd get a couple of her male friends to intimidate me. One of them saw me and wanted no parts and kept things friendly. Another one of them asked to speak to me, and I told him what was up. I could see that he sized me up and decided to keep it friendly too. I actually heard him tell Gina that he was not about to push up on me. See, Gina saw me everyday, so my muscles growing and the fat disappearing wasn't noticeable, but to those that weren't around me a lot or hadn't seen me in a long time, it was a shock to them. I wasn't fat anymore and could rep 225 lbs on the bench press and run 7 miles with no problem, when just a year before, I could barely run 20 feet. I went from 245 lbs, to 185 lbs and no longer needed blood pressure medication.

I COULD HAVE BEEN A KILLER

The graduation party went off without any incidents. I noticed that something was going on and no one was telling me. I won't keep you in suspense. Gina was in the process of moving and wasn't going to tell me. She was planning on being gone while I was out, moving out completely all at once within a couple hour period of time, and me coming home and the house being locked up with the locks changed. I even asked her because I noticed the garage was becoming less and less full. She told me that she was just putting things in storage for Spring cleaning. My instincts knew better. I was already planning on moving and Anjolie and I were moving to southern California. I had already given her mom a 45 day advance written notice as family court said I had to do, and had a move-out date. Finally, Gina served me with paperwork. Not legally, but the information was the same. Little did she know, we would have been out sooner, but when I found out her plans to stiff me once again, I decided it was time for payback. I didn't move out when I planned to. Instead, I pushed it back another month, as I didn't have a time limit and my friend that I was moving in with could wait another month. I wrote Gina a response letter by email informing her that she did not give me proper notice and that I needed a proper three month notice as per landlord/tenant law requires. She did not expect this, so now the property managers had to get involved. They offered to pay me to leave and I turned it down. They were actually kicking her out because her son was causing problems and they got a lot of complaints from neighbors. Incidents involved smoking weed and guns, which turned out to be pellet guns that they were shooting at cars and houses. But guess what? I warned Gina this was going on, but she had the nerve to get mad at me for intervening and me having to put hands on my disrespectful nephew. How ironic. He was 6'4" and 18. I'm 5'8" and 40 at the time. Her oldest daughter even sided with me over pretty much everything. I told Gina that if I wanted to hurt her son, I would have punched him when I had him down, and told her that unlike how she did my 7 y/o daughter who was defenseless, I only wrestled him to the couch to let him know who's boss. I never struck him. He even confirmed that I could have but didn't. Gina tried to blame me for her being kicked out, but she didn't know that I had already seen the notice she was given and why she was given it. I will admit, I was in complete revenge mode. I could have left, but didn't. It would backfire on me a little, but a price I was willing to pay just to cause her hardship. Gina moved out and I was served legal papers by the property manager. Me not moving out constituted Gina not moving out, so we both got served. She cut off all the utilities, which I expected and prepared for. I just had the utilities cut on in my name that same day. I was already prepared for that. It may have been the next day that everything was cut back on, but not a full 24 hour period. During this week, CPS came. They said they tried making contact several times before then, but Gina told them purposely the wrong times that I'd be home. At this time, Anjolie was visiting her mom for the weekend and CPS wanted to inspect my living arrangements. They saw that all the utilities were on and said they received a report stating otherwise. But, they already had a court order to remove my daughter from my care temporarily until we went back to court. This is how narcissistic Gina is. She thought that just because she moved out, that I suddenly couldn't function as an adult. If she cuts the power off, I would be without power. How stupid does that sound? Gina even went as far as to write a letter to Sheray to use against me. It was full of lies that I was easily able to disprove. Once again another sister sided with my daughter's mom. I'm tired of this sisterhood nonsense, especially when it's against men in our own family. This thwarted us moving to the Los Angeles area. I wasn't moving without my daughter, so I stayed and fought. I would visit my daughter while she was at

Boys-N-Girls club through the fence, then I had my day in court. What neither of us realized was, the mediator had us investigated. She actually followed and filmed us. I went to all of the appointments with the mediator, and Sheray didn't show up to any of them. I then learned that the mediator, who over the years was always trying to side with Sheray, finally took my side and even apologized. She said the very first day she followed Sheray, she had her on video, fighting on the front lawn. She told me that all of the unbelievable things I told her about Sheray turned out to be true and she has it all on video. It was then that not only did I get full custody back, but her mom had supervised visitation. Sheray showed up late to court and had fraudulent text messages that she pieced together to make it seem like I was saying things I didn't say. I brought with me 7 years of text messages printed out. The court saw how she was lying, and on the last page of the new custody orders, the mediator put on it all the deceptive things Sheray had done and that I had been right all along and that I was the only one doing things by the book. The judge told Sheray that she's lucky she isn't being arrested, and that he never wants to see her in his courtroom again. That was the last time Sheray tried to take me to court again. Sheray will get her own chapter, but I had to include her in this, as this would be the first and only time she would team up with my sister against me, and they failed miserably. To this day, Gina cannot face me. We did interact a couple of times recently, but she stopped returning my texts. I bet it's the guilt. You see, all that she did, backfired on her. Gina and I went to eviction court. What she wasn't expecting was, for one, I couldn't be evicted as I wasn't listed on the lease agreement. She also wasn't expecting that I had video of her son using a key to get into the home after she already turned in "all" the keys, and while I was still living there. Because of this, the judge told her that she also had not moved. Gina now had a blemish on her credit report. She had an eviction on her record that would last for the next 7 years, and that's all that I wanted to accomplish and didn't care how it affected me. I moved back to Modesto and rented from a friend. I worked at an Amazon warehouse, got my CDL, and life went on. Now to get into the story about how Gina would cause chaos between me and my family back in Buffalo, NY. To All that are reading this, I never got a chance to tell my side of the story because I really didn't care, but now you're about to know the truth from the person that remained silent all these years.

CHAPTER THIRTEEN
LIES & BETRAYAL

Kay, her son, and I moved into the house. I guess it's time to tell you how it is I met her. It was 2001, and I was still recovering from my knee surgery and had a few pounds extra on me. I was driving my brand new 2001 Chevrolet Prizm Lsi, and I made a left turn onto 14th Street and I saw this really pretty, short haired redbone girl standing at the bus stop. I was feeling good about myself, though I was self conscious about my weight. I had never really been the type to pull over to talk to a girl, but had I not done it this time, I would have been torturing myself for a long time. She was actually on the phone, but we had made eye contact as I turned the corner. It was a positive affirmation for me that she was interested in me. I pulled over, got out of the car and asked if I could talk to her. She told the person she was talking to that she would call them back because someone wanted to talk to her. We talked, exchanged numbers and we started exchanging texts that day. We immediately met up the next day, and we were officially a couple. We had gone on several road trips, went out several times, took the couples picture, ironically wearing the same outfit that I wore to the Monterey Bay Aquarium, and she happened to have a sweatsuit the same exact color and also made from velour, so this was a sign that we should wear that. We went to the mall and had professional pictures taken. I had just proposed to her after buying her a ring that I bid on on a website. It wasn't diamond, but it was a really nice ring, and the stone was a sky blue, the same blue as our sweatsuits, which was also her birthstone, and she was so proud to be my fiancé, as I will never forget her addressing me by saying "of course, my future husband."

I think Kay and I may have been better for each other under the right circumstances. She and I both had numerous unresolved family issues and traumas. I don't want to divulge hers as I honestly don't know what happened to her mom, as it was a subject she stayed away from. I never pushed the issue because I had my own unresolved issues with my mother that I never wanted to talk about. I honestly think our circumstances were the same. My memory may be off, but I think her mom may have left them with their dad (she had sisters), and I think she later passed away. I was also heartbroken to find out that Kay's dad passed away 10 years ago. I haven't had contact with Kay since around 2007, and that was only through social media. We were toxic together. There was never any physical abuse or anything like that. She nor I ever threatened each other like that. She just got into her feelings a lot and would take her issues out on everyone around her. She was a yeller. She has a son, and she yelled at him a lot. I do admit, he did act up quite a bit and was with his dad and his dad's family a lot, and I think he picked up a lot of their qualities, so when he was around us, he acted out. I honestly don't think he was bad. He was just a boy and was hyper. I think Kay yelled at me a lot because she became distrustful of me and may have thought I was cheating on her, which I have no reason to lie, I wasn't, well, not until after I learned that she had been cheating on me the entire time we were together, from the first day we met. She refused to fess up to it to the day we last spoke on the subject. I wasn't perfect, we all know this, but I tried. I wish Kay trusted me more though. I remember going to her family's house for Thanksgiving. All of her sisters were there. Her family was dominated by women. I only briefly met her dad's side of the family in Shasta, and I didn't know the dynamics of her mom's side of the family. The house we were at was her aunt's, but I don't think she was her aunt by blood. We had a good time and there were no incidents. Maybe a couple of very minor arguments between a couple of the sisters or something. The day ends and most of us are spending the night at Kay's aunt's house. I was sleeping on the couch downstairs by myself. I sensed someone was in the living room with me and I woke up, and it was Kay's sister. Her sister had several children and she was very attractive. Her only real flaw was from when she was shot in the head and almost lost her life. Her eye area had some scarring and she may have been a little off in the head, but she was normal functioning just like anyone else. There was a lot of bickering amongst the sisters and they often clicked up. Her family dynamic was quite familiar, so I understood. So I saw Kay's sister in the living room and she was wearing nothing but a long white t-shirt. She was standing over me. Maybe she was whispering my name or something to wake me up, I don't know. I just woke up to her standing there, and her sister, my fiancé, Kay, standing at the bottom of the stairs asking what she was doing in the living room with her man while he's trying to sleep. I think Kay knew her sister well and didn't quite fall asleep because she didn't trust her and followed her down the stairs to see that she was up to no good. I happened to wake up as this was going on. After they bickered momentarily and Kay said she would address her in the morning, I just put my head down to go back to sleep, figuring Kay would somehow think I was complacent in whatever was going on, which I wasn't. I barely said more than a few words to her sister the entire day because I already knew better. The next day came and Kay and her sister argued but it didn't come to blows. Kay did say things like she knew she would try to sleep with me because she's known for that, hence all the kids I guess. Kay and I left together. I told her that I really had no idea what was going on. She believed me I think, and she told me that her sister was like that and she didn't trust her, and that's why they don't get along. I'm going to skip many details of our relationship and just get to the parts that caused tension. It wasn't her child's father. He and I got along and were cordial whenever they exchanged their son. It wasn't her son. I was willing to be a stepfather and after spending a couple days around us after spending the weekend at his dad's, he would calm back down and be respectful. This is why I say he was just behaving like that side of the family, because he only acted like that for a couple days, and it was always when he came back from over there. The tension between Kay and I was due to the incident with my sister. I could tell that Kay would have preferred that she and I would have bought the house in Shasta, but she was happy either way. It was the fact that I became stressed after my sister did what she did in regards to the house. That put extra pressure on Kay because I asked her if she could at least pay a utility bill, which she wasn't willing to do. I never dwelled on that, but perhaps I should have. She never even gave me the opportunity to dwell on it. It was just the 3 of us in that house, and her son was mostly with his dad. Kay was tired of commuting from Modesto to downtown Oakland every day. It came to a point that she literally disappeared from me for 3 weeks. She wouldn't return my texts or answer my calls. I would go to her house and she was never there, or at least that's what I was told. I gave up and decided to move on. That's when I started seeing someone else, but not as far as a serious relationship. I told her that

I just broke up with my fiancé and wasn't looking for anything and just wanted to have fun. Someone to go to the movies with. I was just trying to move on. I had done everything I could to talk to Kay to resolve whatever it was that was bothering her, though I had a feeling it was the commute and the quietness of the house. She was used to chaos all around her, and perhaps the quiet became too noisy for her.

Well, after 3 weeks passed, it was Kay's dad that actually contacted me. He loved me and was happy that I was with his daughter. He came over to visit the first day we moved into the house and was in my bedroom while I was setting up the bed that was just delivered days before. He was so excited that his daughter was about to live the American dream and was engaged and moving into such a big brand new home in a suburban neighborhood. He expressed this to me with a big smile. He was a jolly guy. Kay's dad was White and her mom was Black and he had so many children to take care of, living in a Black community on a limited income, it had to be hard for him. Kay and I being together was a stress that he could relieve himself of, so when he called me during his daughter's absence from me, you can understand why. He told me that he felt badly for how she was treating me and he didn't understand it himself. He assured me that he would talk to her and get her to call me back to discuss what was going on in her head. I did tell him that I was planning to move on if I didn't hear from her within the next day or so. I didn't tell him that I was already done and I was so tired of being abandoned with no explanation. I was tired of people just disappearing and not returning my calls or telling me why. No note, no calls, no texts, nothing for me to resolve.

Kay called me the next day. She said she was just under a lot of pressure and pretty much all of the reasons I mentioned. But those were only partial truths. One of the reasons was because I wanted a child. She knew this when we first met, but she said because her son was so bad, she didn't want anymore kids because she just couldn't handle it and she was already struggling. I told her that I wanted a kid and I was going to have one, with or without her. I gave her a car. The very one that I was driving when I first met her. She came over on the weekend. She had a smile on her face and told me that she was ready to have a baby with me. She didn't seem pressured and if anything seemed happy about her decision. I welcomed her back into our home with open arms. We were back together and did attempt to have a child together. One day, I got a call from the girl that I was dealing with during the absence of Kay. She said she was pregnant, and this is my daughter's mom. My emotions were all over the place at this moment. I had just gotten back with my lady and we were now trying to have a baby, and now this. I was happy and sad at the same time. Yes, I would have preferred to have been with Kay, in our home, and have a baby out of love, but instead, it was with someone that I had no feelings for. I was on the freeway on my way to work when I decided to call my fiancé and tell her the news. I actually cried when I told her and that Usher song "Confessions" was playing in my head the entire time. So did I cheat on Kay? I don't know. I guess if you consider that I was done with being abandoned and chose to get with someone else in her absence out of loneliness, then yes, I cheated. This is why it's important to communicate with the ones you love. You never know when they're at their breaking point. But it gets deeper...

The day I was moving into my house, the person that was helping me move, was her "best friend." She had a male best friend and I always had a problem with that, but she told me that I was wrong for trying to make her choose between someone that she knew for years before we even met, so I just dealt with it. We were driving the U-Haul truck on the long journey from Antioch to

Modesto. This is when I learned the true dynamics of the relationship between the two of them. You see, she had not known him for years before she met me. She met him the day before I met her. She just chose me over him and decided he would be on the side. He told me that it was him on the phone with her when I pulled over to talk to her and that I won her over him, but that they were indeed dating because he slipped up and said that she broke up with him after they had been dating a while. Doing the math, if Kay and I were dating from the 2nd day we met and were officially boyfriend and girlfriend, and she just met him the day before me, then she was indeed cheating on me and lying to me about the dynamics of our relationship the entire time. So during the conversation when I told Kay that I got someone pregnant, I told her that we could still be together, but she decided to break up. She accused me of cheating on her. She was trying to do the math in her head and it had only been maybe 5 or 6 weeks since she first left me, I just had to have cheated on her, but that wasn't the case. You see, I told her that I knew the entire time from the day her "best friend" helped me move in, that I knew she had been cheating on me the entire time, so I in fact wasn't the one cheating on her. She tried to deny it, but she really didn't deny it if that makes any sense to you. It was one of those "why would he say that? I can't believe he would say that! It's you that cheated on me, stop trying to change the subject" type of conversations. One of the, if not the only problem I ever had with Kay, was her relationship with this guy. She would tell him things that she wouldn't open up to me about, and I honestly mean this...I would rather you share your body with someone and it not mean anything, than for you to share your mind and soul with someone else but not share those things with me. That means you were either talking about me, or you didn't trust me with the information that you were sharing. I tried to deal with this. I tried to forgive their relationship, over and over again. I tried. I really did. I was the most faithful person in the world to her, and I must confess, I lied in this chapter to you all. I did that on purpose, because this is something I tried to convince myself of when I knew she was out there cheating on me with her "best friend." After her friend told me what he told me, I did grow distrustful and I did want to break up with her, but I loved her so much and I could only see the excitement in her father's face when he expressed the excitement of our engagement to me. I didn't want to let him down. I was just always hoping that Kay would come out and be truthful to me about her relationship with this other guy named "Whisper," so that I could tell her that I knew already and that I forgive her because we're all human and we all make mistakes, and that she doesn't belong to me or anyone else for that matter. My confession is, I did cheat on her, but I never considered it cheating. When I first moved to Modesto, I met someone that was a waitress at a restaurant in Modesto. She was beautiful, and I was vulnerable after just learning that I was being cheated on for the entirety of my relationship with Kay. Well, this waitress told me that she was married and had 3 kids. The way she said it was more so asking if I was OK with that dynamic. I didn't know how to respond, but before I could, she told me that she had a sister that I would be interested in. Before I could finish my meal, her sister showed up to the restaurant and was waiting to meet me in the parking lot. She was nice and had a nice figure, but I didn't find her as visually appealing as her sister, whom I learned months later wasn't really her sister. I'm so frustrated and over people calling people family that isn't really family. My daughter has this same issue and I've had to explain to her over and over again how important it is to tell people the truth about family dynamics. For example, if something were to happen and she needed a kidney, it's important for me to know that her cousin isn't really her cousin.

Sheray's sister, Amber, was disappointed that I had gotten her sister pregnant. She told me that she didn't introduce us for that, which led me to realize it was an excuse for Amber and I to be together. Amber and I did eventually date, though briefly. This was after she and her husband separated though. He was a nice guy and I wasn't going to steal his wife from him. He took care of their two kids they shared after the divorce, and Amber left her older daughter with her (Amber's) mom and Amber moved to Germany. I ended up treating her daughter like my own and tried to convey to Amber that she was wrong and needed to come get her daughter. Amber evidently didn't know about my involvement in her daughter's life. You see, Amber's mom was tired and even stated that she was tired and couldn't take care of Amber's daughter, so she left her with Sheray, and whenever I picked up my daughter, I also picked up Amber's daughter. I guess Amber had developed such a disdain for me, that she got the desired push that she needed in order for her to pick up her daughter. I was happy about this. Her daughter moved to Germany with her. They both became fluent in German. There was a lot of contention between Amber, Sheray and I, and Amber would tell me things about Sheray. When Sheray and I would argue, I would spill the beans, but Amber was playing both sides. I did not want to leave Kay for this complicated relationship. I closed off all possibilities of us ever getting back together with her, not because I had a baby with someone else, but because of social media and me being behind in the new text lingo. I remember spilling my guts to Kay and one of her responses was "LMAO." In all honesty, that was my first time seeing that expression and I was totally unfamiliar with shortened texts. I thought she was calling me lame or something. I asked her what she meant and I didn't get a response from her. I was upset that I just finished spilling my guts to her and opening up to her about my mother, and "LMAO" was her response. After a couple more times of her acting weird towards me after we broke up and tried to remain friends, I went on her Facebook page and posted on her timeline about how I was able to sleep with her the first night we met, and how she was verbally and physically abusive towards her son. That wasn't totally without warrant. She did a good job of smearing my name to her friends and family on and off social media already, and still would not confess to cheating on me. I asked her to put myself and her male best friend, Whisper, on a three-way call and we could hammer it out, but she refused. She would constantly tell me how I wouldn't admit to cheating, but she herself would not admit to it either. I would have definitely admitted to my indiscretions had she admitted to hers that she did first and for much longer. In fact, I would have never had any indiscretions had she not been lying to me. Do I feel badly that I posted that message on her Facebook page? Yes. I tried communicating with her over the years just to resolve things and to see if she's OK. I apologized over and over again. I admit, she was done with me. I would text her and call her, and she would only respond to fuss at me and tell me to leave her alone. She ended up getting married and having a daughter. I know this because I guess I stalked her social media a little, not from a bad place, but just to see what she was up to. Her info was public, so why not? They bought a house together and eventually either separated or divorced. I was actually happy for her. I do admit that I still care for her. I knew where she lived but I never went over there, though I did pass down her street a couple times when I happened to be in the neighborhood. I never went over there specifically looking for her, literally only when I was in the neighborhood. I wouldn't stop and wait for her to come out or anything. I would just pass by, hoping to see her outside so that I could act like it was a big coincidence. I do know that I could have run into her had I waited for her to come out or come home from work. I do know she still works at the same place she always has. Like I said, sometimes I look people up online. A stalker is at an entirely different level, so don't think that of me, though I used the word, it was only a figure of speech. Had I been a stalker, I most definitely would have run into her. If I do ever see her, it will be out of pure coincidence. I do go back and forth on whether I want to get in contact with her about what I'm writing about her in this memoir. Though I didn't use her real name, I would like her to be able to offer a rebuttal to anything I have to say, and also to give her an opportunity to come forth with the truth, as I did. I honestly want the best for her and truly hope that she's happy. I don't know why, but I just get this feeling of incredible sadness from her and I just hope that I am not a source of those feelings and that she has truly moved on from me and not just avoiding me because of the guilt that she feels or thinking that I truly need for her to confess to me what it is I already know. It was me at that time that I wanted her to admit to her indiscretions, but I don't need that from her now. Just don't accuse me of cheating if you're not going to confess to yours. Ironically, I voluntarily decided to return her private photo album she made just for me, and when I dropped it off, she was with Whisper. I was in my brand new 2005 Pontiac GTO with custom rims. She tried to get me jealous, but I was unfazed. He got the girl, I got my freedom and a new whip to replace her, and frankly, my car never yelled at me, just everyone else out of its 5" Borla exhaust tips. Kay couldn't be too upset. I gave her a car with low miles and it was relatively new. Not even 4 years old.

CHAPTER FOURTEEN
180° TO CRAZY

Now let's talk about Sheray. I would use her real name, except I'm not out of consideration for my daughter. You may ask me why I had a child with her if I have so many negative things to say about her. You know, I get tired of seeing or hearing people say this kind of thing to people when they see them going through it with their other half. "Well, you deserve it, you chose him." That's one of the most ignorant things anyone can utter out of their mouth. People like to pick and choose who they say these things to and try to say the context is different when you bring up other scenarios. For example, if a woman gets physically abused by her husband, you don't hear people say "well, you chose him." In the hood, you might hear people say something like "well, you wanted someone who acts tough and could protect you. You wanted a thug. You wanted someone in the streets that had guns and his friends were afraid of him." We say that when a girl gets run through, then she hits that wall to where she's older with a bunch of kids, now she wants that nice guy that she turned down 20 years ago. Sheray wasn't anything like she is now. I wasn't religious and she knew this. She was heavily into church, which I found out was more like a cult than anything else. They weren't allowed to watch television or listen to music that wasn't religious. The women couldn't wear pants or short dresses or short skirts, and they weren't allowed to party or drink. She was quite proper. The moment she got pregnant is when she started acting differently. I will try to keep this chapter as short as possible because there is just too much to say really. Put it this way, it would be a miracle if the police weren't needed during one of our exchanges of our daughter. It got bad, and I was never the aggressor, but guess what? Whenever there's a conflict between a man and a woman, the man is likely the one going away in cuffs, and that has happened a few times. I even would record the incidents on camera. It started before cell phone cameras got good, but they still functioned. One incident I was arrested during, I had the entire thing on camera. It showed her being the aggressor. It showed me walking down the stairs trying to get away from her, and it showed her assaulting me, but guess what? The police weren't interested in seeing my video. It was my word vs hers. She even admitted in her statement that she followed me out the apartment and went after me as I was trying to leave, but that didn't matter. Back then, it was "nab a Black man at all cost." I'm not even kidding. I think it may have happened 3 times that I was arrested and none of the times was I ever convicted even after the prosecution was trying to take it the distance. I always had my proof. I remember once, they were so hell bent on arresting me, all the witnesses around were on my side and would not let them take me without resistance. The police were so mad that they told me they weren't going to press charges on Sheray, even though everyone reported to the police that she was the one attacking me. They said "if we arrest her, we're going to arrest you too." I told them "do it then, arrest both of us because I'm pressing charges." They literally left without arresting anyone, so this is what I'm dealing with. I spent tens of thousands on attorneys and associated fees. I had an account for my daughter that started out with $50k in it. I had to deplete that money because of her mom. Her mom blamed me and told me that I should have just taken the charges without fighting. I was not about to have a criminal record just because her mom wanted to make false accusations against me. I could write several pages just talking about the times police had to be called because Sheray would act off the rails. I'll say this as many times as necessary, fellas, always record when around people like this. Sheray was so off the rails, her own family and friends wouldn't side with her against me. I remember one time the windows of my 1977 Cadillac Seville were busted out, my 2002 Monte Carlo SS was keyed, and I forget which car, but my tires got poked out. Sheray's godparents told me and even wrote me a statement stating that it was Sheray that did it. They said that she admitted it to them. Do you think she got arrested? No. I don't understand why the law protects women to this degree, and people wonder why men get paid more. Maybe it's because women don't have to deal with the long arm of the lopsided law the way men do. I'm not trying to be sexist here, but that is something to consider.

Sheray's was and still is a terrible mother. Hear me out. I'm going to mention a few things here, and just a few. Just realize, for every one story I mention, there are 10 more stories I'm not going to tell just for the sake of trying to keep this book less than 500 pages. Anjolie was about 2½ years old. I would go to pick her up from her mom's after I got off of work, which would be around midnight. A quick side note that goes along with the chapter about having a degree doesn't make you intelligent, Sheray brought up the fact that I picked Anjolie up after work, as if it's a bad thing that a father picks his child up. Sheray was just trying to lessen the time I spent with her so that she could win a child support claim against me. The judge actually tried to side with her and say wouldn't it be more appropriate to pick her up at 4 a.m., which was the time I'd have to pick her up so that her mom could go to work. The judge's reasoning was that it's too cold at midnight for a child that age. But guess what, it is far colder at 4 a.m. You have dew point to contend with. Everyone with basic knowledge should know the coldest times of the day, and either the judge was that stupid, or she thought I was. I had to explain to the judge the failure of her logic.

The apartment complex she lived in was enclosed and surrounded by parking lots. There were no gates though. I got there one time and Sheray's door was wide open. I peek my head in and I don't see or hear anyone. I didn't want to just walk in because I didn't want to be accused of breaking and entering. I heard a voice calling my name. I looked behind me from the 2nd floor porch and it was Lori. She told me my daughter was over there and to come get her. I made my way over there and Lori told me that she needed to talk to me. Lori was married to a guy by the name of Phil. They were heavy into church also. Lori was also really good friends with Sheray and they babysat each other's kids. Remember I said none of her friends and family would side with her? Well this is true in this case too. Don't get me wrong, there were maybe 3 or 4 of her ratchet ass friends that would side with her, but they were all drunks and prostitutes, and I had to get into it with one of them for kissing my daughter on her cheek. This is because she was a prostitute. I was so upset that Sheray would let her hooker and drug addict friends kiss my daughter and I had to be the one to tell them not to kiss my daughter. Anyways, Lori invited me into her apartment which was adjacent to Sheray's. She told me that she wasn't babysitting Anjolie, but several times over the past, Anjolie would make her way down Sheray's stairs and up Lori's stairs, and into her apartment if she saw the door was open.

If the door wasn't open, she would just wander around the apartment complex and Lori or Phil would have to get her and bring her in because they were unable to wake up Sheray or Sheray was nowhere to be found. Lori told me she wouldn't normally get involved in our business, but this was too serious to let slide. She said that Sheray has no business having children and that she would write me a statement for court or for CPS, in which she did. No, that wasn't enough to get awarded full custody, nor was the time I went to pick my daughter up at around the age of 4, and there were butcher knives, scissors, and all kinds of sharp objects all over the place, and I had it all on video. There was a glass table with the sharp squared edges that was eye height to my daughter. I broke it on purpose once when Sheray and I got into it. This was because I kept asking her to get rid of that table and she refused to. I got arrested and the prosecutor, my attorney, and I met up and I told the prosecutor the truth. I picked up one of those heavy candles in glass and smashed it on the table because I was afraid it was going to poke my daughter's eye out. The prosecutor told me that she was glad I told the truth about that and she dropped the charges. She said she didn't blame me and commended me on risking what I did in order to keep my daughter safe. So you think I'm exaggerating about how dangerous her mom was for my daughter to be with? Ok, I got a call from the emergency department that my daughter was there because Anjolie's arm was sliced open. It was literally halfway through her arm and her mom was going to try to hide it from me to act like it was more minor than it actually was. There were many incidents where my daughter had to go to the emergency room while with her mother, and they were all from injuries due to negligence. Not once did my daughter ever get hurt around me, unless you want to include her spraining her ankle once at the playground.

If you recall I talked about Monica and how I came home from work super early and I overheard her coaching Sheray on how she could get me for my money, well she ended up trying and succeeding. I had to have Sheray evicted and I found paperwork in one of the drawers of the headboard to the bed I let her use while living there. It was welfare paperwork for the County. The date was current, but it had her old address on it. I read it and it was a summary of facts along with an approval notice. In the statement of facts, Sheray said she didn't know anything about me except where I worked. SHE WAS LIVING IN MY HOUSE. This was one of the things I showed my sister the next day that Sheray was in denial of. Well, Sheray had a friend that went to the same church that worked for the County in the Family Services/Welfare department that helped to push her paperwork through. After I contacted the Welfare Fraud division, we were in constant contact because they wanted to go after her. I submitted my proof and they prosecuted her. Sad thing is, I'm not sure if her fraud against me is what got her prosecuted, but they found something else. She ended up being convicted of welfare fraud and perjury. What's crazy is, they let her stay on welfare and I ended up having to pay child support even though my daughter lived with me most of the time, and I still pay arrears to this day. I still owe around $1700. I must have paid over $50k over the years. How is it that they make a man struggle and pay child support for a child he has custody of and is living with him just because he makes a lot of money? I was basically financially taking care of her other two kids. I actually didn't get ordered to pay child support until I hired an attorney to represent me. I did fine on my own acting as my own attorney. It wasn't until my daughter was 7 that I decided to lawyer up. Attorney's are crooked. It's like they cut back room deals in order to win other cases. I got railroaded. My child support was $987/mo., but then eventually got cut to $666/mo after I appealed the amount. They were trying to send me a message. Just to show how lopsided the system is against men, I never received one red penny from Sheray for child support when Anjolie was living with me full time. The system didn't go after her like they went after me. There was one time that they tried getting in contact with me in regards to locating Sheray. They didn't specify why, and I can't remember if they said they were the Department of Child Support, or if they were CPS. I knew how to find her, but I didn't share any information with them because at this point, it was useless and I wanted Sheray to be able to spend money on her daughter. She did send her a couple of gifts over the years, but it wasn't much. She had the nerve to call me a deadbeat (go figure), but she never ever gave me a damn thing. Most of Sheray's money was spent on weed and probably other things related. If you were to pop up at her house right now, she'd either be at work, sleeping after a long shift, or smoking weed. Weed isn't free and she was always broke, yet always smoking.

    I tried to file an appeal on a few occasions. I remember living in Buffalo and being contacted by the Child Support division because I was behind in payments. I expressed my frustration to her and she listened. She looked at my case and said that if what I was saying was true, that I could get all of my money back. She sent me the paperwork, I filled it out, and I heard nothing. I would fill out this paperwork a couple more times and submit it properly. Each time, I heard nothing. It was as if I never filed it. This is that crooked crap. The County is full of straight up crooks. They know most people don't have the resources to fight them so they commit illegal acts to screw us over.

    I remember it was my daughter's 4th birthday. We were having a party at the park. Sheray and I got into it of course and she threatened me with her family and her boyfriend. Her family got there and they were on my side. They told her that she was lucky that I'm her child's father and her sister told her that she wishes her child's father was 1/10th the man I was. They all began to get on Sheray's case. Her boyfriend gets there wanting to "talk to me." He thought he was going to "little bro" me, but what he didn't realize is, I was no punk, and like I said before, I had been hitting the weights. Let's just say he didn't want any problems after he saw I wanted all the smoke. I'm not having any man check me at all, much less at my daughter's birthday party. Her family had to hold me back and prevent me from going after him after he left. Believe it or not, he and I never really had any problems after that. Sheray has another child's father that she tried to have check me over the phone, and after I told him it was up when I saw him, he apologized to me because he didn't know what type of person Sheray was and he started having the same problems with her. We became cool after that and actually hung out a couple of times.

I have a couple more stories to tell you about her and then I'm ending this chapter. As I've stated, there are many many stories, but in the spirit of keeping this short as possible, I won't tell those stories. We were living in Buffalo and I sent Anjolie to California to visit her mom for the holidays. Would you believe that I got a text from my daughter right after her mom picked her up from the airport saying that CPS was trying to get in contact with me? She literally just picked her up from the Sacramento airport and didn't even get to her mom's. They left a number for me to call. I called and they asked where my daughter lived. I told them with me in Buffalo, NY. They said that was good and not to send my daughter out there because the situation was dangerous. I told them they needed to tell me because if I was going to keep my daughter from over there, it would have to be a good reason. He ended up telling me with reluctance. You see, they were literally in the middle of taking her other kids out of the house. She had two sons and she was also taking care of a few other kids for her friend, and CPS took them all out and put them into Foster Care. This lasted 2 years. Sheray actually called me crying and telling me that she'll send Anjolie back on the plane the next day. I told her that it was my decision and that Anjolie has a phone and I don't want to do that to her, and just to lay low for the next 10 days until it was time to come back home. I don't want to get into all of the reasons why the kids were taken out of the home, but just use your imagination and common sense from all of the things I told you about her before, and apply that. One last story I will tell you that let me know that I had to micromanage my daughter's interactions when with her mom is when my daughter had bruised ribs. She must have been about 6. She didn't want to tell me why, then after a long talk, she told me that JP would tickle her until it hurt. I told her mom about this and her mom, instead of siding with me to confront JP, she decided to argue with me about it. You see, she would send our daughter to this guy's house to be babysat while she went out to party or work. Why would you pick your daughter up from me on the weekend just to have someone else babysit her? She never told me about this, and whenever Sheray would tell me that Anjolie was up the street, she made it seem like Anjolie was being babysat by a lady. This was JP's mother, but it was often JP instead of his mother. We all know about how child predators play the tickle game in order to get their feels on, so you can imagine my fury when I went over there to confront him. He was supposed to be some tough guy, but you're never tougher than the father of a girl who was touched the wrong way. He wouldn't answer or come outside. One day I saw him and I pulled over. He actually acted real soft at that point. "Hey man, I don't want no problems [sic]. You go your way, I go mine" is what he said. I was heated and I don't know how it is I composed myself to not attack this man. Luck would have it that his kids were all taken out of the home due to abuse and sexual abuse allegations. Now you see the issues I had to deal with left and right whenever around Sheray?

I know I said one last story, but there are two more that I really must include that I would never forgive myself for if I didn't. Sheray had a friend that got her a job at the Dollar Tree. He was a dope dealer, pimp, and anything else you associate with being a bad guy. One day I got a call from him. He told me he needed to see me in person, so I actually took off of work and went to his house. He told me that he had problems with Sheray and it was probably a good idea to not have my daughter over there. He told me he was telling me because from everything he heard, I was a good guy and he didn't want anything happening to my daughter. He probably heard the stories of how I'm a good guy, but with a bad side when it came to my daughter being put in danger. What Sheray will never admit to is, I saved her life. He and I had a long talk, and whatever problems they had, were set aside. Here's where the other story ties in. There was a couple, Moe and Dee. Moe was the guy and he and Dee shared children together. One day, in the very garage that everyone would hang out in, shots were fired, and Dee was struck in the chest and killed. The garage door was closed and the person that fired the shots had no idea who was in there and where they were seated. This could have easily been my daughter, as she was often over there. Sheray had lots of enemies and she was constantly getting into it with people. Whenever my daughter was with her mom I found it hard to sleep. I knew that at any moment I could get a call saying that something happened to my daughter, as it has happened before. Sheray was known for taking my daughter to the emergency room with me not finding out until months or even years later. I happened to request records from the hospital and saw several instances of my daughter being brought in and I had no idea. The judge did not find this amusing either. Anyways, These were mutual friends of Sheray and I. We just happened to know them separately. This was just up the street from where Sheray lived that she and the kids would all be at. It was incidents like these that told me that I had to get my daughter away from there, so before any of you say I took her from her mom, understand that I saved her from Foster care, and possibly saved her life. Hell, I literally saved my daughter's life on the day that she was born.

They had to do a C-section because the umbilical cord was wrapped around her neck. After Anjole was born, I noticed she was breathing funny. I know, babies have an irregular breathing pattern, and I knew this, but I know the difference between struggling for breaths, and an infant's breathing pattern. I told the nurse of my concern and I was brushed off and told "breathing pattern, blah blah blah." Guess who wanted to argue with me when I insisted it wasn't normal? Yep, Sheray. I went to the nursing station and told them I made good money and could afford a really good attorney, and if they didn't give my daughter chest x-rays and put me at ease, if something were to happen to my daughter, I would sue the shit out of them. They didn't fight me and had x-rays done. They found out that my daughter's lungs were more than halfway full of fluid and that she also had jaundice. This is one thing that Sheray will deny. Another thing she will deny, which let's me know she knew better was, she likes to take credit for naming our daughter. She was trying to name her after every foreign car and liquor in the book. Both Amber and I would not allow it. Though the name I gave her in this book is not real, and for her protection, it is a combination of her first and middle name. Amber, Sheray and I decided to come up with a list of 10 names each, and Amber would pick the best name from that list. Amber immediately picked the name that I came up with. You can only imagine the displeasure Sheray had that I had the better name. Sheray just had to try to come up with some way to put her twist on her name. She didn't want to spell it in the traditional manner. She added hyphens and silent letters that had no business there.

Amber and I talked sense into her. I made the argument that we don't want to make it difficult on her in life and that if she wants to change her name or spelling later, then that's up to her, but we won't make it difficult for anyone that has to read her name, or make it so that she has to constantly correct someone's spelling or pronunciation. Amber agreed, and Sheray didn't put up a fight. She knew that if she made it difficult, it was for her own selfish reason. We stuck with that. As many issues as Amber and I have had in the past, they were never serious or blown out of proportion. I have always been grateful for her always being able to talk sense into Sheray.

When I sent Anjolie back to California to visit for Christmas during the pandemic, I told her that she could stay there if she chose to because I knew she was depressed. She said she wanted to stay if I was going to move back, but if I wasn't going to move back, then she wouldn't stay. I told her I would move back and that I would see her soon. I was there two months later. I sacrificed a lot for my daughter and my hope is that one day she will realize it. I say this because I know she harbors some resentment towards me for decisions that I made for her better well being. I actually gave Anjolie the choice of moving to Buffalo in the first place. I knew she recognized all of the things that were going on around her. She saw more with her mom than I did and I saw a lot. She made up her mind that she wanted to move. She had visited Buffalo with me during the Summer. I drove a big rig across the country and took Anjolie with me. When we visited family in Buffalo, everyone was really welcoming and Anjolie loved it. The food in Buffalo is excellent and has even been rated as 3rd in the world by National Geographic for best places to visit for food. One of my favorite people was Aunt Debbie. I mentioned before that she did a lot for me and we shared a special bond. While out there visiting, Aunt Debbie suggested that if we were planning on moving to

Buffalo, that we stay with her because she had a nice home that she was renting but in the process of buying. She showed us around, showed us where our rooms would be, and around the neighborhood. I told other members of the family that we may be moving back to Buffalo, and they were all excited. No one offered any insight or advice. They knew of my plans of moving in with Aunt Debbie, but no one said anything. You see, Aunt Debbie wasn't the same. Our family suffers from mental illness. I don't know if she's bi-polar, schizophrenic, both, or what, but she believed a lot of conspiracies and was heavily into that sovereign citizens thing. She had electronic devices throughout her house that would block cell phone signals from being able to penetrate, and she would drink her own urine. This is crazy because she has been a registered nurse her entire life. I don't understand how she would think this could be healthy. A simple Google search would tell you that there are no benefits to drinking your own urine and in fact, the harm that it can cause outweighs the fact that there are no benefits. My cousin told me a story of where Aunt Debbie made her famous Christmas Tree cake and everyone got sick and was vomiting. I honestly believe it's because she used urine as an ingredient, and the rest of the family believes the same thing. Aunt Debbie is the mother of another cousin that I was close to. Serina is very intelligent and a go-getter. She had a son at the very young age of 14. Usually when people have kids at a young age, it ruins their lives, but in this case, it pushed her into wanting more out of life. She strived for more and her priorities changed. I bring this up because Demone passed away in 2008. He was murdered for being in the wrong place at the wrong time and wearing jewelry that they probably thought looked valuable, but was nothing more than costume jewelry. He was shot. I don't want to give details any further than that, but you can imagine what that does to a family. Demone and his mom were inseparable. This goes the same for his grandmother, Aunt Debbie. When he passed, I think this caused more trauma than one might think. Both Serina and her mom haven't been the same ever since. When I say mental illness runs in the family, I don't think it's genetic. I think it's more so that we are susceptible when triggered by trauma. It could also be genetic as I do have a couple of relatives that just seemed to grow mentally ill out of nowhere and no trauma that caused it. I use them as examples because they had seemingly good lives.

No one warned me that moving in with Aunt Debbie was a bad move. I feel as though someone could have said to me that she was mentally ill and could flip on me at any moment. They all had the opportunity, but none of them took it. Debbie and I agreed that I would move in with her. I told her when, and told her I would give her an exact date soon. I was still driving truck and only planned on driving truck for a year. I was just using truck driving as a tool to see the country not only for free, but to get paid while doing it. It was also a way to slowly move my belongings from California to Buffalo. I also couldn't keep driving truck as leaving my daughter with her mom wasn't a good idea and I knew it was causing her harm, but I had to do something in order to be able to get us out of the rut we were in and truck driving wasn't going to be permanent.

I gave Aunt Debbie a date in November. We did talk on the phone here and there, and she was aware and agreed on the date. I would send her texts every now and then to remind her and to make sure everything was all good. The date grew closer and closer and I put in my notice to the trucking company I was working for. I had already landed a local trucking job in Buffalo that had a run from Buffalo to Niagara Falls, and I had a start date for that which was in the middle of December. I informed my aunt of this because I didn't want her to think that I was just sitting on my ass for three weeks doing nothing. I had enough money to last me until my first paycheck and as long as I wasn't wasting my money, I'd be fine. I did inform my daughter that we wouldn't see family like she did when we visited and they were just putting up a front because we were visiting. She said she understood that, and I made this clear before she decided that she wanted to move to Buffalo.

I left Sheray my car, as I had no use for it unless I planned on driving it across the country, which I was not going to do. It was a 1999 Ford Crown Victoria unmarked detective car. It was in good condition, so it's not like I was leaving her a burden. Anjolie and I caught the plane and arrived in Buffalo. I called and texted Aunt Debbie, as I did let her know the date was solid and that we had tickets already. She acknowledged it, but when we got to the airport, I heard nothing from her. I called and texted several times. She said she would be there to pick us up, but now that we're there, she's not responding. It was late and I was getting nervous, and I was now having second thoughts and regrets, especially after already having many experiences with family leaving me hanging with no explanation. We ended up deciding to catch an Uber to her house and hoping she would answer the door, which she did. That was a $40 Uber ride that I certainly wish I didn't have to take. We got there and she did indeed answer the door. She said she didn't know that I was coming. I told her that we communicated about it several times and we discussed the date and even talked about it very recently. Her response was disturbing. She said she didn't know if I was serious or not. I think I just dropped the subject at that point. My thinking is, someone doesn't joke about things like that. Why would I say I turned in my two weeks notice and bought plane tickets? Why would I have brought several items to her house throughout the Summer for when I got there? I just didn't understand her logic. She welcomed us in, showed us to our rooms and we chatted for a long time that night, and now that we were there, everything seemed good. In the morning, she gave me information about the school so that I could enroll Anjolie immediately. Anjolie was going to school within the next couple of days, now the only thing left was to pass time until it was time for me to go to training for my new job. I was scheduled to spend a week in Ohio, which is normal for a trucking company to have the new recruits travel to their headquarters for training. The same thing was done for the trucking company I was previously working for. Aunt Debbie started getting agitated. I just somehow could tell. You just get a feeling from someone when something's wrong. She was hanging up Christmas decorations and I asked to help her, and she was short with me and just said no and had a cold look on her face. This was the feeling over the next couple of days and I was thinking it was because I was hanging around the house a lot. I didn't want to go anywhere because I was trying not to spend any money. I explained to her that my training started in 10 days and there was nothing for me to do but to hang around. Going out costs money, even if you go places that are free, you end up spending, and after buying two plane tickets and not working for a couple of weeks, I couldn't take that chance. She actually called me lazy and she thought that I would come out here and work. She was hoping for me to contribute to the rent and bills. I couldn't make my starting date for work change. It had to be something else that she was agitated about because we already agreed to everything, including when I was going to start paying bills. I was going to start contributing immediately after training. I started thinking back to what could have possibly made her agitated with me. Her son was selling a car, and I needed to buy a car. I was looking online for one, but you don't just buy a car just because someone you know is selling one. It was a 2005 Jaguar. I had a short list of vehicles I was willing to buy. I'm a car guy and I do research, plus I wasn't planning on buying one until after I started work. I had a settlement check I was waiting on that I was going to use to make the purchase, and it was in its final stages of being sent to me. I already signed the agreement, and the judge already approved of the settlement amount. I did not want a Jaguar. I wanted a hatchback with AWD, especially being that we get a large amount of snow and live close to Lake Erie. Aunt Debbie got really upset with me that I wouldn't buy the car from her son. It wasn't personal, but am I the only one that only spends that kind of money on things that I actually want? I know the cars that are money pits and bad for Buffalo winters. There was a reason why he was selling it. He bought it because of the brand name, as many people make the mistake of doing. He found out that it was a money pit, and was looking for a sucker to dump it off on. That sucker wasn't going to be me. This had to be the reason Aunt Debbie was upset with me. I had only been there maybe 10 days, and already things were bad. Aunt Debbie and I never had any bad exchanges or anything. I just couldn't figure it out. The only other thing is I wouldn't conform to her diet. She's a vegan and I wasn't planning on becoming one too. She was trying to get us to only use the products that she uses and consumes, and that's just not how things work. Aunt Debbie also seemed a little upset that she and I shared different methods of raising a child. I know she has far more experience than I did, but I can't call hers any better than mine. One of her children was a high school dropout. The other and a baby at 14. Aunt Debbie said a couple of things that highly offended me, and rather hypocritical at that. She said to me that my daughter is retarded. Anjolie didn't always respond the way in which she should have, but it has nothing to do with retardation or being slow. It's just that her mind always wandered off. She's quite brilliant if I'm honest. I say Aunt Debbie is hypocritical because her children didn't quite respond to her the way one would expect either, especially coming from someone so judgmental. Judge your kids first. Her son is far from stupid, and I would never call him that just because he dropped out of high school. He actually enrolled into college and was taking classes with no high school diploma, and no GED. His college found out and kicked him out. I will admit, like I said, there were many many many times that I have said something to my daughter, and she totally got the wrong thing out of what I said. She probably has a diagnosis of something, but definitely not retardation. She is in college right now and she has done mostly well in school. She did struggle with difficult classes such as robotics and math, but that's far from retarded. She more so shuts down when she's not interested in what it is you have to say. She is a little self centered but not conceited. She has to be interested in order for her to pay attention.

Anjolie does come off as a bit lazy too. This was a new trait that started almost immediately after receiving her 2nd HPV vaccination. I'm not trying to be this big conspiracy theorist, but you have to realize that vaccination experiments have been done on people in the past, most infamously, the Tuskegee experiments, which is another reason people are apprehensive about vaccines. So, my daughter had a doctor that I did not like, and I was in the midst of changing her Primary Care Physician, but she still needed to go to checkups. This doctor seemed far too eager to give her the HPV vaccine. I understand that it's important, but the way this doctor acted about it seemed like he had something up his sleeve and I just didn't trust him at this point. I specifically told this doctor that I didn't want her to receive the vaccine just yet and that her mom was bringing her to the next appointment, and not to administer the vaccine, specifically because I was waiting on her hematologist to give the okay, due to her also having cyclic neutropenia. I also told the mother that the doctor seemed aggressive with wanting to give her the vaccination, and to not let him. I already explained my reasons to her. I had full medical decisions over her, and the doctor's office had this in their files. The mom is nothing more than the person bringing her to her appointment, and they are to only communicate with me about any medications and treatments. I knew better than to trust her mother with following simple instructions, but once again, just like trying to invent a strange new way to spell her name, she felt as though she needed to have some sense of control over the situation and she allowed the doctor to give Anjolie the vaccination. Anjolie was 7, and she went from pretty good at math, to totally not interested and started struggling, even doing the same math that she excelled at the previous year. Not retarded, but there was a drop in performance. That's something I will never forgive her mom for. I would have sued the doctor, but life got in the way, and being the breadwinner, I had to work and just didn't have time to go through the motions. I've always had to deal with the fact that men do not have the same rights as women when it comes to children. It is always assumed that the woman is the primary and doesn't need proof of custody when picking a child up. I can't tell you how many times I had to present court orders in order to pick my daughter up from school, yet they never asked the mom for anything. They would let her go to the office and make changes without doing any kinds of checks whatsoever. She would change who is and isn't allowed to pick her up. She would add people that I never heard of, and she has even gone as far as taking me off the list of people allowed to pick her up, AND I'M THE PRIMARY AND SOLE DECISION MAKER. I had to threaten a couple of her schools with lawsuits if they allowed her to make changes again. Her schools would make me submit my court orders to the district office, the secretary, main office, and the records office. After receiving the paperwork saying the mom has no authority to make any decisions for school, medical, or anything at all, then I would still have to threaten them with a lawsuit. It wasn't any different with hospitals. It got to the point that Sheray took Anjolie into the hospital so many times, they knew right away to contact me to let me know my daughter was being seen for an injury or illness. I had to go through the same thing with the two main hospitals, alerting me if my daughter arrived for any reason. I would show them the court orders, and show them the hospital records of all the times my daughter had been to the emergency room without my knowledge. The hospitals finally would alert me every time. It's amazing how many times her mom tried to cover up the fact that my daughter got injured due to negligence and didn't tell me.

Back to life with Aunt Debbie. It was not even two weeks into living there that she told me she wanted us out. I was confused and asked her to give me time to find a place and to start working. She didn't care, she wanted me out, but Buffalo was now a strange land to me, and you don't invite someone to move across the country and live with you just to kick them out because you don't share the same diet or you're in desperate need of money and think I should be paying you the last little bit of money I had left, leaving me with no money while out of State for training. I drew a line and refused to leave. Remember, family isn't family, and I couldn't just show up at someone's house and ask for boarding. Yes, I'm well aware that she has rights as the primary tenant, but understand my position. I had no idea what the hell was going on and why it was going on, but I would soon find out.

CHAPTER FIFTEEN
BACK TO BENNY

Debbie would call her best friend and buddy, Benny. Yes, my father Benny. Debbie would leave for work super early in the mornings. She was a nurse aid on the bus for children with special needs. I suppose she thought she was qualified to say my daughter had special needs because she worked directly with them. Her leaving in the mornings that early gave Anjolie and I plenty of time to have the house to ourselves and get ready for school. I would walk her to school with no problem, but coming home would be an issue as sometimes Debbie and I would arrive at the same time, sometimes she would beat me there, but mostly I would beat her there. I had a key and she had not changed the locks. She would have to get permission from the landlord in order to do so, so I really wasn't worried about that. One day, Anjolie and I got home from school, and I just felt something in the air. There was a white conversion van parked up the street, and as Anjolie and I walked up the driveway to get to the front door, this van sped from its parking spot and ran us out of the driveway. It almost hit us. It was Benny. He's in his 70s, but he is very healthy and doesn't physically look to be as old as he was at the time. He could be an imposing figure for anyone and has often threatened people, including his own family, with violence. There was an instance where he was going after his own brother with a hammer, and his brother had to pull a gun out on him in order to stop his charge. There were a few more instances where he got into physical altercations with his brothers, and he always got beat up. He was basically all bark and no bite.

He jumped out of the van, and that's when I realized it was him. He ran to the door and blocked me from going inside. My daughter is on the lawn crying. I pulled out my phone to call the police but my battery was actually dead, so I asked Anjolie to call 911. This is because I saw he had keys between the knuckles of all his fingers and this was a punk tactic that I saw him use before on one of my uncles he was getting into it with. He actually punched me lightly in the back of my head, but my only concern was keeping him from getting to my daughter because he actually made a threat against her. Debbie made a threat against her too by saying to me "and if you know what's good for her, you'd keep her away from me because I will hurt her." I don't have to tell you that the gloves are off when you threaten my daughter. That goes for anyone. Aunt, father, friend, sister, or anyone. You threaten my daughter, that could be the beginning of the ending for you. At this point, Both Benny and his sister were on my list of people that I wouldn't mind if they were "Thanos snapped" away from existence. And I honestly still feel this way. After Benny realized that he could not physically overpower me, he ran into the house as Anjolie and I stood outside waiting for the police to arrive. I still had my back to the front door, now talking to my daughter who had seemingly calmed down. I could tell that she was still distraught though, but she was no longer crying and she was talking to me with a normal tone. I was telling her that she had no reason to fear him because he was unable to overpower me. I actually was telling her that he underestimated me because I worked out and he wasn't stronger than me, and she said she could tell, then she started pointing behind me. It was Benny, standing behind the closed door with a psycho look on his face. I looked at him and said, "you know what's up. You keep that door closed because you know what's up." Before he got into the house, he did manage to snatch my keys from me, but the cops now arrived and they made him leave after learning that Anjolie and I lived there and he didn't. The problem is, he left with my keys. The cops didn't want to do anything about him assaulting me and running my daughter and I down in the driveway. They said it was his word against ours. That was a load of nonsense. My daughter told them what happened and it matched what I said. We're now in the house and he left. Anjolie and I just stayed in my room when Debbie got home. I was working on finding us a place to stay and it was going to be a couple of days before I could make anything happen. I recalled something Benny said while he was behind the door of the house. He said to me "you should have just paid her the money from the settlement and none of this would have happened." See, this is where the delusion comes in. People will make up in their own minds whatever it is they want to believe and not use logic. I did tell Debbie that I was expecting my settlement check at any time and that I had already given them the address to her house. The problem is, I can't make them mail it out any sooner or on time for that matter, and I can't make it magically get there. Trust me, I was depending on that money and it was part of the timing of us moving to Buffalo. They gave me a date that it would be mailed, and it just didn't come when they said it would come. For whatever reason, Debbie and Benny thought I had the money already and was just trying to use her for a free place to stay and would run off after it came. For one, it wasn't that much money. It was somewhere around $5,000. Yes, I was shopping for a used car in anticipation of the check, but that's what I do. I don't wait until I have money in hand to start researching. All of this because of some weird conspiracy theory? I could not believe my favorite aunt was acting like this. I was totally thrown by this. I did, however, expect this coming from my father. He did things in the past that let me know that he is only out for himself, will use you, and is not to be trusted.

Debbie gets home and she is yelling and banging on things, and just outright acting crazy. She knew the only way to get us out of there immediately is to make it a hostile environment. There was no hostility before, just an uneasiness, but now it was hostile. She barged into Anjolie's room and opened up the drawers and started throwing her stuff out of the 2nd story window into the backyard. Then she went into my room and started doing the same thing. That's when I called my uncle, Sam. I previously called him "Sal" but at this point, I feel comfortable calling him by his real name, as I don't really have anything bad to say about him really. I do have a reservation about his choice of loyalty to his friends over family, but I won't hold that against him as the incident I'm referring to isn't that serious. It was enough to let me know that favors from him come with a price and that price is never paid, no matter how much time goes by and no matter how much you've done to repay him. Uncle Sal is on the phone and he's hearing what's going on in the background, and he could not believe what he was hearing. It totally baffled him.

I sent Anjolie to the backyard to recover our belongings and Debbie tried to stop her and went after her, but like I said...my daughter...I grabbed Debbie and threw her down to the floor. She then realized that she wasn't going to overpower me and that she crossed the line. She immediately went into "help, get off me" mode. Uncle Sal heard this and he assured me that I had every right to defend myself and my daughter. Uncle Sal also called the police. I tried calling them, but I can't recall exactly what happened. Either way, they showed back up and it was a different set of police from earlier, and I learned why the other police were uninterested in filing charges or arresting Benny. It was because it was the end of their shift. That should never be an excuse for not doing your job. That's why they get paid the big bucks, right? Why should someone else get better assistance than I just because they called at 12:00 and I called at 2:30? The police are now asking everyone what happened, and they said to me yes, I have the right to be there, but because of the seriousness of the situation, we could no longer be there. They were sensitive to the situation, but they did say some things that set me off a bit. They had the nerve to try to act like I wasn't a good father for putting my daughter in this situation, as if they knew. I did tell them we had nowhere to go, so they brought us to a hotel and the city had funding for situations like this. They paid for one night, but we had to be out the next day by 10:00 a.m.. This is when the officer did and said something again that ticked me off. He spoke to my daughter as if I weren't there and made me out to be a bad father and said something to the order of "it's too bad that she has a father like me not making good decisions." Oh yes, I went off on that officer and he honestly had nothing to say. He thought I was just going to sit there and let him talk bad about me to my daughter? He couldn't tell me what it was I did wrong other than trusting my family. My family is messed up. That's not something I decided on. When he was talking to her, he made her cry, and that's what pissed me off. She was doing just fine until then.

Uncle Sal called to check on us and I informed him of what happened and where we were. He told me that he was renting a place for he and his wife's business, but they weren't actually using it and that his lease was up the next month and he wasn't planning on renewing it. He told me that we could stay there for the next couple of weeks and that he would talk to the landlord, who was an old high school friend of his, and that maybe he could rent the place to us. Uncle Sal was doing us a really big favor, but it also worked out for him because he couldn't afford to keep the place anymore. It was a money pit that they weren't using. He claimed to be rich, so I was confused as to why he couldn't afford it. I later found out he was claiming his wealth because of some "your birth certificate is worth $3,000,000/sovereign citizen" nonsense. It was more plausible to claim to be rich because he bought his house a long time ago and it was a year away from being paid off, and it was a really big and nice home. That being said, Uncle Sal was so very caring and helpful. He picked us up from the motel and brought us to his place he was renting. He went home and came back with a king sized air mattress and space heater. He and his wife's things were still there. She organized parties and made all of the favors and decorations. I helped clear the stuff out and we made the place our own. I met up with the property owner and he asked to see my proof that I was expecting a settlement soon. I showed him the proof, so he gave me a contract to sign saying that I would pay him the $750/mo out of my settlement check. At this point, we weren't staying there for free, and I also had to pay for the time we were already there, so Uncle Sal didn't do me that favor. I had to pay Uncle Sal for that time, which I did. One would think that it's no longer a favor if they're charging you for it. I ended up having to go to the County for benefits because now I could no longer go to Ohio for training and I couldn't accept the job because Debbie was no longer going to babysit for me while out of town as she previously agreed to do. Other family members heard about what happened and that's when suddenly everyone was a library of information. "I thought you knew that Debbie was crazy!" I received this same sentiment from pretty much everyone

I COULD HAVE BEEN A KILLER

that I talked to after this. I find it odd that none of these people warned me about her before I moved in with her. I told everyone of our plans months ahead of time, and not a single person told me that Debbie was actually taken into a mental ward against her will on a couple of occasions. Had I known this, I definitely would have made other plans. It's not hard finding a place to rent in Buffalo. What's hard is when you have to do it suddenly and you've been living across the country for the past three decades. Now mind you, I did say that I was a vengeful person, and I still somewhat am, though I let people bury themselves more so these days. I wondered how it was that Debbie was working with kids with special needs, knowing what her background is with her psychological diagnosis. She was on meds and wasn't taking them. She had made some comments about the kids on the bus she was working on that let me know that she shouldn't be around them. I forget which entity it was that I called, but I did call and inform them of her disposition. I'm sure they did their investigation and took appropriate action. I never followed up, but I learned that she was being kicked out of her place that she claimed she was in the process of buying. Yes, she originally told me that she was the owner of the home. Keep that in mind when I tell you that she's delusional. I would drive over there and park a couple of streets away to see if I could see her, primarily because I was wondering if she still lived there. The way the neighborhood was situated, if you're parked across the grass field, you had a clear view up several different streets and could even see a couple of streets over. There was a for sale sign on the lawn and I saw another woman enter and exit the house. I approached the woman and told her I was looking for my aunt that lived there fairly recently, and the woman said she had no idea who I was talking about and that she had been living there for a long time. I don't know why people feel the need to lie. I wanted to tell the lady that she was lying because I lived there just a few months ago, so she couldn't have lived there for that long. It was a White woman and the area was a bit racist, so she was just telling me anything for me to go away. Well, I now knew that Debbie had indeed been kicked out because she hadn't been paying rent and was far behind. She was using the fact that she used to date the owner of the property or that he liked her. It was her own daughter that told me that she was being kicked out. This is the underhanded shit I'm talking about with my family. Serina and her mom were at odds with each other. Serina was either dating or just going out with the owner of the home and he was feeding Serina information about her own mother, and Serina would tell me things. I have no issues at all with Serina, but she did have an issue with me. Her issue was that I didn't want to get in the middle of the family war going on. There were different factions of people against other factions of people. It was so complicated that I couldn't keep up with it. All I knew was, I hadn't been around any of them much at all over the past 30 years and unless someone did something to me directly, I had no problems with them, but, if I'm speaking to the enemy of someone, I'm not to be trusted, so smut must be put on my name in order to make me not believable. I wasn't sharing any information with anyone. If I was told something, it stayed with me. Serina and Benny were besties. Benny and Debbie were besties, but Serina and her mother weren't speaking. Go figure. They spent a lot of time together, so should I say the same thing to her? She was mad because I had no problem speaking to El, but I'm not supposed to have a problem with her speaking to Benny. Such hypocrisy. It wasn't enough for me to have a problem with her though. I would tell her things about my father, which I purposely call only by his first name, and I honestly didn't care if she went back and told him what I said. You see, I'm the type of person that wouldn't say anything behind your back that I didn't already say to your face.

Not "wouldn't" say to your face, but that I didn't ALREADY say to your face. I already expressed myself to him and didn't care what he thought or had to say about it. I let it be known that I did not care for him, about him, and in fact hated him, and didn't care, and I still don't care if something horrible were to ever happen to him, and I said that to his own brothers and sisters, and I don't care how it is they feel about that. Come to think of it, I remember saying that to Shawna and hearing the noise in her silence. I could tell that she was offended, but I really didn't care and I even doubled down on what I said. Benny had never been there for Shawna nor Gina, so it baffles me why they would feel the need to ever be offended by my disdain for him, and this will lead full circle to Gina and how she never really let things go in our dealings over the house debacle.

Debbie said to me that Benny told her what happened with the house and that I cheated Gina out of $50,000. Of course I defended myself and told her the truth. Whether she believed it or not, I didn't care. Whether she told Benny what I said, I cared even less. I was more upset that Gina was causing me problems all of these years later by telling people these lies as if I would never find out. I had it in my right mind to sue her for defamation of character, especially being that it caused both my daughter and I great hardship. Debbie also told me that she knew in advance "what happened" and that I must be stupid to believe that I was going to do the same thing to her by letting me move in. So the truth comes out. They came up with some crazy conspiracy that I was into using people for places to stay to not pay them. Their belief that I cheated Gina out of $50,000, coupled with their theory that I already received my settlement check, had them believing all of these things about me. Of course none of them ever asked me about it or asked for proof. They just believe whatever clever story someone concocts, and that's all there is to it.

My grandmother passed away while I was there visiting. Anjolie and I were at the truck stop just waking up and getting ready to go visit her. It was in 2017. I hadn't heard the news yet. Aunt Meta called me and asked me if I was sitting down. I of course always made jokes of things and she told me this wasn't funny and that I needed to be sitting down. I sat down and told her I was ready for the news. She asked me where I was. I told her we were at the truck stop and just got to Buffalo the night before and we were getting dressed to go over to see grandma. She then asked if I had been over there that morning and I told her I was planning on going over there and I was just waiting on Suhan to lend me his car so that I could go there. Suhan was Demone's father. Even if he wasn't his biological father as he claimed, he still raised him as his own, but wasn't really involved until Demone was a bit older. This is when Aunt Meta told me that Grandma passed away that morning. I was shocked and caught off guard. Even just after hearing the bad news, I began to wonder why she asked me if I had been over there that morning. She wasn't the only person to ask me that either. It was a running theory that I went over there that morning and somehow poisoned her. Wouldn't you know that Benny and Debbie also believed this theory, and this would play into how they treated me when I moved out there. My grandmother had a lot of worldly possessions. Everything from expensive jewelry, fake jewelry, fur coats, lots of clothes, cars, furniture, etc.. One thing she promised me was that she wanted me to have the marble table set with the coffee tables that matched. She said this the Summer before when Anjolie and I were visiting and she met my daughter for the first time and it was in front of Aunt Sonya. I did really want those items, but I wasn't willing to fight over them like everyone else was fighting over her possessions. Aunt Meta took the marble table set. I told her that it belonged to me and that she could verify that with Aunt Sonya. Aunt Sonya confirmed that she did indeed want me to have that set. I told Aunt Meta that she could keep it and that I didn't care enough about material possessions that I didn't buy, to fight over them. She didn't say thank you or anything. She just happily kept them. Uncle El, Aunt Sonya, and Aunt Meta were left as the executive committee over what happened to grandma's possessions once she passed, and Uncle El was made final executor. They set a day to where everyone would come over and lay claim to whatever it was that they wanted. I have no doubts that the three of them had already gone in and taken what it is that they wanted to keep for themselves, as the case is made with the marble table set. Aunt Meta informed me of the date and I told her I was not going to show up because I did not want to be a part of all the mess that I could see unfolding. It was already a mess when everyone met at the house immediately after her passing. Benny was upset because he was the eldest and should have had a say in what happens, and he made a big deal out of that. He and Uncle Sal got into it. Uncle El kept calm about everything and didn't get involved in any of the nonsense. Everyone seemed to be upset at him and against him because he was favored and made executor. There were all kinds of rumors floating around about him, including one wild conspiracy theory thought up by Serina that he was a clone because he had three careers and there was no way he could do all of those things. I am not going to disclose what Uncle El primarily did for a living, but let's just say he didn't need three jobs. One of his jobs was his private transportation and security business. The other was a passion job that he was just interested in and eventually took seriously. The main job is secret. Let's just say he wielded a lot of power.

It seemed like the entirety of the family was against him. I let him know that people were talking badly about him, and I also told him that I wasn't going to say who was saying what, but I didn't believe any of it and that he could count on me to have his back, and that I set anyone straight that said something bad about him. I wasn't trying to gain any favor at all. I was genuine about it. I wasn't expecting to get anything from it as my name was already tainted and I didn't know who believed what about me and having anything to do with my grandmother's death. When it came to everyone picking and fighting over my grandmother's possessions, I told the three executors I only wanted one single item. They asked me what it was, and they were quite shocked when I told them what it was, and I still have it to this day. There was an iron pole that my grandmother used to keep her bedroom window propped open. That pole was older than me. I remember using the pole to go and rescue Aunt Debbie one day when she called the house looking for help because her young son's father was beating on her. I was a teenager and no one else was there. It was just me and my friend, Marcus. I grabbed that pole and Marcus rode his bike with me on the handlebars the several blocks from Minnesota and Bailey, to Berkshire, Parkridge and East Amherst where she lived. Her boyfriend's family was downstairs in a car while he was up there beating on her. Aunt Debbie was shocked to see that I came to her rescue against this behemoth of a man, and I was all of 140 lbs. I entered the apartment with the iron pole in hand and my friend Marcus. I threatened him and he was shocked. His family came upstairs and pleaded that I don't harm Eddie. Where was their consideration for harm when he was there beating on a woman? He quickly left with them and Aunt Debbie was happy to know that my friend and I had come to her rescue. That was short lived because she soon got back with him and resented me for getting involved. I now know why Uncle El didn't do anything to Suhan when he beat the living daylights out of my cousin Serina. Whenever you help family, it backfires. I should have known she would be unappreciative. I remember I used to babysit her son while she went to work. I was good with kids. They listened to me. Little Eddie was bad, but not with me. Only with her. One time, she asked me if I was abusing him or something because I was the only person that he would listen to. I was a nanny for four years. It started out with two little girls, then the lady I was babysitting for got pregnant again, and I was then babysitting three little girls. I got the babysitting gig because my crazy aunt, the one that made me memorize the Bible, used to babysit for a young lady and could no longer do it and suggested I replace her, which I did. I did so well that Sonja suggested me to her friend, Valda, and that's how that happened. But I once again digress. Aunt Meta, Uncle El, and Aunt Sonya were shocked that all I wanted was that pole. I went to the house the day after everyone left. I got the pole, and left. I think it baffles them to this day. Well, there was still the issue of her house. I seemed to be the only candidate to receive the house. Everyone else either already had a house and couldn't afford another expense, or they didn't have a job and couldn't afford the house. I thought the house was paid for, but I learned that grandma took a couple of loans out on the house, including one big loan to bail Benny out of jail and pay his legal expenses. Also, another aunt of mine was stealing money out of her bank account. This was the same one that had the nerve to accuse me of having sex with her foster daughter in the kitchen. I got the phone call that the three of them decided I should have the house. I actually turned it down and I'm glad I did. You see, I was no longer the nice and friendly BJ. Not after all of the conspiracies put on me and the way I was treated. Benny would often move into the basement of the house whenever he lost his job or apartment, and Uncle Arnold would do the same. I was warned by several family members that it would become a big problem that I would have to deal with. If I were to take the house, no one would be living there except for Anjolie and myself. So many people were mad that it was decided the house would go to me and the hate started from there. Correction, the hate picked up and amplified from there. I seemed to be the only person that indeed wasn't trying to profit off of my grandmother's death. By that, I mean fighting over her possessions, including what I was promised. It seems to be true that the person with the least intentions wins out. After the deadline came for me to decide and secure a loan, they decided to put the house up for sale. Initially, they said that if I didn't take the house, that they would split the mortgage as they had been doing, but they put it up for sale. I guess they didn't lie, because they split the mortgage until it was sold. I then kind of regretted not taking the house because I wanted to keep it in the family for personal reasons. It was the house that I had so many memories in, just as they did, but I had this belief that my mother could still be alive and that she could come there looking for me one day, being that it was the house that she left us at. This was the house that I used to sit in the sun porch looking out the window, waiting for her to come back. I just couldn't let it go.

Now back to Benny. It was back in 2004 and Sheray was pregnant with Anjolie. Benny got in contact with me and wanted to come visit. We had a non-existent relationship. It had been so many years that we had even spoken, but suddenly he wants to be in my life. I was weary, but I gave him a second chance. A third or fourth actually. He told me that he wanted to move out here to get away from it all. I told him he could visit, but I had a child on the way and I didn't have room nor the mental bandwidth to have him living there. The time that he was coming out to visit was literally the same time I was on a small vacation and would be in Las Vegas. I was still into music and producing albums. I used to go to Vegas every couple of weeks to clear my mind and just because I liked the drive. I had a 2002 Chevy Monte Carlo SS that I had done a lot of custom work to. I told him not to come to California until I came back from Las Vegas. I had a friend that lived in Vegas and I would visit her often. She used to live right up the street from me in Oakland on Madison St. and we always remained friends. I get to Las Vegas and I get a call from Benny telling me that he had a surprise for me. His surprise was that he was in Vegas waiting on me. This was not good news and I found it to be quite irritating to be honest. I was quite pissed. I didn't really know this man and I already expressed to him that I wanted to be alone in Vegas after he suggested that we meet there. I was very clear about that. I ended up picking him up from the Greyhound station. I didn't act excited to see him at all. I already had my hotel room booked. I always stayed at the Rio, which was my favorite place in Vegas. Before he arrived, he told me that he had money. This was because I told him that I didn't have money to take care of him. He told me not to worry because he owned several cars from the collision shop he owned and that he was in the process of selling them. I forget the number, but I think it was something like $20,000 that he made from the sale of his cars. By this time, I told him that if he had money and could find a job when he got to California, then he could stay there, just as long as I wasn't coming out of pocket. I know that sounds cold, but I had no feelings for this man and he was honestly a stranger to me. I hadn't seen him since I was a teen. I don't even remember seeing him in 2004 when I came to Buffalo twice for two different weddings. One of them was Uncle El's wedding to his high school sweetheart, which happens to be the sister of the famous Melyssa Ford. We sat at the same table during the reception. She was cool and she had just gained fame from starring as a video vixen in Nelly's music video. She is now a co-host on the Joe Budden podcast. We used to be Facebook friends, but she either closed her account or deleted me. I don't know which, but I never held that against her. When she got into her near fatal car accident in California, I spent countless hours reviewing traffic cam footage trying to find the truck that did it.

So we're in Vegas and now I had to cancel my plans with my ex-girlfriend, Dawn, not to be confused with Dawn Robinson who also moved from Oakland to Las Vegas. Remember, Benny said he had a lot of money from selling his cars. I guess he thought he would be staying with me in my hotel room. No, not happening. I cannot express to you how much this man was a stranger to me and I was only even dealing with him because he is my biological. I asked him where he was staying, and he said he assumed it would be with me. I had a suite, but I planned on having company, and even if I didn't, I wasn't sharing my space with him. I asked if he planned on staying at the same hotel, and he said yes. There was some kind of standoff as he was waiting for me to volunteer to pay for it. I had a feeling this is what was happening, so I said I'll drive there and I would check in and bring my stuff to my room as he checked himself in. There were two separate lines for reservations and checking in. After I took my stuff to my room, which included my music producing equipment and clothes, one piece of equipment being a Korg Triton Extreme 88 key synthesizer and monitors, he comes to my room and says he's going to stay at a motel instead because he didn't want to waste his money on a room where I was staying. I guess he thought he could sway me into going against my conditions for him moving out here. He just totally put me in a bad mood. I didn't even contact Dawn to meet up with her. He was just too needy. I'm honestly still pissed about that and it was 20 years ago, down to the month. I found him to be repulsive and the most irritating person on the planet and I knew I made a big mistake. This man was trying to teach me about things that I had already mastered. He wanted to teach me how to drive, how to avoid scams in Vegas, being that he lived there and was married there for several years. He was a limousine driver and did collision work and custom car paint jobs, and according to him, was rated as the best in the business out there, which I didn't doubt because he was quite excellent and I witnessed his work first hand. I drove him to his motel that night and was relieved to be by myself. The next morning, I had breakfast and was just trying to relax before contending with him. I honestly wasn't planning on seeing him at all and was just going to ignore him and go about my business. Why let him ruin my weekend in Vegas, right? He called me and kept calling. I kept ignoring him. He's a grown ass man. He does not need me to pick him up. Las Vegas is his old stomping grounds and he wasn't supposed to be there anyways, so why should I give a shit? I couldn't turn off my phone because I still planned on meeting up with Dawn and I still had people that I needed to keep in contact with, namely Sheray, who was carrying my daughter. He would not stop calling me. Call after call after call. I finally answered and was audibly irritated. I thought maybe he had gotten arrested in Vegas again. He spent a few years in prison in Vegas for domestic abuse. "BJ, you're not going to believe what happened to me?" I'm thinking to myself, "oh no, what is it?" He goes on with this story that went something like this.... "I woke up and went to have breakfast. Now you know every place of business out here has slot machines and cards. I saw this one guy playing cards and he kept winning. He won a lot of money, so I decided to get in on the action, and I lost all of my money." I told him that he should have known better and that's how they get you. They act like someone is winning in order to draw the next sucker. I told him that after that long lecture he gave me on how not to fall for any scams, that he had a lot of nerve. I honestly didn't believe his story to begin with and if I wasn't regretting letting him come out there to live with me before, I would be even more regretful now. So now I have to end my trip and check out early. I wasn't about to pay for his stay in Vegas, nor was I concerned with how or if he paid for his room. He has all of his luggage and I have all of my things driving in a two door coupe. It was raining and it was a long drive home. He didn't even offer to drive, but he wanted to criticize my driving and wanted to teach me how to drive. I had some really good rain tires on my car and I probably was going faster than he was comfortable with, but I didn't give two shits. It was cramped and I couldn't sit how I wanted to sit. I couldn't listen to my music, because...extra person, extra luggage. I just wanted to get home. We finally arrived after what felt like forever, notwithstanding a small argument along the way. He sees the huge house I had and I guess he thought he struck gold. I was tired. The next day, I was out all day. I didn't want to be around him. I introduced him to Monica. I left a phone book out and opened it to the collision repair shops page. There wasn't much in the fridge, as I wasn't expecting him, plus I wasn't going to supply him with food anyways. He was supposed to have $20,000, right? I told him he wasn't going to see me until the following weekend. That was the weekend he was supposed to come anyway, and I still had to work. I leave in the morning, take the 2 hour commute to work, work 10 to 12 hours, then take the 1 1/2 hour commute home. 77 miles each direction. It's faster coming home than getting there. I didn't leave him any money, nor did I leave him the keys to any of my cars. I don't know what it was he was thinking, but he didn't do any of that stuff for me and he didn't earn the right to be taken care of by me. I was forcing him to stick to the agreement, and personally, if he didn't find a job or if I sensed he wasn't even looking, I was going to ask him to leave and I would have paid for his bus ticket home and a cab to get to the bus station. Well, we didn't even make it to the next weekend. I came home on a Friday and Monica was in the kitchen. It was the end of the week and I was off on weekends. I asked where my father was, and she said that he left. I thought he went out for the day. She said "no, he left. He packed up his stuff and left. He was complaining that you weren't spending any time with him, wouldn't give him keys to one of your cars, and that there was nothing to eat." I explained everything to her, and she agreed with me. My grandmother called me and told me that he was complaining to her that I was disrespecting him and yelling at him and that he wasn't going to have some kid talking to him that way? I was a 30 y/o kid that had his own home, a nice one at that, and a few really nice cars. He never owned a home or even tried, but he wanted to talk down to me. He made up some stuff that wasn't true. She said that he went to Vegas after leaving my house and he called for her to send for him to come back to Buffalo. This grown ass man was still trying to use people for a place to stay, but I was accused of that. My grandmother said when he went to Vegas, he was hospitalized because I poisoned him or something. There is nothing true about that. She said he came back and his hands were all swollen. I honestly think he went out there and got into trouble and someone probably took a hammer to his hands. But evidently, he got in contact with his ex. The very same person that he did over three years in prison over and things didn't work out with her either. I still find it hard to believe that he complained that I, someone that was gone 14 hours a day during the week, didn't spend any time with him. The person that had my sister and I waiting for him for hours, often, to never show up. The same person that I only lived with for a short period of time. The same person that ran my mother off by physically abusing her and from what I hear, he tried to kill, which is why she disappeared in the first place. I suppose he believed that he succeeded in killing her. I remember the look on his face when he was standing behind the door at Debbie's house and I told him that I know he killed my mother. He didn't respond.

Back in 2018 in Buffalo, my aunt's husband, Uncle Al, which everyone called Stewart, which was his last name, passed away. I went to his viewing and guess who showed up! Benny. I tried my best to stay away from him, and of course this was after that entire incident happened at Debbie's house. One thing I forgot to mention about that incident, my daughter told me that when she went to the backyard to retrieve our belongings, she saw him and another guy hiding in the backyard and the other guy had a gun. They were setting me up to kill me. This is why Debbie was trying to stop Anjolie from going back there. The plan was for me to go back there. Yes, this really happened and they really did create a plan to kill me, and I honestly wish they both would die horrible deaths. I wouldn't do anything to make it happen, but it would be music to my ears if I did indeed find out something happened to them, so when I learned that Benny was having regrets and failing health, I smiled. Even now, I smile thinking of many ways he could meet his demise. There are many things I'm leaving out about him so don't judge me. Just know the fact that he ran my mother off and possibly killed her or tried to kill her, backed by the fact that they had this plot to kill me, is enough for me to want him erased from existence. So when I saw him at the viewing of Uncle Al, he approached me and asked if we could talk. I told him I really didn't have anything to say to him and he insisted. We went to the entrance of the funeral home and he apologized for how he acted and what he did. I tried saying my part, but he just wouldn't fucking shut up. His way of apologizing included telling me that my mother was a whore and that all she did was cheat on him, and that he wasn't really our father, and that our father was Arthur Ash, the famous tennis player. Well, this was debunked by not only the fact that I had many of his physical characteristics, but that I took a DNA Ancestry test that shows me as related to the family. I could not believe that even in him apologizing, he's calling my mother a whore and saying she deserved what happened to her. He basically admitted to killing her. I had it all recorded, but luck would have it that I used a recording app called "AutoBoy Blackbox" and I found out that files easily got corrupted. I had enough of his rant and decided to leave and he walked me to my car and complimented my choice of vehicle, which was a 2005 Subaru Forester. I really was not interested in his fake ass praises, and the only reason I didn't break his face was out of respect for being at Uncle Al's viewing, a man that I had far more respect for than my own biological, and this was the uncle that wouldn't let me around his daughter's after hearing of the fake rape allegations against me. I was happy to reunite with Uncle Al after all those years and for him to accept me and give me the praises that he did, and for him to meet my daughter before he passed. He's one of the few people that I truly miss.

It was this entire fiasco with my Benny that I truly buried him (Benny). All the time we were in Las Vegas and the car ride home, he was literally trying to compete with me, his own son. He wanted to challenge me to a foot race. I'm not kidding. He went on an entire spiel about how the original is better than the offspring at everything. I'm competitive, but not like that. I will only compete if I have to. If someone wants to be the smartest in the room, I'm fine letting them believe that. Maybe they are, but if it doesn't affect me, I really don't care. If someone says they're the fastest in the room, I really don't care. They can be the fastest, even if I believe I am. I haven't been of the age where I felt I had to prove myself to anyone, for many years. Benny was competing on all fronts, and I saw why no one wanted to be around him for more than a couple of hours, if that. He would go on and on about how he's stronger, faster, smarter, and knew more about everything. Do you really think I wanted this man living in my house just to have to hear him yapping about how much better he is than everyone else? Ok, go out and get a job better than mine since you want to compete with me so badly.

I heard from my Aunt Meta that Benny was sick and didn't sound good, like he lost his voice and she made it sound like he might not make it. It was probably COVID as this was before it was a pandemic. She mentioned to me that he was trying to make amends with everyone and that he was regretting that none of his kids liked him and that he did everyone wrong. She alluded to the fact that he wanted to make things right. Look, he already tried that with me once and I wasn't going to fall for it again. He probably was losing his apartment and needed a place to stay and was using his illness to gain sympathy. I told her good, I don't care if he's sick and that I have no wish to make things right with him. I told her that I don't care if he dies, on his deathbed, or has any regrets. Just because he has regrets, that doesn't make things right and it doesn't mean I have to forgive him. My message to her to pass along to him was, he made his bed, lie in it. I already gave him that chance, several times, and each time, he stabbed me in the back. When he does die, I will not care and I won't regret it or have any sorrow.

I got word that Benny and Debbie were at odds with each other, which didn't surprise me in the least bit. No one keeps their alliance with anyone for very long in my family. For example, Uncle Sal and Debbie. Uncle Sal was so surprised by how Debbie was treating me because he was working with her on some sovereign citizen nonsense. They were besties for quite some time and he was mentoring her on how to do certain things and sharing documents he received from City Hall, etc. I'm still unclear on where they stand on the sovereign citizen thing because just after listening to it for a few minutes, I found so many flaws in their arguments that I had no interest in hearing anything further. It's like me being a man of science, and I actually do study different sciences and math and I'm very well versed and well rounded, and I have to sit there and listen to someone tell me how the Earth is flat and we've never been to the moon, and their information is based on a YouTube channel from someone that blocks comments that proves them wrong. I just have no interest in the conversation. Uncle Sal and Debbie fell out with each other because Debbie just had a problem with time and thinking everything had to be on her time. I guess Uncle Sal didn't respond to her in a timely fashion and she said he was ignoring her calls so then she started talking badly about him to whoever would listen to her. One of the things I questioned Debbie about was when she was saying you don't need a driver's license to drive a vehicle, and if you use the correct terminology in court, you'll win. But she still maintains her license, so she doesn't believe that nonsense herself. When I read the law, it says every citizen has the natural right to TRAVEL freely without harassment (I'm paraphrasing). It doesn't mean that you have the right to operate a vehicle wherever you wish to without proving your capabilities to operate such a vessel. I could go on and on about the many flaws with that sovereign citizen stuff, and they do have some good points, but that would almost be an entire book.

CHAPTER SIXTEEN
LOYALTY

If you name any two people in my family, I can point to a time where it was those two people versus everyone else in our family, and I can also show you where those same two people were enemies before, or even after. In fact, this may be the premise of the sequel to this book. I say this because I need you to see how hard it is to get along with anyone when everyone is playing factions. Alliances were changing so often, when I woke up in the morning, I didn't know who it was I was and wasn't supposed to be speaking to. People are so fickle and the same rules they put on some, they don't put on others. For example, I go back to Suhan. As I mentioned previously, Suhan beat my cousin Serina almost to death. This was in the early 90s, maybe 1990 or 91. It may have even been 89, I don't quite remember. I didn't really know him that well and Uncle El was first on the scene when this happened and he was pretty much the enforcer of the family that people feared if he got physical with you, especially being a licensed concealed gun holder. Uncle El took a more diplomatic approach to the situation and I learned a lot from him about how to handle those types of things, but not at the time. I wanted revenge on the person that beat my cousin beyond recognition. My late cousin Gerald and I talked about it and we were upset. I was young and very impressionable. We could not let Suhan slide like that. I don't want to name the entity that we worked with so I won't name any names. I will however, give you specifics about the situation and you can peace it together yourselves. Serina was renting a place that was upstairs from a popular Italian restaurant. Serina had a relationship with the owner of said restaurant. I recall her telling us that he was giving her money and paying her rent. Suhan found out about this relationship and beat the hell out of her. The owner of this restaurant really liked Serina, so he was very upset about the situation too. Knowing this, Gerald and I met up with the owner to express our displeasure. Mind you, Blacks and Italians really didn't intermingle. They were usually very racist towards us, but not all of them. I mean, the Italian owner of a restaurant was openly dating a Black girl. It was like a scene from the Sopranos. Three members of the Italian Mob and two Black teens discussing getting revenge on the person that badly maimed the person we loved. I honestly went there just thinking we were going to teach Suhan a lesson. It turned into a conversation about murder. When I say "I could have been a killer," this isn't actually one of the things I was thinking about when I came up with the title, but I guess even back then, I could have been one. I actually just remembered this incident as I was writing this book. I'm writing in order of memory and jumping back and forth in time based on that, and also when necessary to make connections between memories. This is my version of the movie "Arrival." So the owner of this restaurant and his two buddies, who may have been relatives, mentioned cutting Suhan up and dumping him in a barrel of battery acid. This was the first time I ever even heard of something like this. This actually excited me and I was looking forward to this. The words "kill, murder" or anything directly referring to ending his life was never used. I honestly at the time didn't know they were talking about killing him, and technically, they never said it themselves. When Gerald and I left the restaurant, we were excited and celebrated that we hatched a plan to teach Suhan a well deserved lesson. I honestly thought about it for a while and realized that dumping someone in battery acid would actually kill them and cutting them up would just add to the torture. I talked to Gerald and told him I didn't wish to kill anyone. It was a few days later that I went back to the restaurant and talked to the owner and expressed that we were coming up with a plan to teach Suhan a lesson without killing him. I actually talked the owner out of harming him and told him this was my family and that it was my decision and my revenge to take and for them to stand down. It was some real gangster shit. They respected me and told me they would stay out of it. I remember telling Suhan this story around 2018 and his reaction was weird. I told him I was glad we didn't do anything, and he was in disbelief because he had no idea how close he was to dying way back then. I say all of that to say this, when Suhan and I first reconnected, it was because of the advent of Facebook. He sent me a friend request. I like to keep a low friend count on my page. I have lots of people that I know and I don't have them as friends on Facebook. This is going back to how people put different standards on me than they do everyone else in the family. I didn't accept his request right away. I didn't know what the relationship was between him and my cousin, so I sent her a text and told her that he sent a friend request. She told me to accept it and that she didn't mind and held nothing against him. I can't make this crap up. There were at least 15 other relatives that had him as a friend on Facebook. Serina was a friend on Facebook and we talked on the phone a lot and also texted each other a lot. I stopped hearing from her and when I looked her up on Facebook, I saw that she deleted me. I got a strange friend request from someone named Rene and had a different last name from Serina. I later found out it was Serina and she was hoping I would accept her friend request just so she could spy on me, but I don't care how pretty you are, I'm not one of those people that just accepts friends because I want to see my numbers increase. I'm not fooled, nor easily amused by bolstering numbers. After finally getting in contact with her and asking her what the deal was, she told me that she didn't appreciate that I accepted his friend request, yet and still, she was still friends with everyone else that had him as a mutual friend.

I remember Serina first giving birth to Demone. I remember being in the kitchen of my grandmother's house when I first found out she was even pregnant with him. I saw her belly and asked her what was wrong and why she was getting so big. She laughed and said "you really didn't know? I'm pregnant!" She had a good laugh about that. I was just never in people's business like that. I think I was 11 at the time. I really didn't know about the birds and the bees and about what pregnancy was. I learned all of that from her. I also learned what a period was from her, ironically. I remember coming home from school and seeing lots of blood in the trash bin of the bathroom. I had never seen that much blood on a bandage in my life. I ran out of the bathroom screaming "who got hurt?" Serina, once again (actually before her pregnancy) got a good laugh. "That's mine. I'm on my period," and she explained to me what a period was. This brings back memories because I was the one that had to explain this to my daughter when she had her first pre-period and I had to go to her school to pick her up. Demone was born the night before Christmas. I remember Serina's water breaking and her being rushed to the hospital. She was such a good and dedicated mother. Her mom, Debbie, was so pissed at the situation and often contemplated having Suhan prosecuted for statutory rape, as he was 18 or 19 when he got Serina pregnant. But after Demone was born, Debbie became more docile. She said she didn't want to ruin her grandson's life by having his father thrown in jail. She would often say this to Suhan and really couldn't stand being around him. I found it ironic that her son's father was half her age, and it was even funnier that she said she enjoyed being with him because he had a huge center member, if you know what I mean. It was surprising that she would even discuss something like that with me. I really didn't need to know all of that. Demone got a lot of attention in the family which was both a good thing and a bad thing. Like with me, the men in our family never had any part of his life. They never took him anywhere or had anything to do with his upbringing. Because of this, he spent most of his time around women and started having female mannerisms. Oh, the men had something to say about this! Even back then, I found it strange that they would criticize his female mannerisms, yet never had any hand in helping him to become a man. It was widely thought that Demone was gay, and this was during a time that being gay wasn't accepted. Even his mom and grandmother thought that he was going to be gay. We all accepted him anyway, I mean, he was still a child and had time to grow and become a man. His father recognized it and stepped in. Now that he had a male role model, he started to grow out of his feminine ways.

I was living in California and Demone and I started to communicate more. I was into music and doing well and he was trying to find his way. We actually made serious plans for him to move to California. It was during this time that he was murdered. I carried so much guilt and grief because I felt as though I didn't do enough to expedite his move to California and had I done things sooner, he wouldn't have been there to have been killed. I still can't believe it to this day, so I can only imagine how his mother and grandmother were coping. This wouldn't be the last time that I started to connect with someone and they ended up getting killed. One of my points in this story is, the traumas that happen to people really shape their mental well-being and how the rest of their lives are shaped. This may be, in fact, I'm positive that this is the cause of both Debbie and Serina losing their minds and succumbing to mental illness.

I have a sister that I have yet to mention. We'll call her "Bailey." She also suffered the same unbearable tragedy of losing a child. I never knew any of her two children, though I did meet her oldest son when he was a baby. Bailey had a daughter I will name Teyana. She was so beautiful. She just started making waves as a professional model. She actually turned down an opportunity to be on America's Next Top Model. I was never really connected to Bailey's kids because Bailey and I were never close like that. She was always in another State and hard to find. She often used aliases and would never have the same phone number. When Facebook came out, we eventually connected that way, but the more things change, the more they stay the same. During the time Debbie and I were speaking and making plans for me to move there, evidently the two of them were feuding, so Bailey decided to delete me from her friend's list. Just as I stated previously, this is just how my family is. I had nothing to do with their dispute, but I got caught in the crossfire. She eventually sent me another friend request, but I didn't accept it. I don't play those games. You delete me, keep me deleted. She tried to explain herself, and I understood her explanation, but her explanation was just stupid and I wanted no part of it. When her daughter was killed in a car accident, she reached out to me and I was also distraught for her and I did give us a chance to connect, but Bailey being Bailey, that didn't last long and I'm sure our other sisters played a part in that. They all got together and hung out and said it was a "girls thing." Hey, who am I to be upset about that? That only further solidified the fact that it's women before family. They got together to go to the funeral and I didn't even know when and where the funeral was going to be. By the time I found out, it was too late. I couldn't make last minute plans to be there. I did have to work. Had I planned ahead, it wouldn't have been an issue. Actually, it was a memorial. Bailey couldn't make up her mind on when and where the funeral was going to be held and we were in communications about that, but she went off the radar and left me in the dark, so I ended up missing it. Belle, and this is out of character, did tell me that the funeral was going to be in Los Angeles in a week, but I honestly was upset that Bailey herself didn't tell me and it was apparent that she didn't want me there. The memorial is what everyone went to that I didn't know about until the last minute. This was one of those circumstances of "I thought you told him." Don't ever depend on Belle telling me a damn thing, and the same goes for my other sisters. I'm supposed to be psychic to the point that I just know everything without anyone having to tell me anything I guess.

    I was just warming up to Teyana and sharing her modeling photos and videos. I had been in contact with Isaac, her older brother on Facebook, but we didn't have a "close" relationship. It was just a mutual respect. We were never at odds or anything. I just didn't know him and wasn't around his mother much. I saw an opportunity for us all to come together in Teyana's passing. I started to comment on her photos and I'm not sure if I sent her a friend request. I never did anything for Bailey to block me. I don't get it. I never did anything to have Bailey upset at me. Imagine how I felt to see that she unblocked me and sent me a friend request. I never accepted it and she sent me a message asking why I hadn't accepted her friend request. I told her straight up that I wasn't about to deal with her drama after she unfriended me just because I was talking to a family member that she had a problem with, and all she had to do was come to me directly and voice her concerns. I suppose this plays into her being distant with me when it came to her not inviting me to the "sisters' get together," which should have been a sibling get together. I mean, there were a couple of other people there that weren't even related. I just don't have the patience for the drama anymore. You unfriended me, keep that same energy. I don't know what sets you off so I prefer you to stay away at that point. Her reactions seem to come from what other people say. I honestly don't have time for people like that. I do understand that she just went through a tragedy, but she was this way before the tragedy. Crazy thing is, Bailey and I have the same passion for writing. She has published a couple of books in the past, but she only seemed to surface when she had something to show off. I do feel really badly for her. I could not imagine losing my daughter. I have an old friend that also lost his daughter recently. She was murdered. I watch him on Facebook crashing out all the time. He had a really good job that he was proud of and often posted pictures of him on duty at his roadside construction gig. We have talked on the phone about many different things, but he never brought up his daughter and I never mentioned her either. Some people are only comfortable writing on social media about things like that, which is totally understandable. Sometimes saying things aloud causes an emotional response that we're not willing to show. I will say this, and I do not wish to throw salt on any wounds, but I refused to let my daughter be in a car unless she had her seatbelt on. I would not pull off until I saw her put it on and heard it click. Teyana died because she didn't have her seatbelt on.

 I have an Aunt by the name of Rochelle that lost her son not too long ago. Gerald was my ace growing up. It was he and I that consorted with the Italian Mob to seek revenge on Suhan. He was quite the athlete and broke many records in football and was being scouted by the NFL. He just made some bad life choices as he never went to college. He had NFL scouts coming to his high school games. He played for Seneca High School. His younger brother was even better than him at football. Cory on the other hand did have aspirations to go to college and even moved to California for a brief stint, but made a bad decision to move back to Buffalo, where he and his White girlfriend were at the wrong place at the wrong time. He was in a racist part of town that did not appreciate that he was with "one of theirs." They beat Cory senseless, literally. He lost many of his scruples, and if losing your marbles is a thing, this was it. Corey did end up staying in the field of football and became a scout for the SEC. This alone tells me that had Cory not been beaten the way he had been, he definitely would have been in the NFL. Gerald and I did a lot together growing up. The same way he was an excellent older cousin to me, I was the same for Cory. Gerald and I went on long missions across the city to neighboring cities, usually chasing tail. Gerald was a wild one. If we arrived at a girl's house or were about to meet a girl, if he didn't have gum, a mint, or something to freshen his breath, he always had cologne samples. I remember he sprayed his mouth with cologne in order to approach a girl. It really wasn't necessary. This particular occasion, we were up the street from where I lived at my grandmother's. The 2nd house from the corner was a girl's group home and we often talked to the girls that lived there. They were just happy to talk to guys and his breath wasn't enough of a factor to spray cologne in his mouth. These were the types of life choices he made. He partook in smoking and drinking...a lot! You'd be hard pressed to not catch him doing one or the other, or both. I never saw him taking any drugs, so I'm not going to put that on him, but I wouldn't put it past him either. He was a thrill seeker, and though small in stature, he was a really tough guy. I've seen him beat up much bigger guys than himself, and in fact , the only people in our family as tough or tougher than Gerald, were our older cousin by the name of "Hitman," real name William, Hitman's older brother Dwight, and our Uncle El. Honestly, all of my uncles were pretty tough. It's just that the other two uncles didn't show that side of them unless necessary.

Of course, as we get older and start to live our own lives, we become more distant. I moved to California and didn't keep in contact with Gerald. He went on to father a few children. I hadn't spoken to Gerald from 1993, all the way until 2004 when Uncle El got married, and also that same year when our younger cousin got married. The next time I would see him is when my daughter and I were in town and our grandmother died. He lived in Florida, and he, his younger brother Gary, and his mom came up to pay respects and to be with the family. Gerald didn't look too well and I even questioned his health. He was very thin and had the yellowest eyes I had ever seen. He downplayed everything, but I knew something was wrong and he just refused to get checked out. I remember being on the road 4 years later and finding out while at the gym of my hotel, that Gerald had passed away. I was talking to my sister Shawna on the phone and she was telling me how she was in Florida for a funeral and how she met Gerald's father for the first time, and how he was such a cool guy and she had no idea that he and his wife were so warm and welcoming. Shawna was talking fast. I thought she was saying she met Gerald's father before he passed away and that she went back there for the funeral since she met him and felt close to him or something. Then she said "Gerald." I literally said "wait, what? Who died? It sounded like you said our cousin Gerald died." She told me that she was talking about our cousin Gerald. I had to get confirmation "Rochelle's son, his brothers are Cory and Gary?" She confirmed it was him, and once again, I got the "I thought you knew." That's a recurring theme in my life. If at any time I found out someone in our family died, I would call or text everyone. I don't get that same respect. I sent a text to Uncle El because I knew he and Gerald were also close. Uncle El was shocked to hear that I had not known. I don't think Uncle El believed I didn't know. I haven't confirmed this, but I think he contacted my sister, Belle, to ask her if she told me. I'd bet a dime to a donut that she lied and told him that she did inform me, just as she has lied in the past about the same thing. Uncle El didn't return any of my texts after that, which leads me to believe he had a reason not to believe me. Honestly, if you're going to judge me for not showing up to a funeral, why didn't you tell me of his passing yourself? My question to Belle if I were to ever speak to her again would be, when did she tell me? Show me a call record in her call log to my phone. Show me a text message. The only time we spoke in that time period is when I contacted her to tell her some news that I found out. You see how I don't do her how she does me? I had it in my right mind to not tell her the news, but I did anyway. I will get to that later, but with the news I told her, believe me, she would not have thought about telling me about Gerald's passing. The news I had for her was too overwhelming to even remember her own birthdate. There was absolutely no way I would have said "Belle, (then told her this mega shocker that changes everything)," and then she would say "by the way, Gerald died." It would have been equivalent to me calling to tell you I won the State mega lottery for 1 billion dollars, and you remembering to tell me that McDonald's brought back the Mighty Wings. I guess I care that I wasn't told and I guess I care that people think I constantly act like I didn't know someone passed away, but at the same time, I couldn't care less. Gerald did upset me slightly before he passed, but not nearly enough for me to wish harm upon him. It did play into a narrative that I discussed with my sister Shawna that people that do me wrong seem to die if I think about it hard enough. Maybe people thought that I wished Gerald passed away. There is nothing that he could have done to make me wish that. It would take a lot, and I mean a whole lot, for me to even think ill of him in any way. He has done too much for me in the past for the mistake that he made, to cause me to wish any harm upon him.

His brother Gary on the other hand, I don't care for that little shit at all. As much as he has come at me in the past with the hate, negativity and threats, but not having that same energy when we were at my grandmother's house, I just don't respect him. Grandmother passing or not, you're supposed to invite me around the corner to slug it out. The problem is, he's a little guy. He played like he was tough, and he probably was, but to me none of that mattered. You have to show me. Before I get to what Gerald did, I have to get this story out of the way. I remember when Gary was born. I actually went to his mom's house with my grandparents so that they could get her to the hospital. I even remember meeting his father. He was a really cool guy and he was well to do. Gary never had to struggle. Anything he wanted, he could just ask his dad and his dad would do it for him. Gary was into music, which wasn't shocking. Most of our family had musical talent, and Gary was no different. I supported him and even reposted all of his music on my Facebook page and shared anything I could find related to him, to anyone I could. I even shared it with some of my connects. I'm not going to sit here and lie and say I thought his music was trash, because it wasn't. My problem is, I was also into music and whenever I posted or tagged him in something, he would never respond. He was blatantly ignoring me. Finally, I said something to him. He finally responded as if he were keeping it in for a long time and couldn't contain himself any longer. He told me that he was pissed that I was in California doing well, making all kinds of money and not sending any back to the family. Huh? For one, I don't know what kind of money he thought I was making, and even if he had the numbers right, if he was aware that this is California, not Buffalo New York. The cost of living is not the same. I might make three times what the average salary in Buffalo is, but rent and mortgage is four times what the average rent and mortgage is in Buffalo, at least at the time. Buffalo did start getting more expensive, but at this time, there was a clear difference. Also, I wasn't sending anyone money that never gave a shit about me. Remember, when I informed everyone that I was moving to California, no one showed up or put together a care package for me, yet they threw an entire party for Uncle El when he was going out of State to Pennsylvania for a temporary assignment. What I did as I previously said was, I had opportunities for people to make money. Gary could have easily gone to his dad for money. I never had that. The only thing I could depend on with my father was him not showing up. He showed me what not to be like. Gary and I had a big falling out regarding this entire thing, and he had the nerve to tell me I was worshiping the devil and I was working for Demonds [sic]. Many of our arguments were actually in the comments section of his YouTube video. Gary was changing faces with the wind. Anything he could do to gain a little clout, he would do. He wasn't doing well in the secular genre, so suddenly he became a Christian rapper. Everything he was rapping about was nonsense because I knew differently of him, especially just judging from the way he was coming at me and things he said to me. I tried brushing it off and cutting him off the way I would do anyone that has crossed me, but he did something that I really did not appreciate and I couldn't let slide. Our late cousin, Demone, was working on music with Gary. I respect that and would never get in the way of them collaborating. The problem is, Demone passed away, and Gary started using Demone's rap name as his own. Gary told me it was homage. I had to explain to him that it isn't homage to use his name. He disagreed, but I'll tell you one thing, he stopped using his name.

I can go on and on about how I know people personally that have lost their children due to tragedy. Most times, it could have been avoided just by being a little nosey and a little more intrusive on your children. Stop trying to be their friends all the time. Stop trying to be that cool parent that would rather not embarrass their kids in front of their friends. I don't do that unnecessarily, but if my daughter isn't getting the point when I'm trying to be discreet, then I will say what it is I need to say in front of her friends and cousins. If my daughter is involved in some hoodrat activities, I'm going to put a stop to it, or at least I will try. Maybe she'll get the point and correct herself, and maybe she won't, but I will stay adamant with her.

I have a friend that lost his daughter a couple of years ago. She was murdered. I don't know the details, but either way, it was senseless. It may have been something that was totally out of her control, or it may have been something she was directly involved in. I just don't know and I didn't ask my friend any details. He's already hurting enough, and it shows when we speak on the phone and on his Facebook posts. Another close friend many years ago also lost his daughter to a gun. The crazy thing is, it was the day that they buried Marcus's brother and they all met up at his mom's house after the funeral. She was 14 years old at the time. She and a couple of her younger cousins went into their grandmother's bedroom and opened the drawer where she kept her gun. Marcus's daughter picked the gun up, barrel pointed right at her face, and the gun went off. I had never felt so sad in my life. That was my first experience with a close friend losing their child. It's one of those things where you don't know what to say, nor what not to say. We were friends in real life and this was before social media, so when I moved after that incident with Tommy, we grew a little distant, though I did end up going to a BBQ that he hosted at his house in Stockton where he moved to. I had my daughter with me, and I think it was hard for him to see other people with their daughters. I sent him a friend request on Facebook and he never accepted it. We never had a falling out of any kind, so the only rationale I can think of is because my daughter was the center of my universe and I talked about her a lot, though I was careful to be sensitive around him. Hey, maybe it was my anti-religious sentiments? That couldn't be it because we had a mutual friend that we're both close to that shares the same beliefs as I.

CHAPTER SEVENTEEN
TJ

As far as what it is Gerald did that upset me, there is a lengthy story that leads up to this. Growing up, there was a guy named TJ, short for Troy Johnny Brown, Jr. He lived up the street from us and was the same age as my cousin Serina. So basically, he was about three years older than me. There were a lot of kids that lived in the neighborhood, and it was his mother, Linda, that I ran into in Cleveland at the Greyhound station when I was on my way to California. TJ was tall and towered over everyone else. He didn't hang around people his age, which we all found odd, but he always had the latest video gaming systems and games. He had a large back yard and had things like trampolines, a basketball hoop, water guns, skates, extra bikes, BB guns, and things kids liked playing with.. He had cable television with all of the channels, so a lot of the neighborhood kids liked to go to his house to hang out. This included myself. TJ was a punk though. He was scared to death of Andrew and Marcus's older brother, but not nearly as terrified as he was of my Uncle El. Back in the 80s, being gay wasn't acceptable. I remember being at a convenient store named "Stop-N-Go" with TJ and these well known twins were in there. Their names were Roman and Gabriel. There were rumors as to why they were the way they were, one of them including that their father was gay and molested them. I don't know if it was true or not, but when TJ saw them in the store, he would spew insults at them and call them every derogatory name in the book. Use your imagination. Well, they didn't appreciate it and they jumped him. They left me alone as they knew though I was with him, I didn't agree with his actions. I recall them chasing him around the store and throwing things at him. When we finally left the store, he questioned why I didn't help him and I told him straight up, I didn't agree with his actions and I had no problem with them. The truth would soon come out. Rumors about TJ started floating around the neighborhood that TJ himself had an affinity for the same sex. This was weird because he also would try to compete with me over these two sisters, Toni and Rachel. How could you be gay, but still chasing girls? He also used to brag about having girls at the group home across the street from him. To me, the allegations were just rumors, that is until I found out first hand. Andrew and Marcus told me stories without being direct and I began to wonder why it was he was so afraid of their older brother. One day, we were in his basement playing pool and video games. It was Andrew, Marcus, and myself. There may have been someone else there, but TJ started talking nasty and brought out a couple of porn tapes. We were still in grade school and had not yet gone through puberty and TJ began to tease us about it and questioned if we even had pubic hair yet. Of course, every boy our age strives to have it, but few of us really did, and if we did, it was merely a couple, as in my case. Andrew and Marcus quickly left and I was ready to follow them. I think they knew what was coming, I don't know if it was from personal experience or if they had solid information, but they were out of there. TJ cornered me from leaving and insisted that I prove to him that I had pubic hairs. I was scared and he made me pull my pants down to show him. I quickly pointed out the one hair I had and tried to pull up my pants to run, but he grabbed me and threw me down and tried to give me fellatio. I hit him as hard as I could and ran. He ran after me and pleaded for me not to tell my uncle El. I had never been so terrified in my life. I was too ashamed to tell anyone at that time what had just occurred. I did, however, warn people to not hang around him because I thought he was a pervert. I was doing the same thing Andrew and Marcus did and tried to warn people without being direct.

From that moment on, I stayed far away from TJ, but then I remembered something he said to me not too long ago before that. I was sick due to cyclic neutropenia and I had boils on my butt. I was in the backyard and he came back there. I was sitting on my side and he noticed how I was sitting. He asked me what was wrong and I told him. This dude asked me to show him. I should have known at this point that he was sick, but I guess I was too naive. No, I didn't show him the boils. This entire situation was odd to me because TJ was into church and was even an accomplished self taught piano player. By accomplished, I mean he played piano at his church. I went to a church called "Prince of Peace." TJ would eventually join the same church where he would also play the organ and even shared duties in directing the choir. TJ was not short of ambition, and had he used his powers for good, I could see him being worth several hundred million dollars, and I'll tell you why this is a fact and not speculation in a moment. Before I continue, TJ had a little brother named Robert. I felt sorry for him because to me, it was a very strong opinion that TJ was molesting him. Robert was adopted and he was a very bad kid, but I then grew to understand that he was probably just acting out because of what may have been going on behind closed doors. So,

TJ now went to the same church that I was attending and it was about 6 years later from him attempting what he attempted with me, so I knew about him. It wasn't long before rumors about him floated around in the church. The biggest rumor was about this one boy whom everyone thought to be gay. Being gay doesn't mean you want to be molested, so let me clear that up right now. John John has a sister that at the time was very popular. She was gorgeous and fine in every sense of the word. Her name is Sherry and she was a very gifted singer. She's one of the few girls that I didn't make my way around to, though I was on my way and we did talk about getting together. John John was also in the choir. He started to complain to members of the church that TJ was rubbing on his leg underneath his robe while in the choir stands. No one believed him. Had I heard the rumors, I would have definitely come out and told them of my experience with TJ. I ended up speaking up later saying that I had reason to believe John John, but I was still too ashamed to say why I believed him. Little did TJ know that though they didn't take action against him for the accusations, they were watching him. The church not believing him was a ruse just so that they could catch him. I don't know if they caught him touching John John or if it was someone else, but they caught him and they kicked him out of the church. TJ pleaded with them to let him stay. He had some gaul. I couldn't imagine getting caught doing something like that and wanting to still be around the people that caught me. Honestly, he probably had something planned for revenge. Who knows. TJ left the church and actually started his own church. It was a youth church and he was now an ordained minister. Even scarier, I learned that he got hired into the Buffalo Police Department. I don't know at which capacity, but he was working there and I was told he wore a police uniform. How do they not do enough of an investigation to find out the allegations against him? How did no one go to his place of employment and inform them that their recruit likes to touch on little boys? So, TJ is now a pastor at his own youth church. No one here was older than him. You can Google his full name and put in all the key words and you'll find everything that I'm telling you as valid. It wasn't long before he started back to his ways of old and the rumors would resurface. Things eventually got so bad for him that he would leave the State and he moved to Atlanta. Coincidentally, Andrew and Marcus moved to Atlanta several years before, and I wouldn't be surprised if they ran into each other. TJ ended up starting another church in Atlanta and grew into a Mega Church rather quickly. He was raking in the dough. Being relegated to being called a Mega Church means you are so big and have so many members, that you have now earned that name. TJ was a brilliant person and I don't doubt at all that he was literally a genius. I have known and seen many Pastors that have spent decades trying to grow a church to even just double their original size and have actually gotten smaller. He amassed a MEGA CHURCH in the span of a few years. He knew that the formula was to play off of the youth audience. He saw the trend and did the math. Young adults were looking for something to belong to. Programs that used to exist were one by one being taken away. A perfect example is the after school program at my old grade school called "Lighted Schoolhouse." Gyms, basketball courts, etc. started closing down. YMCA's started losing funding. The skating rinks we used to frequent closed down. There's no memories like USA Skateland and New Skateland and dancing or skating to Salt-N-Pepa. Places to safely meet up and be around other people your age quickly dwindled. I admittedly only went to church on my own for the social setting. I wasn't the only one, so I can only Imagine things not being much different in Atlanta. The word quickly spread that there was a youth church with no adults monitoring them, and because it was a church, the parents of these teens had no problem with letting them go unsupervised. I mean, it's a church for Christ's sake, right? Well, you can read the details of the story on your own by doing a Google search, but good Ole Troy Johnny Brown would soon rear his ugly head as accusations started piling up and one of the boys that he'd been grooming came forward. TJ was arrested, went to trial, and he was given many decades as his sentence, 70 years to be exact. This was 30 years more than the prosecution requested, and with good reason. The details of the case are so egregious, I will not even quote them, nor will I copy and paste them. You'll just have to look it up for yourselves.

So, how does this relate to my cousin Gerald? Well, when my daughter and I were living in Buffalo between late 2017 and early 2021, just before moving back to California, and I literally mean during my last couple of days there, I received a message from TJ. I was absolutely flabbergasted. I still have some of the messages he sent me. It was January 7th, 2021. I ignored his calls and we communicated on Facebook Messenger. I had nothing to say to him. I told him "this can't be the TJ I know because he's in prison." After continuously ignoring the prison allegations and seeing that I wouldn't continue talking to him unless he confirmed it, he said he was still in prison and granted permission to use the internet. I guess they gave him a tablet and low and behold, he started an online prison ministry and he would not only minister to the prisoners there, but also to other people over the internet. Unfortunately, Aunt Rochelle and my cousin Gerald fell for his shenanigans. Gerald gave TJ all of my contact information without my permission, and this was someone I never wanted to hear from ever again. I did speak to Gerald and expressed my displeasure. Gerald told me that TJ was a changed man. I told him that he could believe that bullshit if he wanted, but I knew better and to not ever give him my information ever again. I had to change my phone number because of that. Luckily I was already moving. TJ told me that he knew where I lived because Gerald gave him all of my information. He even told me that he knew I worked for the NFTA and one of his friends worked there and was keeping a tab on me. If I had no other reason to leave Buffalo and quit that job, that would have been the one reason good enough to do so. TJ was, is, and always will be a very dangerous individual. He plays the long game and will convince you of anything he wishes you to believe. I was in shock and awe that my aunt and cousin fell for him and worshiped under his ministry. I told TJ that I moved to St Louis and if he didn't believe me, ask his friend if I was still working at the NFTA. Honestly, I was almost considering staying in Buffalo longer, but the simple fact that TJ had a spy watching me at my place of work, caused me to shut that down and continue with my move.

Gerald and I ended on a bad note, arguing about why he did what he did, yet and still, I have no regrets as it's not my fault that he did what he did, so there's no guilt on my behalf. I did also have a few words for my Aunt Meta as I did tell her not to give my phone number to anyone, including family, and it was from her that Gerald got my phone number. She felt bad about it and apologized. She said she had no idea. I forgave her and left it at that. That's all it takes is to admit to your mistakes and we can move on. It's that simple with me. She and I never discussed that again, though we did talk about TJ and how neither of us could believe that Aunt Rochelle and Gerald would fall for it and consider themselves members of his church, even after me telling them what I told them. No wonder people don't report these activities, because people don't care.

CHAPTER EIGHTEEN
KIDNAPPED

This story here is one of the ones that hurt me the most. I think I was a senior in high school when Uncle Roger told me that he ran into a relative that neither of us ever met. I remember this because I remember the Bills came back from a 4th quarter 32 point deficit against the Houston Oilers and I remember Candy Man had a hit that was still in rotation on the radio. I don't recall exactly, but I believe he said they met at a train station and after talking, they found out they were cousins. It was maybe 2 weeks after he told me about this that I coincidentally met Monique the same way. I don't know how, but when we met, I knew it was her. We are actually distant cousins, like maybe second or third cousins. She has another sister named Janet, and a sister named Iris. There's also her brother, BJ. This was during a time that I briefly lived with my father. I really did not enjoy living with him. I couldn't stand the fact that he tried to act like he had a hand in raising me and had the inherent right to tell me what to do, where I could go, when I had to be back, etc...I used my bike to get around and I remember asking for permission to go visit my cousin. I was asking out of respect and had he said no, I would have probably packed my belongings and moved back out the very next day. But he tried to act like he cared and asked for info about who this cousin was. I explained that I just met them not long ago and we grew close. He had a speculative look on his face and told me to go but not to stay out too late. I didn't like being home anyways as he and Linda, his new wife, were always arguing. Linda has a son named Desmond which was a pretty good kid, but they tried to force him on me as my brother. I have a real brother that I have never met that I never called my brother. In fact, and this is the first time I've actually thought about it, but I have two brothers, none of which I have ever met. Well, two that I know of. If I can excommunicate a blood sister that I've known my entire life, I have no problem in not claiming brothers that I have never met. Am I a bad guy for that?

I would often go to visit Monique and we would sit there and watch television and movies on her father's home made projector, which I thought was the coolest thing in the world. In fact, it's because of him that I started using projectors rather than regular televisions. I now use AR/VR glasses, as they are the next logical progression in content consumption and gaming. Her younger brother, BJ, was too young for me to grow an attachment to, but because we went by the same name, we got a kick out of it. He told me I used to call him Gismo. Sometimes their parents would call for him and I'd answer. I went over there one day and Monique wasn't home, but Iris was. She was only a couple of years younger than me and instead of me not hanging around, Iris and I would hang out and get to know each other. She would sit on my handlebars and ride with me to the store and around the neighborhood. I just loved having cousins that lived relatively close that I could hang out with and their parents welcomed me as part of the family. Well, one day Monique and Iris made the newspaper. I guess Monique had mental issues and I don't want to butcher the story, but Monique allegedly kidnapped her own sister and held her for a $20,000 ransom from their father. I don't really know the outcome of that story, but what I do know is it brought back memories from when I was in grade school. I was in the 7th grade and I was in love with this girl named Shadia. After the school year ended, I noticed that I would never see her anymore at the family owned corner store. I finally asked her sister, who was in the same class as me, why Shadia hasn't been around. She looked at me and kind of laughed and said to me "You didn't hear? She got sold for $20,000 and a mini van." That actually hurt my feelings. I know I didn't really have a shot at dating her, primarily because her parents probably wouldn't allow her to date outside of her race, but I was still hurt because I had just started becoming successful in dating people that had previously told me no before. I think I grew up a little and I grew into my looks. I did have a couple girls that were in high school tell me that I had a nice butt and they loved the texture of my hair, so I thought maybe, just maybe, I had a shot at Shadia. So, back to Iris and Monique. I felt so badly for both of them, and also their parents. It wasn't long after that when Iris would be kidnapped again. It made the news, but I was first told by Uncle Roger what happened. This time it was more serious. Iris was missing, like for real this time. The rumors were that her cousin, we'll call him Deandre, had some kind of Arabic connection and found a buyer, and that Deandre and Iris's dad sold Iris to an Arabian Prince. This didn't seem far-fetched to me because Shadia was sold and she's Arabic. When I tell you I was distraught, I called Aunt Sonya and told her what happened and I cried like a baby on the phone. Deandre owned a beauty salon, which he still does. I went there to ask him if he knew anything about what was going on, and he claimed to know nothing about it nor have anything to do with it. I was told that the FBI had already contacted him, which is where the rumors may have started that he had something to do with it. Iris's dad went on the run, and if I recall correctly, he was somewhere in Ohio in hiding. I learned that he is half Arabic, which lead everyone to believe the story of Iris being kidnapped and sold by her own father.

One of the rumors that surfaced is that she would keep in touch with Deandre and write him letters that she was being treated well, and that every Valentines day, her husband would buy her a pink Rolls Royce, and that she had several children. I think she may have only been 14 or 15, so this was appalling to me, but being my cousin had a baby at 14, it wasn't beyond belief. Several years went by and she still wasn't found. So how was she able to write Deandre letters? He would deny that he received letters from her, but the rumor was that she didn't contact him directly and that there was someone that would forward him any correspondence from her so that they could make sure she didn't give them any information about her location. The only thing we knew is that she was somewhere in Saudi Arabia. I actually just checked my messages with BJ and he said she was living in Dubai, then somehow got back to the United States and was living in Atlanta, and that her family went to pick her up from there in 1998 and took her to Florida. He said she was kind of an extremist and it took a long time to get her out of it. Between the four of them, they have a ton of kids. BJ has 6, Monique has 3, Janet has 9, and Iris has 8. He first contacted me in May of 2016 and I asked him to have Iris contact me. He said she wasn't doing too well so it would be a long shot, but maybe since it's been an additional 8 years, she's ready to talk. I just wanted her to hear from me that I did everything I could to find her, though I was unsuccessful.

Here's a disclaimer, I don't know the full or true story of what happened to Iris. I only told the version of the story that was told to me at the time, and until I'm given new information, this is what I know as truth, but all of it is still alleged.

I bring all of these tragedies of people losing their children up for a reason. I suppose I may have been overprotective, but it's not without reason. I always gave my daughter long talks. I always made sure she was safe. I still allowed her to go to parties and have fun. I wasn't one of those fathers that kept a close leash on my daughter because I know personally what happens when you're too strict on your kids. It's the preacher's daughter syndrome. I was the guy that got to the preacher's daughter, and I didn't want my daughter falling for someone like myself at her age. I tried to teach her as much as possible. Even when she was in the 7th and 8th grades, I allowed her to be home alone while I was at work. I trusted her. I did everything I could for my daughter, but you know teens these days, they know better than you, as so they think. I know you can say this about any generation, but things are truly different these days. We're in an era of change, the woke movement, technology, cancel culture, and a host of other things that we didn't have to worry about when I was young. We never had to worry about getting canceled for saying something before this generation. Whatever happened to "sticks and stones may break my bones but words will never hurt me?" It's the exact opposite now, and if you're born before the 90s, you probably missed the training session and made some "mistakes" with your children. Hey, we're the generation that climbed ice mountains with pick axes after walking across a salt lake on bare feet for 30 miles, then swimming in a river of alcohol just to get to kindergarten, right? Me, seeing what I've seen, knowing what I know, experiencing what I've experienced, just wanted nothing more than to keep my daughter safe, even if it meant keeping her away from her own family. I always told her "I'd rather you hate me now but appreciate me later." She never really believed me. Anjolie was and is very impressionable. She's like a chameleon. Anjolie was very trusting of people. She's been this way since she was old enough to walk, and she was walking about when she was just a year old. She was maybe 3 when we were at the mall. There was this interactive light show that shined from the ceiling to the floor. For example, there would be a koi pond, and the fish would run as the kids stepped on them and the water would ripple. One day, I was sitting on the floor leaning against the store window while keeping busy on my flip phone. It may have appeared as if I were too distracted to be paying attention to my daughter, but my mind is like a military aircraft radar. I could see everything my daughter was doing, so when this hispanic boy walked up to her and grabbed her hand and started walking away with her, I saw the entire thing. He couldn't have been more than 10. He looked at her, so I know he knew what he was doing. He turned the corner with her and that's when I decided to see how far he was going with her. I followed behind for about one minute before I asked him where he was going with my daughter. He looked shocked as if he knew he was caught, let go of her hand and picked up his pace and disappeared off with the rest of his group, probably to find another victim. I immediately went to the security booth which was located right near the light show. I described what just occurred and that it was obviously deliberate. The security officers were uninterested and did nothing, which caused me to believe they were part of this kidnapping organization. I called the police to report it and they were also uninterested, even after I told them I think the mall security was in on it. Maybe the police were afraid of real work, or maybe they would have responded differently if we had blonde hair and blue eyes, or maybe they were on two payrolls, but if I weren't already super protective of my daughter, my instincts were even sharper and showed no signs of letting up. Anjolie picks up the habits of whatever authority figure she's around. When she was around me, she did well in school. When she was with her mom, she missed a lot of school. Her mom would even have her stay home from school so that Anjolie could babysit for her while she went to work. I tried my best to put a stop to that. Her mom would have her lying to me a lot. I could tell when she was lying, but what can I do about it? I tried all I could. I gave her all that I could. We've done well financially, and we've been poor. I landed a job that paid a lot of money, and I would deposit $100 a week onto Anjolie's Cash App card. I would constantly tell her to only spend half of it. I wasn't going to stop giving her money. I wanted her to either learn a good lesson, or learn a hard lesson. I constantly checked her balance and noticed she was just squandering her money on stupid things. She should have had thousands of dollars saved, but she'd only have like $20. I still kept giving her money, even against my best friend's advice. I would tell my best friend that I knew she was right, but I had a bigger lesson that I wanted to teach her, and also at the same time, prevent her from blaming me for her not having anything. I knew the money wasn't going to keep coming. I was cutting it off at 18 unless she went to college. I would constantly remind her that she either needed to save, or get a weekend job. Did she listen? I won't leave you hanging. You know the answer to that. No, and this leads me into this next chapter,

CHAPTER NINETEEN
GETTING TO KNOW YOUR HEROES

Anjolie was into K-Pop music. Her favorite group was BTS. BlackPink was a close second, though for a while she hated them because one of them used the "N" word in one of her songs. I had to explain to her that people make mistakes, and her being South Korean and not really knowing our culture, probably only knew us from videos and social media. She didn't call someone the "N" word, she used it in a way that we use as a term of endearment. We actually argued about that and she got mad and sassy at me. I told her she can act mad all she wants and miss out on great music because of a stupid mistake, or she could understand that we all make mistakes and that one day she will make a mistake and want forgiveness. She came to her senses, because when BlackPink came to the United States on their tour, do you think Anjolie didn't want to go? Yeah, she wanted to go. She would have missed out had she not come to her senses, because I wouldn't have bought the tickets and drove several hours to pick her up and to drop her off. I would have made her lay in the bed she made. My job had me stationed in the Los Angeles area and Anjolie was living a 7 hour drive north of L.A., in Modesto. She told me about the concert and I paid almost $2,000 for the tickets. If you add in all expenses, it cost me over $3,000 for the concert, plus the time I took off from work, plus 28 hours of driving to pick her up, drop her off, and to come back to where I was stationed. We had floor seats very close to the stage. It was funny because when we first got there, we were in the wrong section. After moving a couple of times, we figured out that we were in the section right next to the stage. I still have a clip of the concert as my lock screen on my phone where one of the members of BlackPink pointed directly at me while I was taking a video of them. My daughter had on a very expensive body suit made by Nike, and I also was wearing a Nike outfit, and we both matched the "BlackPink" theme. It was probably the most fun she had ever had and the night went off without a hitch. It was also the first concert she had ever gone to.

Anjolie was also wearing her class ring. I spent over $1,800 on that ring. I know, you can get a class ring for much less than that, but I wanted my daughter to have what I never had. I didn't even have so much as a yearbook. She got the most expensive optioned class ring that was available. It's 18k gold, with the Mother of Pearl stone setting, and diamonds on the band. It has all of the etching and engravings you can get, with her name and year of graduation on it.

I also bought Anjolie the iPhone 13 Pro Max with the Apple watch of her choice. When the iPhone 14 Pro Max came out with the Dynamic Island, I bought her that one also. Not to mention, she had tons of new sneakers and shoes. Really nice name brand shoes, not that off brand crap. I'm talking Off-White Nike. That's a brand collaboration, not a color. They were actually Lakers colors, and I bought her a limited edition Michael Kors purse that matched them exactly, and that wasn't cheap. She was known as best dressed in school. She was very popular, and almost everyone loved her. When a relative had a birthday, I made sure that Anjolie would bring a nice gift. Whenever Anjolie had a birthday, I always made sure she had a party. I did it all. I raised her most of her life, took her to all of her appointments, went to most of her after school activities, recorded most of her memorable moments on camera, went to most of her parent teacher conferences, met up with the school and parents of children that were bullying her, and much much more. I made sure she was able to go on the trip to perform in DC at the big parade. I bought her tickets to Disneyland and gave her some spending money for her class trip. I got up super early in the morning, even though I had to be at work, to make sure she got there on time and didn't miss the bus because her mom was notorious for forgetting or not being on time to almost everything. I can go on and on and on with the things I did for my daughter that no one has ever done for me. I did these things unconditionally. It wasn't an investment. I only wanted some appreciation, but really didn't expect it all that much. This leads me into the story where Anjolie learned the biggest lesson of her life thus far.

    I think we all have that member of our family that we gravitate towards more than anyone else. For me, it was my sister Gina. We already know how she let me down. She was my hero that I met and found out she wasn't really what I always imagined her to be. Well, let me give her some credit, she probably more so transformed into the monster she became. For Anjolie, her hero was her aunt, Tashia. I never interfered with her relationship with her aunt. She admired her, and as long as it was from the distance that it was, I was perfectly fine with it. Tashia would pop in and out of town and they'd hang out. Fine. A couple of times, I drove Anjolie and her cousin who's only two weeks younger than her, to go and visit Tashia. I would drive them 7 hours to Reseda, CA, drive 8 hours back home, then make the same trip again to pick them up after the weekend. I had no problem with that. It's not like they were moving in with her or going to be around her long enough to be in any kind of danger. Honestly, I had no reason to believe they were in any kind of danger at that point. I learned during these interactions that there was something funny about Tashia. She had many of the same symptoms as my Aunt Debbie. I mean IDENTICAL. I remember on one of the trips when I was picking up Anjolie from over there, Anjolie called me and told me that Tashia wanted to give me a massage. I thought that was not only strange, but highly inappropriate for someone to have my child pass me that kind of message. I told Anjolie to tell her I declined her offer. I even told Anjolie that there was a hidden reason why she wanted to give me a massage so badly. Her "job" was a masseuse, but I knew better. Tashia is a prostitute. Let's be clear. At this point, I was only speculating based on what I've seen and heard while around her, but I would confirm it later by acting like I wanted to become one of her clients. For the record, I only wanted proof in writing and never planned on following through with anything, as after I got the written proof, I ended all communications with her. After I conveyed the message that I did not want her massaging me, Anjolie told me that Tashia had a special all natural drink for me. I naturally grew suspicious and thought of every scenario that I could think of as to why she was either trying to put her hands on me, or have me consume a liquid. I assumed she was trying to drug me by either rubbing something on my skin, probably scopolamine, aka dragon's breath, or some other kind of drug. I get to her apartment and Tashia insists that I stay for a little bit. I told her I was a little tired from all the driving that I had been doing, then going straight to work only to get a total of maybe 4 hours of sleep the entire weekend. So when I got to the apartment, she gave me a drink in a small shot glass. I was hesitant. I already left all of my valuables in the car at the charging station under her building, and

I hid my car key on my person where she wouldn't find it. I was prepared for her to try to rob me. The drink had a very strange flavor to me. It definitely had wheat grass in it, which has that horrible sewer taste to it. I was already really tired, but I felt even more tired after that. I had my alarm on my phone set to go off every 15 minutes to vibrate. I took a half hour nap after crashing out on her couch. My thinking was to tell her I was already super tired to offset her thinking that whatever drink she was giving me to take advantage of me, actually worked. I also had a couple of Red Bulls to stop me from sleeping for too long. Whatever she had planned, didn't work as I rested, but was well aware of what was going on around me and I would wake up every time someone came near me. We all ended up going out to eat that day. Tashia was very controlling and as I stated, I observed many similarities between her and my aunt. I mean, I couldn't even drive without her telling me what lane to be in and where to start merging. I've been a professional driver for many years and have driven across the country several times. I have been in every State other than Alaska and Maine, and in every major city. Basically, I know how to find my way around and don't need a backseat driver. I know the right turn is coming, but she wants me to change lanes when she wants me to. She wants me to hit the brakes when she says. She wants me to accelerate when she sees fit. You see where I'm going with this, right? I even told her to stop. I had no interest in being with her and that's something that she wasn't used to. I guess she used her looks on so many men and it worked that she thought she could have her way with me easily, but I'm no simp. It seemed like she was trying hard to show my daughter that she could have me if she wanted me, but I truly did not want her and was not overtaken by her looks. I was seeing someone already for one, and secondly, she was way prettier and sexier than she. It wasn't even close, and I wasn't going to ruin a relationship for someone that's the sister of my daughter's mom. I remember we were outside eating at a popular mall where a lot of celebrities frequented. Tashia pointed out a guy that I was familiar with and he and I had a mutual friend. Tashia knew him as the guy that had a sex tape. She didn't know that he was a very famous battle rapper. My daughter knew him as the guy that's on "Wild-N-Out." She also didn't know he was a battle rapper. I turned around and said, "Oh, that's Hitman Holla. He's a battle rapper!" I sent our mutual friend a text message and he told me to tell Hitman to Holla at him. I spoke to him briefly and had my meal. I guess the point of my story is, she found out I was no lame and also knew people. My daughter started to tell her aunt that I knew all kinds of celebrities. My daughter found it funny that I would talk about who I know and who I had connections with, then for her to see it in person. "Yo wuddup Hitman, Chris told me to tell you wussup and to Holla at him." Tashia was trying to show my daughter that she could turn me into a simp, but I showed my daughter that I was no simp and that actually made Tashia attracted to me.

On the ride home, I pointed things out to Anjolie and she said that she noticed. I didn't say much bad about her aunt. I just pointed out that I was annoyed at how annoying I found her and that someone's looks doesn't make me act out of character. The entire interaction with Tashia turned into it seeming like she was really trying to interview me for a relationship. If I'm wrong, I'm wrong, but I don't think so. It was after this experience that I started to become weary of Tashia. It was several months later and I was at a new job, stationed in Los Angeles. I lived in a really nice hotel. I contacted Tashia to see if she wanted to meet up. I made sure it was all on text. I don't want to say too much, but she told me because of the distance, that she had an additional fee. That was all I needed. She confirmed to me that she was a prostitute just by negotiating the price. I now knew that my daughter had to be careful around her. I wasn't going to stop Anjolie from being around her, I just knew to keep an eye on the situation.

Anjolie expressed to me that she wanted to move to L.A. when she turned 18. She would look up the cost of living and apartments for rent, etc. I had to remind her that she needed a job to pay rent. She seemed to think that she could get by without having a job and that she could just earn money the way her aunt earned money, but she really didn't understand that her aunt wasn't making money the way she was claiming to. My daughter seemed to be looking for shortcuts. I'll be honest, being a masseuse is usually a gateway into other things that include house calls. Not always, but more often than not. I'm not saying this for brick and mortar businesses, just the house call variety. I don't believe you have to go to college in order to be successful, and I do believe college in the United States is a racket, but if you can keep the cost of going low or even free, you should go. It wasn't an option for Anjolie to not go or to fall for one of those "assistant" certifications. Tashia was constantly trying to convince us that this was a good career path. I can't tell you how many times I had to tell Tashia she's not Anjolie's parent and to stay in her lane. "But I think it's best"...SHUT UP, IT DOESN'T MATTER WHAT YOU THINK. I found out she was letting Anjolie drive without having a learners permit. I couldn't get my daughter to actually go and take the test for a permit, yet her aunt and her mom would constantly let her drive. Her mom and I recently got into a spat and she brought up the fact that I wouldn't let her drive. She shut up after I said "not without a permit. She lives with you now, why haven't you taken her to get it?" She was doing nothing to make her study for the permit test, which is probably why Anjolie hasn't gone to take the test yet. I told Anjolie I wasn't going to make her do anything and that I was tired of reminding her, so if she didn't want to get her license, fine, but don't drive without one, or don't get behind the wheel with her mom and aunt without a permit. Her family just doesn't seem to understand this concept. Honestly, my hands are washed on this.

Time goes on and Anjolie graduates. What she failed to realize or believe was, she almost didn't graduate. Her grades started slipping once she moved in with her mom. She had to go to Summer School, and even ESS, which is Extended Summer School, and she almost failed ESS. Her mom was leading her on to believe it wasn't important and none of them realized the many phone calls and meetings I had with her Principal and teachers to give her 2nd and 3rd chances to complete her work. Anjolie almost didn't graduate. I had to take over, pick her up from school, make sure she did her work by calling her everyday and signing in online to see if her work was complete. None of it was working. Anjolie was not taking school seriously. I had to message her Principal and instructors of the classes she was failing and suggest that they give her one last chance because I was about to take drastic measures. I told them that she will no longer be allowed to be in any extracurricular activities until she passed her classes and turned in all of her work. Luckily, I was in charge of that and her mom had no say. She was almost unable to go on the trip to DC and I had her taken out of her dance class and off the Cheerleading team. Anjolie was angry at me about this, but I bet you one thing, she completed her work and passed her classes.

Summer comes and it's graduation time. Her aunt Tashia comes up from Reseda and while Anjolie and I are driving and making plans, she gets a text from Tashia, and Tashia was in a brand new C8 Corvette convertible. She throws a monkey wrench in our plans. Tashia tells me she wants to take Anjolie out for graduation. I had to tell her that she's not her mom and that graduation is for her mom and dad to spend time with her. I told her that she did nothing to help her graduate, she went to zero parent teacher conferences, she didn't have any of the hardships, pay for anything, sacrifice anything, have to leave work because the school called, basically nothing, and if she wants to take Anjolie out for graduation, it'll have to be another time. I saw that Anjolie wanted to hang out with her hero, so I gave in and let her for a couple hours. It was from this point on that the little respect I had for her aunt had dwindled even more. Tashia told me that she wanted to take Anjolie driving, and she said this in front of my daughter. I told her then and there, no. For one, no permit. secondly, definitely not a C8 Corvette, which is far too powerful. Also, there were a ton of police out and traffic was heavy. Everyone was graduating that day. There was just no way. Her mom even got mad at me for this. We went from getting along to her talking out the side of her neck. This made it so that I no longer felt comfortable with being at her mom's house for the after graduation dinner. I had to tell my daughter I was leaving because of how her mom was acting and I wasn't going to risk an incident. I told my daughter that she should have told her aunt no and that it shouldn't have come down to me. Of course, after I left, I know they all had nothing but bad things to say about me. Her mom realized that she was at fault for me not staying for dinner. Before you think to yourself that I should have stuck around and stuck it out, remember the earlier chapters. I learned my lesson and I wasn't going to let those lessons be for nothing. My daughter is 18 and she's going to have to learn to take some responsibility. I know that they went out driving. I also told her aunt that if anything happens to my daughter, I would take legal action, so if they did go out driving, that's the risk she's taking.

School's out and my daughter sends me a text asking if I still had the projector that we had in Buffalo because she was moving to Los Angeles the next day with her aunt. There were talks of this before that and I expressed my displeasure with it because Tashia was selling her a pipe dream and I knew it wasn't going to be what

Anjolie thought it would be. I never said that she couldn't go. It wasn't for me to decide. It's just my job to warn her. I didn't want to have to tell my daughter what it is I found out about her aunt, and it wasn't just the fact that she sells her body for money. I got upset at my daughter for not telling me until the day before she was moving, and why she would keep that from me. Although I was against it, I could have helped her move and given her money, but I took a lot of time off work so I didn't have extra money for her. She told me that she didn't want to tell me because I had been trying to stop her from going and I was being nothing but negative. This wasn't true. In fact, before this, I talked to her aunt and told her that Anjolie needs to enroll into college and that since she was adamant on her moving with her, she wasn't going to charge her rent, and since she was trying so hard to act like a parent and that I didn't exist, she would have to provide for her. Tashia told me that she wasn't charging her rent and that she wasn't going to make her work. I already knew this was a lie. I'm very observant. She acts like I don't remember her trying to convince Anjolie to move there to take over her apartment while she left for the Summer across the country, so that she wouldn't lose her place. She was trying to use my daughter. Anjolie and I got into it big time. She actually told me that I was just trying to stop her from having a life. She told me I was harassing her, to leave her alone, to stop texting her, and basically talking to me with such utter disrespect through texting that I genuinely believed that it was her aunt talking to me. There was no way my daughter was coming at me like this. This is when I started "talking to Tashia." This is when I told her that I knew she was a prostitute and drugged men and robbed people, and that she was into drug running. I looked her up. She's wanted in two States for armed robbery, burglary, drug possession, and prostitution. On her paperwork, it says that she is a career criminal and it shows warrants. My daughter didn't believe me and moved to Reseda with her aunt anyways. I even showed her all of the texts where I was supporting her moving if that's what she wanted to do, but she had to go to college. Her aunt was trying to get her enrolled into some nursing assistant 6 month school. I sent Anjolie all the information showing that they don't make a lot of money and that the turnaround rate was high, and most of them regret taking that path. Thank goodness she actually listened to that.

Here's one of the problems that I had, and this is where the big falling out with my niece, Elana, and her mother, Shawna occurred. I asked Anjolie for the address, and she told me her aunt didn't want me to have the address. There's no reason for that unless you're trying to hide something. Her aunt knew I knew what was going on. She did not want me showing up at the door. She was trying to groom my daughter into her lifestyle. She mentally kidnapped her. I learned later that even her mother said it wasn't right that they were keeping her address from me and making it seem like I was some type of bad guy. I was the only person in her family that wasn't a criminal and the only man giving her good advice. None of the women on my side of the family would ever call or text Anjolie or try to guide her in the right direction. Anjolie needed a woman without a criminal record to give her advice. As much as I have done for my sister and my niece, you would think they would do me one favor without having selfish motives. For some reason, they didn't believe the seriousness of the situation. Why do people think I need to lie about a situation? They thought I was exaggerating and thought I should just let Anjolie make her own mistakes. I explained that I'm fine with that, but not if her life is on the line and that her aunt is trying to sex traffic her. No, they didn't believe that. I asked for one thing... To tell Anjolie that she was wrong for speaking to me the way that she did, and to tell her that she needs to apologize and give me her address. Both of them had pretty much the same response. They didn't want to tell her that and that they'd rather take the "I'm your friend, you can count on me" approach. They said they didn't want to scare her off and ruin their relationship with her. I tried reminding them that this isn't about them, it's about her well being and her relationship with me. They did not care. All that I have done for them. Things went left when I said to Shawna, who passed the message along to her daughter... "How many times over the years have I begged the two of you to keep in contact with Anjolie? How many times have you given me excuses as to why you haven't? How many times have any of you EVER called or texted Anjolie, or even invited her anywhere in the past 18 years? ZERO, and now you suddenly want to preserve your non-existent relationship with her? The only times you have ever seen or talked to her is when I brought her over. Neither of you treat your other nieces like that." Shawna's response in the past has always been that she doesn't keep in contact with her other niece's either. I had to remind her that it's because she sees them all the time. She's always visiting them. She keeps in contact with them so that she doesn't have to call or text them. I found it ironic that every time I was over there, they would share information on updates about them or knew what was going on in their lives. They didn't know my daughter was a dancer, but they knew our other niece likes to make Tik-Toks of dancing? Shawna warned me to be careful of my next words, and I told her I don't care because I now know how she feels and I'm tired of dancing for their attention. I let her know that she's fake and that she doesn't care about me nor my daughter and to stop pretending. I told my daughter that they'll probably now keep in contact with her for a little while, but it'll die off after a while, and that they were doing it just because they knew I was right, but not to be disappointed because it's not going to last long. I'll save you the wait, I was right. I had to send them both messages... "When's the last time you heard from your cousin/niece?"

Elana tried to act like she knew what was best for Anjolie because she's a female. Elana has never even raised or had to take care of anything alive and breathing, knew nothing of my daughter, which I raised myself, but had the unmitigated gaul to tell me she knew what was best. Have your own children and then know what's best. I couldn't get one favor because these two selfish girls want to be selfish. They saw the opportunity to side with a female over a male, and regardless of the thousands I have spent on them, the favors I have done for them, to wipe that out just to somehow win? And I don't care if they read this and feel a way. I have absolutely no hopes or wishes to resolve any relationships with either of them. I'm more done with them than they pretend to be done with me. If they ever tried to reconnect with me, I would turn it down. I'm in a much happier space without them in it. I would tell my niece the same thing she told me. "Fuck off". I have never cursed at my niece or talked to her with such disrespect. Need I repeat all that I've done for her? One of them being, getting into a fight with a guy twice my size over disrespecting her and my other niece and nephew? It's as I previously stated, when people know they've done you wrong, they can no longer look you in the eyes and can't talk to you. They avoid you at all costs and make it seem like you're the problem. But wait, I haven't even gotten to the kicker yet. I kind of skipped ahead a couple of months. Let me rewind a bit and tell you what got us to this exact point.

I did my due diligence and found out where my daughter and her aunt moved to. I even went as far as sending her a screenshot of the apartment building and the address and apartment number. I had to send it from a different number because my daughter blocked me. I also sent her a picture of her aunt's criminal record and the charges and warrants she was wanted for. I didn't get a response and I didn't expect one. I know she saw it. Someone informed me that my daughter was back in town, and that she had been in town for a couple of weeks. I didn't say anything, but my daughter was somewhat gullible and I used a burner number to text her and act like I was a friend of a friend. I used that as an opportunity for this made up character to make her realize how lucky Anjolie was to have a father like me because she barely knew who her own father was. What reunited my daughter and I was, if you notice the front and back cover of this book, I drew this while I was angry and upset. I was in San Francisco after a day of doing Uber and having to stop because I just wasn't in my right mind. I drew this picture on my folding phone using the S Pen attachment. I had no purpose in drawing it. I hadn't planned on writing this book or using it as a cover design. It was just something that I ended up drawing out of anger and self therapy. This picture is a true representation of something I was going through at the moment. It was the child coming out and expressing sadness and anger. The pictures are a representation of everything I was feeling at the time. I looked at it, then sent it to Anjolie from another burner number. She of course asked who it was and I told her to guess. I asked her if she knew what the picture meant, and she said that she thinks so and actually got some of it right. She asked who I was, I told her to guess, and she said "my dad?" I said yes, and she responded that she figured. She continued to text me back and forth and I knew she was ready to reunite with me. She told me that she had been thinking about contacting me lately which is why she didn't block me again. I knew that I had to figure out a way to get through to her and that words weren't working. I guess this is what it means when they say a picture is worth a thousand words. This was a few weeks after she was in Modesto visiting and didn't contact me. I saw her at the mall but she didn't see me. I didn't bother her though. I left without her knowing I was there. I just had a strange feeling that she moved back. I traded in the black Tesla that I had for a red one, and it wasn't so that I could spy, it's just that the black one started having lots of issues. Because of this, I know Anjolie wouldn't recognize the car if I were to drive by her mother's house. I did notice that she was in town for a couple of weeks and I was just waiting for her to tell me that she moved back. Well, one day she told me that she moved back. I asked her why, and she told me straight up. "You were right. You were right about everything. Even my mom said you were." I asked her for details. She said I was right about her being controlling and hard to get along with and that her friendly personna was an act. She said Tashia was trying to control her diet and wouldn't let her have friends. I was right about her boyfriend, about her, and she even told me that Tashia drugged her. You read that right. She drugged her. Anjolie said the very first day she moved in, she put something in her drink that made her woozy. Anjolie told me Tashia laughed about it and told her she drugged her and thought it was funny. She told me that she and Tashia got into a lot of verbal altercations that almost got physical, and on the last occasion, she kicked her out late on a Friday and that my daughter had to call some guy she met at school to pick her up and take her to a hotel and pay for it. I didn't question my daughter and asked her what happened. I figure I would wait until she was ready to talk about it. There's a lot I'm leaving out for the sake of not making this too drawn out and long, but when I say I was right about everything, I mean everything. When I say I could have been a killer, I probably would have been had I seen her aunt any time close to this incident. Anjolie's mom tried fussing at me about something and I had to remind her that it is she that allowed our daughter to be put in this predicament. She actually shut up after that, which is rare. I really wish I wasn't right. What saddened me the most is that Anjolie said that she hates her aunt and wishes that she never sees her again. I saw this coming, and this is exactly what I was trying to prevent. What comes to mind is, you never want to meet your heroes. By meeting them, I really mean you don't want to get to know them, because you find that they are just as messed up as everyone else. I guess if there's a bright side, my daughter now listens to me and takes my advice. She believes me when I try to warn her about something and she doesn't want to learn the hard way anymore. I'm reminded of when I used to fix phones for a side gig back in 2014 or 2015. I got a call to fix a phone at a tattoo shop, and Bushwick Bill was there. The entire shop stunk like hard drugs, and he and the owner were taking turns going to the back room and taking hits. Bushwick Bill was super intelligent. He's one of the most intelligent people I ever met, if I'm honest. I had no idea he was that brilliant. He taught me about book publishing and the ins and outs of it. He thoroughly went through fine details of what to do and what not to do, and what to look out for, and what to avoid. I gave him a copy of my book. He invited me to hang with him at his show in Modesto, but I declined. This was only because that's not my environment. I don't hang around drugs and people that are high. No matter how highly I think of someone, I refuse to purposely put myself in a bad situation, and this was a lesson I was trying to teach my daughter. Rest Easy Bushwick Bill. He was a cool friend that I had to stay away from.

 This is what led to the last words between Elana, Shawna, and I. I texted both of them to let them know what happened. Elana's response was "well at least she's alive." I responded, "no thanks to any of you. She could have died, and her aunt was trying to groom her for sex trafficking, and that's your response?" I forget what her response after that was, but I told her that I really didn't care, and my niece called me an unappreciative prick, and told me to fuck off. Unappreciative? She did nothing for me to appreciate. I asked her to do and say something, in her own words, but in alignment to my sentiments, and instead of doing that, she took the opportunity to be selfish. No, I do not appreciate that. What was I supposed to appreciate? Her using the situation to hijack my relationship with my daughter? If you ask me to drop you off at Target because you're too tired to drive and I agree to take you, then along the way you fall asleep, but instead of taking you to Target, I drive an extra 3 miles to Walmart and drop you off, you get out not realizing I took you further to the wrong store and in a bad neighborhood, just because I gave you a ride, did I really do you a favor? This little twat had the nerve to tell me that I was no perfect dad and that this was basically my fault. This coming from someone that like I said, never had to raise anything except for her skirt and her hand. And yes, I was right, she and her mom stopped communicating with Anjolie as they had before. They were only doing it to try to prove me wrong, but a lie is hard to keep up. If you have never texted or called her on your own free will and accord in 18 years, I know for a fact that you're not going to keep up the charade for long. I don't care about burning bridges. None of them have ever done anything for me either way and whenever I was in real need, they were never there. I needed a place to stay just for a few days many years ago, but they didn't have the room, but when someone else got out of jail, they had space for her to stay. They only have a problem with men, which is why they both have problems with the men they have. Yes, I know about it. All said and done, my daughter did survive and she did learn a valuable lesson, but almost at the cost of being groomed, drugged and kidnapped. At least she now knows that her dad has her back and has always only looked out for her best interest. I don't know if she realizes how many relationships I have ended because I needed to relocate her or relocate myself to be close to her. I don't know if she realizes the good jobs that I left behind for the same purposes. One day she will, but I'm not going to throw it in her face. Maybe one day she'll have children of her own and realize the sacrifices. God knows, my niece doesn't know. I had Elana on a pedestal, but then there was an earthquake and I just don't give a damn anymore. I will tell you that Elana was there for me at one point, but I begin to wonder if it's just because of the juiciness of the situation and the thrill of being on the front line and knowing something other people didn't know. I begin to wonder if it was just the intrinsic power that she held, is the reason why she was there during this situation, or maybe she just felt obligated. Or maybe she was being genuine. Probably the latter, but as long as she gets her way, it's all good.

CHAPTER TWENTY
IF I COULD BE WHERE YOU ARE

I'm at work at one of the Los Angeles COVID test site locations. I'm playing tennis with the nurse and at this point, I was still very overweight, but I had been exercising and had a good wind and agility. I played several games of tennis against a couple of different people. I was wearing an all black uniform that included all black jeans. I got a call from Uncle Roger which is strange because we really didn't talk that much. I braced myself for bad news, such as grandma being hospitalized or even having passed away. I think he could tell by the nervousness in my voice when I answered. He immediately assured me that he wasn't calling with bad news and that he could tell by my voice that I was worried. I think he even anticipated that his call would evoke fear and worry so he was prepared to immediately calm me down. After he assured me that he wasn't calling with the news that I thought he was calling about, he told me that he had news for me and that he was told not to tell me until they found out more information, but he just didn't feel comfortable leaving me in the dark. Let me rewind a little.

It was on Mother's Day in 2022. I had to bring in my shuttle for maintenance from Los Angeles to Modesto. I was in the parking lot resting in a rental that the company made available, as they had several for us to use when coming into town. I get depressed every holiday, including Mother's day and my birthdays. I was listening to Pandora radio. I have a few stations set as my regular stations for music. One being Enya. They played a lot of classical and ethereal music which I enjoy a lot. My playlist is crazy. It ranges from hardcore hip-hop to Beethoven. One of Enya's songs came on that I had never heard before, called 'If I Could Be Where You Are.' It's probably the saddest song I have ever heard in my life. I hardly ever cry, and I had been trying to just let the tension out. I would always fall asleep before being able to cry, but this song did it for me. I never cried so hard before. I'm not a religious person at all, but I believe we are all spiritually connected. I do believe in a universal being, and that we are all part of that universal consciousness. I do believe in the power of prayer, or as I call it, meditation. The difference to me is, prayer is towards one being and you're asking for something and have no real control over the outcome. Meditation is to the universe and you, being part of the universe, are trying to manifest the results yourself. I asked for answers and for relief. I had to know what happened. I had to know where my mother was and if she was dead. You see, it was 2014 when I got a message and a friend request from someone named Debra. She claimed to know my sister and I because she was our mother's best friend and she used to babysit us. I do actually remember our neighbor and her daughter babysitting us. I remember the entire layout of the house, including the velvet paintings on the wall. I remember one of the velvet paintings was of a black panther, and another was of a man and woman's bust, one higher than the other and they both had afros with a pick. I remember the chair that was by the front door that her mom would sit on and just stare outside. I remember her feeding us pickled pigs feet out of a jar. I actually enjoyed the flavor, but I would not eat that today. Children don't know better. Everything this lady was telling me, I remembered. I just didn't remember her face. I remember objects quite well though. She told me that my mother was murdered just a couple of years after she left us at our grandmother's house and that she was sorry to give us that news. Any news regarding my mother was welcome and I was happy to be in touch with someone that was close to her and willing to share information about her. After our conversation, I did my due diligence to find out more details. Debra told me that my mother went to Boston with some of her girlfriends and went missing. Then Debra's mom was contacted by the Boston Police Department asking for dental and medical records. Debra said that the last thing she heard was that her mom said it was a match and that the Boston Police Department said that she was brutally murdered. I contacted the Boston Police Department and told them who I was and why I was calling. I honestly didn't think they would be helpful nor even interested in helping me, especially it being obvious that during this time period, everything was in written files. The detective I spoke to did say that they had begun transferring everything over to digital and there may be a chance that he could find digital records of the case. I gave him every possible name that she could have used. I also gave him date ranges. He checked on the computer and said he didn't see anything that matched. I could tell that he really wanted to help me and wanted me to have closure, so he told me to give him a couple of weeks and that he would personally go through all of the records to try to find a match. I know unsolved deaths require dedication and manpower, and I'm sure they had a large caseload, but he really wanted to help me. I got a call from him a few days later. He assured me that he went through all the records that even slightly might match this case, and he said there were no matching cases even closely similar during that time period nor any time around it give or take a few years. I could tell that he was actually trying to find this information, and he even told me he had several people helping him. Like my uncle, I think he sensed the urgency and pain in my voice when I first called. I could tell that he was sorry that he couldn't help me. I assured him that he was of big help and gave me hope that she was still alive. No one had ever found her remains or anything pertaining to her. I recall being told by my grandmother that the FBI was even looking for her and turned up nothing. Several family members concluded that she wanted to disappear and Aunt Debbie even said that she wanted to live a single life and talked about leaving one day. Debbie said she always convinced her not to do so, and when she did leave, she knew that she wasn't coming back.

At this point, I began to question who this Debra lady was and if she was really who she said she was. She never asked for money or anything, so what was her motive in contacting us to tell us some lie about my mother's body being found? Days, weeks, months, and years went by and Debra never asked for anything. I told her that the police never found anything and that they even contacted the FBI for me and that the FBI hadn't found any information either. I forgot to mention that earlier. The Police Detective did tell me he got the FBI involved. I'm thinking that solving a 35 y/o missing persons case was important. This was only a year after the Boston Marathon bombing, so maybe they had an excess of people on staff at the time. I grew weary on who this Debra lady was, and her motivation. There was one recurring thought about her. It was that she was still in contact with my mother and that she wanted to mislead us by concocting this story with my mother so that we wouldn't find her. But why now? Well, I kept Debra as a friend on Facebook, but I blocked her from being able to see any of my posts, as I didn't want her to be able to report to my mother anything about me. If my mother wanted to know how I was doing, she could do it herself.

So back to when my uncle called me as I was playing tennis. Oh, and this was the first time I ever played tennis. I was 48 and actually pretty good at it. It makes me think that I could have been a professional tennis player. I also got a good laugh to myself out of it because of the "Arthur Ashe is your real dad" rumors. Uncle Roger told me that his mother's sister called her and he knew it was serious because they really didn't communicate that much. I'll refer to her as "Aunt Connie." Aunt Connie told my grandmother that a tribal investigator contacted her about someone that was seeking information about her (Connie) father. The investigator didn't have much information other than this person that contacted him was looking for pictures and it was possible that this person was trying to get tribal benefits. Aunt Connie wasn't familiar with my mother, but she knew of my grandmother's story and that she once had a daughter. She told my grandmother that the name sounded familiar, and that it was someone named "[redacted]." I don't want to disclose the name for privacy purposes, but the first name matched my mother's. The last name was unfamiliar, and that's all we had to work with. The only other bit of information that the investigator was able to share was that this person lives in East Chicago, IN. So basically, I had a first name that was a match, an unfamiliar yet common last name, and a city.

I ended my tennis playing and walked around for a bit and became a bit reserved. My mind was all over the place as you could imagine. I did some quick Google searches with this information that I now had and there were no matching results. I then just sat on the shuttle and thought about how I could proceed. I was pretty good at finding people with very little information. This would be my biggest challenge yet though, being that this person had been missing for 43 years. Most other people that I tried finding at least had some form of social media presence, even if it was LinkedIn. Even people that refused to have Twitter accounts, Facebook, Instagram, or any of the traditional social media accounts, could be found as long as they had a bill in their name. Even if they didn't, as long as their name was on a lease, I could find them. I have found people that did none of that, though I had to keep checking back after several months. People know how to wipe their names from the internet by using special services or by doing it the hard way and doing searches on themselves and telling each organization that had their name listed, to delete their information. This being said, I found absolutely nothing on this person. But then I got lucky. I saw something that gave me hope. There was someone with her name that was listed as an employee of a local casino. I got in contact with the casino and the person I was in contact with was just like the detective from the Boston Police Department. She really wanted to help me. She gave me her personal phone number and email. I sent her an old picture of my mother. The weekend passed and she got back to me with information that the person I was looking for wasn't her. I started looking for addresses with the last name of the person I had. I did tenant searches for everyone with this very common last name and anyone with that name and where they lived. There were so many results that I knew I had my work cut out for me. I sent out several emails to tens of dozens of people. I sent Facebook messages to everyone that I didn't have an email for. If your last name was [redacted], you probably got a message from me.

After I did my due diligence of looking for and contacting any person that may know her, I looked up marriage certificates. I paid for different companies to give me information and I found a name buried within some information. There was an odd name that was married to someone with the name of the person that I was looking for. An odd name is a good thing when looking for someone. If you can't find the person you're looking for, if there's someone connected to them, just look for that person. After doing the same internet searches for this person with the odd name, I found several other people connected to him. I then emailed or sent Facebook messages to all of those people. About a week goes by and I get an email from someone. I cannot tell you his name because he's the son of the person and they have the same odd name. He told me that he knew the person that I was looking for and that he's my brother. This part is very emotional for me and I actually had to take a small breather before continuing. I just did a little digging into the emails, and it was on 5/22/2022 that I thought I was contacting my mother's husband, but it was in fact his son. It was the very next day that he replied to me informing me that we were brothers. He told me that our mother was alive and well, though she had been through a lot. He told me that she doesn't know that we're in contact so he didn't want to give me her phone number, but he would talk to her and he assured me that he would put us in contact and not to worry because my search was over and he wasn't going to leave me hanging. He told me that he knew of me and had been wanting to find me. I do believe him, but I imagine our mother did her best to hide us from him. Had she wanted to find us, all she ever had to do was go to the house where she left us. All she had to do was type in my name to any search bar. She could find my name on any social media platform. I don't have a common name, and the one that I used all my life isn't the one that I'm using for this book. Basically, she knew how to find me. I knew she was about to get the shock of her life when her son told her that the jig was up. He told me that it wasn't up to her anymore and that me finding him was all he needed. I think he was just as excited as I was.

I'll call him "Gregory." Gregory gave her my phone number. I wasn't really ready to speak to her to be honest. I found out what it was that I always wanted to know, but now it wasn't speculation. Can you imagine having something like this happening to you? My entire life, every night, I went to bed wondering where my mother was and if she was dead or alive. Almost every movie or television show I watched, there was something that reminded me of my mother. Exactly two weeks before this, I was crying my eyes out asking that the universe give me an answer. You might think that I did this every year, if not every day. No, I always tried to go to sleep without thinking about it. I never asked the universe for answers. I was being somewhat of a hypocrite I guess. If I were to believe in some kind of spiritual connection between everyone and the universe, then why was I not asking the universe for answers out of the earnest of my heart? So yes, this was the first time I actually did this. That Mother's day sitting in the rental car of the company parking lot, after the hard cry, I felt somber. Something different was in the air and I honestly felt that I was going to have some kind of resolution.

My mother emailed me. I'm not going to get into the details of that email, but she basically said that she needed time to wrap her head around things and that she would call me soon, but to give her a few days. Hey, what's a few days compared to 43 years? I don't remember exactly how long after, but I woke up in the morning to a voicemail. According to my call log, she called at around 3 in the morning. She left a voicemail. Before clicking on it to hear it, I just stared at my phone. I was about to hear my mother's voice for the first time in 43 years. I was 5 the last time that I heard from her. I clicked on the voicemail and heard her. I closed my eyes and cried. She sounded hardened and scratchy, but I imagine she went through a lot, and according to the lifestyle she lived before disappearing, she likely did a lot of drinking, smoking, and maybe even hard drugs. I still don't know her story. I, to this date, haven't spoken to her. We texted a lot. She would promise to call me, then she'd call, but my phone wouldn't ring. I asked her about this and she admitted to using an app that would bypass ringing and go straight to anyone's voicemail.

Many people would question if this was really her, or if it was someone playing a long scam. No, it's her. She sent me several pictures of her and her son. I sent her several pictures of my daughter and I, and also some pictures I had of her from when she was young. It's most definitely her. In some of our texts, she would talk a lot about how she had a hard life but wouldn't get into detail. The one thing she kept going back to is that she had another son other than the one that contacted me. She said that he died when he was 7. Whenever I asked her why she left and never came back, she wouldn't respond and it would be days before I heard from her again. She didn't contact me again until I told her I wouldn't ask her anything she wasn't ready to volunteer to me herself, and then she responded. I was ok with this arrangement because I figured she'd eventually come around to telling me. Days turned into weeks and she would never explain herself other than she had a hard life. She would keep coming around to tell me that she had a difficult time after losing her son when he was 7. I told her that way before then, she lost a son when he was 5, and he is here now. This would only cause her to keep withdrawing from me. It was around this time that things would take a dark turn for me and I could feel myself declining mentally, becoming withdrawn. I had lost a great deal of weight because I no longer turned to food for comfort to get my mind off of wondering where my mother was. In a period of about 7 months, I went from 225 lbs, down to 176 lbs., but after realizing my mother cared more about her son that died physically and not about the one that was dying mentally, I began to be more depressed than I ever was. During this entire ordeal, I literally questioned whether I was in reality or not. I honestly didn't know, and even now as I write this book, do not know if I'm living in reality or if I died and I'm living some kind of twisted hell. I actually mean this literally. I cannot tell what reality is. Because of this, I just try to do the right thing. I look for things that I was never able to do in dreams, but only can do in reality as we know it. I see signs that nothing has changed, but I also see signs that a lot has changed. It seems like 95% of the population has become stupid. I keep picturing this meme in my head where several kids are in a swimming pool. All but one boy has peed in the pool, but they all surround him and laugh at him for not peeing in the pool. This is really how I see the world, and this is why I feel like I'm not in the same reality as I was once in. I often think that I died in that rental car in the parking lot and that's how the universe was able to grant me answers, by sending me to an alternate reality where I found my mother.

Just eight days before my brother contacted me about his mother being the person I was looking for, another great tragedy happened. This was the mass shooting at Tops grocery store in Buffalo. I personally knew two of the people, and one of the other people killed was a high school classmate's mother. His name is Wayne. We were never close friends, but we've been friends on Facebook for many years, though we have few interactions. I remember opening up Facebook the day after the shooting and saw his post saying "she's gone, I can't believe it, my mother's gone." That hit me hard. I said this every day, several times per day ever since she left. He didn't say why, but I had a feeling. It became evident that day after I was glued to the news. I sent him a long message giving him my condolences, but he never responded. One of the other people I knew was the security guard that was also a retired police officer. We weren't close either, but I often talked to him because I worked for the NFTA, Paratransit, and

Tops was one of the most frequent pickup/drop-off locations. While waiting, or even going there to use the restroom, or just to have lunch, I would often talk to him. He was a very kind person and didn't deserve what happened to him. I had one family member that passed away in that shooting. Aunt Pearl Young. We weren't close over the years, but when I was young, she was one of my favorite people at the church. She and my grandmother ran a food pantry together. Also, they did most of the cooking together for church events. I always referred to her as "Aunt Pearl." She didn't give off the air of snootiness like most of the other ladies at the church. We went to "Good Samaritan Church of God in Christ" on Leroy Ave, not far off of Kensington Ave. They're located at a different location now, but I switched to a church on Kensington Ave because they were bigger and had a lot of people my age there, and it was walking distance from my grandmother's church. I remember as I got older, I would ride with my grandparents to their church, but would walk to Prince of Peace. If they weren't running late, they'd just drop me off along the way. Aunt Pearl had a couple of children of her own that I was close to growing up, and a cousin that I went to grade school with. We've all been in contact with each other on Facebook and actually interacted a lot over the years, so I felt really bad. Aunt Pearl was always so nice to me, and though I hadn't seen her since I was a teenager, I thought about her all the time. Whenever I passed the church on Leroy, or whenever I even just thought about that church, or even just interacted with my cousins on that side of the family, I thought of her and her smile every time she saw me. I recall the times my grandmother would make me come with her to Aunt Pearl's house in the suburbs. She had a really nice house. Very high ceilings with huge windows is all I can recall. It was a very open floor plan and I imagined myself living in a house like that when I got older.

I'm bringing this tragedy up because it not only happened just a week before finding my mother, but it seemed like so many people lost their mother's that month of May, yet I found mine. I couldn't help but to feel guilty. I would often think to myself, and I still think it, that in order for me to find my mother, others would have to lose theirs. You'll have a hard time convincing me otherwise. If I could change things, I would. If I had to go back to the universe where I didn't know the fate of my mother so that I could bring back the mothers of all the people that lost them that month, I would. One of the irony's is that I inherited my immune disorder from her. Every 21 days, I get sick and I'm forced to think of her. I couldn't get her out of my mind if I wanted to. One of the first things I asked her was, how she coped with her illness. Her response was "I haven't been sick since I was a teenager and left my mother's house." How is it that she deserved to be illness free and alive, but all of these bad things were happening to me and those around me that I love? I also feel guilty because Gregory doesn't deserve for me to have these thoughts about his mother. He wants me as a brother so badly, but I cannot be that right now. I have a lot of healing to do. I know he understands, and he seems to be very wise and often gives me words of encouragement. I do plan on visiting them one day, but the time just isn't yet. I will say this, though I was unable to get help by going to a therapist that seemed to make things worse, getting most of my thoughts out in this book has helped me a lot and hopefully it will help me to be a functioning member of society once again as right now, between my physical and mental health, I feel debilitated. I guess one of the thing's holding me back from healing is, I wish she would actually put in just a little effort to make things right between us. Don't call me and send it straight to voicemail. I know I'm not alone in how I feel about talking to her at the moment because her own mother and brother haven't had any correspondence with her either. She and my sister texted back and forth. I don't think they spoke on the phone either, but last I communicated with our mother, she said Belle stopped messaging her. I guess part of that is my fault, but I don't feel bad about it. My sister, the one that has done nothing except stab me in the back our entire lives, told her that she better not disappear again and hurt her little brother. You better believe when I heard she was using me as a scapegoat to protect her own feelings, I texted her and laid in on her. I reminded her that she never gave two shits about me ever, and to keep me out of her frame of reference, so when she talks to our mother, keep the subject on them. Belle did not care about anyone hurting my feelings when in fact she has been hurting my feelings for 4 decades.

As for my mother, don't call me at 3 in the morning. Call me when you know I'm awake, even if I am living in a form of hell. Meet me in my reality. Get to know what you created.

Lastly, I sent my aunt Meta a text message telling her that I found my mother. I had also told her years before that I believed my father killed my mother and explained my reasons why. After I told her that I found my mother, rather than expressing any sentiments for me and understanding the implications, she managed to say, "You owe your father an apology." An apology for accusing him of murder? Do I owe him an apology for him trying but failing to kill her? Is the apology for him not being there most of my life? Or is it for the abuse I had to endure when he was around? Or maybe I owe him an apology for causing my mother to want to fake her own death just to get away from him... No, Aunt Meta, you owe me an apology—not only for your insensitive reaction to the news I shared with you but also for when you accused me of having ulterior motives when I offered to buy your daughter's car from her. You owe me an apology for taking the marble table set that Grandma gave me. To Benny, just hurry up and die already. I'm not going to do it just because you tried to end my life. This book is about healing, but I'm fine with our bond being broken and not caring for you whatsoever. I choose to let you live in misery. I thought about ending you, but it was just my imagination running away with me. Just know that I could have. My daughter saved you. I could have been a killer. I was almost yours.

I will try to end this on a positive note. There are people that I have known and also people that I met and only talked to once that give me hope for humanity. I may not like people as a whole anymore, but some people still give me hope. No need for last names, but Jovanna has always been there for me and never switched up on me over the years. Daniella, I only met once when I was driving for Uber, but she was a bright light and had the best smile. You could see her soul shine through and her aura shine through so brilliantly. My high school friends, too many to name. My beautiful, brilliant daughter, Anjolie, shines bright enough to stop time itself. My boy Jonathan L Taylor, Laurie and Wayne McDonald, Tim Parker (Rest in Paradise my friend), and Carmen Thornton, (Rest in Paradise). There are a few more I'm sure, and one that didn't want to be named, so I'll give her a pseudonym, LaTasha Tudor, thank you for everything.

I would like to send a special thanks to Simon Jakops and XG. Your music has turned my black heart red and given me life once again. Jurin, Chisa, Hinata, Harvey, Juria, Maya, Cocona.... Alphaz on deck...

– Benjamin Smart, aka Alpha Supreme!

EPILOGUE

I believe we all have choices. We may not believe we choose the circumstances we are born into, but if you go to the beginning of this book, I believe we do. Regardless, we have certain other choices once we're old enough to think for ourselves. There's a quote that I love from Star Trek said by Lieutenant Data..." Every sentient being knows the difference between right and wrong." Are we in control of our thoughts and actions? To an extent, yes. I think the outcome of everything is predetermined, but how we get there is up to us. If there's a bomb that's supposed to destroy a country, it will happen, but your part in it going off is up to you. I think there's patterns we must recognize and paths we must follow. I think life is a giant puzzle to be solved. None of this matters when it comes to our day to day lives. We can try to complicate things by evoking some higher being and all kinds of philosophies, but when it comes down to it, most of us don't care about those things when we see mass murders. The person that did it had a choice. We can blame it on their upbringing. We can say they need help and they didn't know what they were doing, but the bottom line is, people that choose to take a life other than to protect themselves or others, don't belong around those that choose to be civil. In contrast, we can study the frontal lobes of these killers, and they seem to have a smaller lobe than those that aren't killers, so maybe they aren't in control at all! We can blame it on their parents and the doctors that misdiagnosed them or prescribed them the wrong medication. That doesn't mean they should roam free either. There are many people that I wish weren't amongst the living, but I'm not going to take their lives. Many people annoy or irritate me. From the person that took the life of a child, to the person that walked out the toilet stall from going number 2 and didn't wash their hands... I don't think any of those people should exist, but the fact is that they're part of this world and we must navigate this existence knowing that they also exist.

I walk this planet knowing some of the best people I know are hypocrites. Let's take Thanos for example. If you ask 100 people if he was the good guy or the bad guy, 98 of them will say he's the bad guy. Then when you show them that he's no different than the God in the Bible they worship so greatly, they don't want to talk to you anymore. This is one of the things that makes me a loner. I will have no problem pointing out your hypocrisies. I know in order to have friends, you have to be able to lie. I just can't. When I see or hear people say "I'm blessed and highly favored" or "God is good... all the time." I will say to them, what about those kids with no food and horrible bacteria and diseases. They were born on the side of the planet that didn't teach them your religion. What about the families that can't pay their rent, car notes, mortgages, or even have food? Why is it that you're blessed and highly favored? What makes you more deserving than anyone else? I don't like those people. They don't think about the world outside of themselves. Don't confuse me for hating them or their religion, because I know many religious people that don't act like they're more deserving than others. They realize there are bad people in this world that are also "blessed and highly favored" if you're equating that to your possessions and/or success.

Everything I wrote about is true. If you read the manifesto of the several mass murderers in our history, they all placed blame on one thing or another. Bottom line is, they were probably born evil, or they just made bad decisions. I can't speak on being born evil, but I have had enough bad things happen to me to cause me to want to take a life or two, but I made the choice not to. I don't care how big or small my frontal lobe is. I hold onto hope. I choose to lead by example and show my daughter the right path. Money doesn't cause someone to be happy. You can barely survive financially and still be happy. You can be wealthy and still be depressed. How many times can you travel the world before you get bored? How many cars can you buy before you get tired of driving the coast or showing off to your friends that you don't know if they're there for the money or truly are your friends? I've had those "fair-weather friends." When it comes down to it, there are only a few people that I know have been there for me even in my darkest times, and none of them share my blood. The ones that were there, I don't need to name. They're there when I call them, even if I haven't talked to them in many years. We talk as if no time has passed. These people are my light. My daughter is my light and why I live. I will try to end this on a positive note. There are people that I have known and also people that I met and only talked to once that give me hope for humanity. I may not like people as a whole anymore, but some people still give me hope.

I have given you many reasons why I could have made really bad decisions. I've had tens of dozens of reasons to wipe certain people from existence, but I chose to let those people live in their personal hells and not give them a fresh start or an easy way out.

You're going to watch me live. You're not going to kill my spirit, even if my spirit is in a dark place, for I know it's temporary. When I did the artwork you see in this book, I was in a really dark place. It is full of symbolism and riddles , and I invite any of you to discuss and decode what they are and what they mean. I want this to be a topic of discussion in classrooms around the world, from grade schools, to universities.

 I am happy that I have had the experiences that I've had. Maybe my stories will help that one person. This world isn't fair and we must learn how to navigate it without adding to the chaos. You never know what can set someone off. One of the things that bothers me the most out of anything is when I was sexually harassed by a woman at work. I reported it and not only were my claims ignored, but the company I worked for tried to retaliate against me. Also, what kind of life are you living if you have nothing to strive for? Nothing to hope for? No adversities to overcome? What is it that you contributed to mankind? You lack wisdom. I equate it to a person that grew up poor getting their lights turned off with no source of income. They figure out what to do. They can see the light at the end of the tunnel. But let that person born into wealth lose their wealth and get their lights cut off. For them, it becomes more than literal, it becomes symbolic of the state of mind they are now in. Darkness with dark thoughts. It's not hard to slip into darkness when the world is geared towards capitalism and not humanity. Nothing is designed for someone to rise to the top unless it's by chance. For example... You can't get a driver's license or ID without a home address. You can't get a home address without a driver's license or ID. You can't get a car without a job. You can't get a job that pays enough for the cost of living unless you have a car to travel. You can't get an apartment with bad credit. Your credit goes from good to bad when you lose your income. It's cheap to eat the foods that are killing us. It's expensive to buy healthy food. I can go on forever, but things are just designed to keep the masses from thriving. Capitalism needs consumers, and poor people are the biggest consumers. Both literally and metaphorically, I could have been a killer, but I chose to write The Book of Benjamin instead.

www.ingramcontent.com/pod-product-compliance
Lightning Source LLC
Chambersburg PA
CBHW032028290426
44110CB00012B/720